D0282891

ONLINE TRADING

Other titles in the *SFO Personal Investor Series:*

SFO Personal Investor Series: Technical Analysis

Learn firsthand from the founders of technical analysis. A collection of the top technical articles from *SFO*, The Official Journal for Personal Investing, this book will teach you the basics and more advanced tools from the most revered names in the field, including Gerald Appel, John Bollinger, Thomas Bulkowski, Nina Cooper, Brian Dolan, Philip Gotthelf, Adam Grimes, Michael Kahn, Peter Kaplan, Cynthia Kase, Jeffrey Kennedy, Tracy Knudsen, Steven Landis, Kira McCaffrey Brecht, Lawrence McMillan, Bernard Mitchell, John Murphy, Steve Nison, Mark Pankin, Sam Seiden, Ken Shaleen, Brian Shannon, Christopher Terry, Ken Tower, and Russell R. Wasendorf, Sr.

SFO Personal Investor Series: Psychology of Trading

A collection of the best psychology-related articles from *SFO*, The Official Journal for Personal Investing, this book will help you assess what kind of trading is right for you and how to manage your personal mind games. Learn about the most effective psychology strategies from the top trading psychologists and behavioral economists in the industry, including, Linda Bradford Raschke, Eliot Brenner, Terry Burnham, John F. Carter, Mark Cook, Flavia Cymbalista, Mike Elvin, John Forman, Doug Foster, Richard Friesen, Ned Gandevani, Kyle Handley, Philippa Huckle, Peter Kaplan, Adrienne Laris Toghraie, Ilan Levy-Mayer, Desmond MacRae, Gail Osten, Bernie Schaeffer, Denise Shull, Brett Steenbarger, Christopher Terry, Van K. Tharp, Toni Turner, and Russell R. Wasendorf, Sr.

SFO Personal Investor Series:
ONLINE TRADING

INTRODUCTION BY:
RUSSELL R. WASENDORF, SR.

EDITED BY:
LAURA SETHER

W&A
PUBLISHING

P.O. Box 849, Cedar Falls, Iowa 50613
www.w-apublishing.com

Published by W&A Publishing, P.O. Box 849, Cedar Falls, Iowa 50613. www.w-apublishing.com

SFO, (Stocks, Futures and Options magazine, The Official Journal for Personal Investing), is dedicated to the education and professional advancement of personal investing. For subscription services go to www.sfomag.com.

In the publication of this book, every effort has been made to offer the most current, correct and clearly expressed information possible. Nonetheless, inadvertent errors can occur, and rules and regulations governing personal finance and investing often change. The advice and strategies contained herein may not be suitable for your situation, and there is a risk of loss trading stocks, commodity futures, options and foreign exchange products. Neither the publisher nor authors shall be liable for any loss of profit or any other commercial damages, including but not limited to special, incidental, consequential, or other damages, that are incurred as a consequence of the use and application, directly or indirectly, of any information presented in this book. If legal, tax advice or other expert assistance is required, the services of a professional should be sought.

Library of Congress Control Number: 2007920278
ISBN: 978-1-934354-00-1
ISBN-10: 1-934354-00-7

Printed in the United States of America.

14 13 12 11 10 09 08   2 3 4 5

CONTENTS

INTRODUCTION

BY RUSSELL R. WASENDORF, SR.

The beauty of online trading is that you can do it virtually any-place and at any time. To the XBox videogame generation, who cut their teeth on a joystick and computer mouse, flexibility has become the norm. Gen X'ers, impatient with the old ways of doing things that their Baby Boomer parents tolerated for years, gobbled up technology on all fronts.

Today, for those X'ers and Ys with moxie and the means to trade, nothing less than a 24/7 mentality is acceptable. And then, of course, these whiz kids in turn have helped their parents turn the corner and embrace innovation. Even old dogs are learning new tricks. Instant gratification is the watchword. Enter online trading.

Traders today can connect directly to an electronic trading platform from the comfort of their own homes. Many exchanges have made the time aspect of trading nearly irrelevant, with markets available around the clock for the worldwide trader with insomnia. Not only that. The limited number of markets acces-sible electronically just ten years ago pales in comparison to the wide array listed today. And, unlike ten years ago, fully electronic exchanges in both securities and futures are challenging the few traditional exchanges and even taking their business away.

Early acceptance of electronic trading, however, was slow. When the Chicago Mercantile Exchange (CME) launched GLOBEX in 1992 and the Chicago Board of Trade (CBOT) also began offer-ing electronic trading in 1994, volume on the new systems amount-ed to less then one percent of total volume for their first year. Given those numbers, open outcry, or face to face trading, did not seem in danger of losing traders' support. However, electronic trading on each exchange has grown meteorically since it began, and both exchanges now boast approximately 75 percent of their volume traded online, reflecting the 24-hour, automated, 21st century.

By the end of 2006, all major exchanges in the U.S. have the majority of their volume trading online. Even the most stalwart floor trading exchange, the New York Stock Exchange (NYSE), has rapidly become electrified. The purchase of the CBOT by the CME is likely to quicken the move away from the old world of floor trading.

Online trading has not only changed the way customers enter orders; it has fundamentally changed the investment world. Customers have gained far greater control over the way their orders are handled. This empowerment has dramatically democratized the markets like never before. Trading parity, or the leveling of the playing field, should be considered a basic customer right. It is hard to justify giving one class of investor an advantage over another, but that's the way it has been for decades at the world's exchanges.

Futures exchanges, in particular, have had a history of offering uneven access to their markets, with exchange insiders at a distinct advantage. Traders on the trading floor could see firsthand who was trading, the price of their transactions and the size of their bids and offers. For outsiders this important information was either delayed or not available. Of course, with the majority of trades now executed online, this edge is rapidly shrinking, but even today, some floor traders are clinging to pit trading, unwilling to give up this special privilege.

Online trading leveled the playing field among market participants. The technology that facilitated online trading carried with it some other spectacular improvements for investors and brokerages.

A GODSEND FOR BROKERAGES

For brokerage firms, who function as trading intermediaries, online trading has been a godsend. Online order entry systems have solved many of the most serious challenges vexing brokerage firms. For decades brokerages firms suffered the substantial cost of errors, broker fraud and facilities management—three very expensive problems, which often had a crippling effect on firms.

The traditional order entry system of telephoning a broker to transmit the order to the exchange floor was fraught with potential errors. The customer could misspeak, the broker could mishear, the order could be miscommunicated to the floor, and so on. In the end the firm would invariably pay for any error. The technologies of online trading have enabled the market to efficiently handle a large volume of transactions with fewer staff and far fewer errors. For many firms online orders are not just seamlessly transacted but seamlessly booked and posted, resulting in straight-through processing. Less human involvement means fewer human errors.

Broker fraud, including unauthorized trading, high-pressure sales and churning, could cost firms dearly. Not only are firms liable for the cost of reparation, they are potentially responsible for punitive damages and/or regulatory penalties. In fact, in the years leading up to the development of online trading, futures brokerage firms increasingly abandoned the personal trader, due in part to broker liability. Brokerages could have tolerated small order sizes, but the liability created by brokers interfacing with personal traders often became untenable. During the 1980s and 90s several brokerage firms were dealt a death toll in the aftermath of broker misconduct.

The cost of maintaining trading floor operations and other elements of facilities management has been compounded by the increasing demand for lower commissions. Firms were caught in the middle; the cost of interfacing with the trading floors at traditional exchanges rising, while to stay competitive, brokerage firms lowered transaction rates.

Considering this trifecta, some brokerage firms were forced out of business. Today there are fewer than half as many firms as there were a little over fifteen years ago. For hundreds of brokerages, technological solutions came too late.

Online order entry turned these liabilities into assets. Since customers input their own orders, broker error and broker fraud have been virtually eliminated. Since online trades are routed directly into an electronic trading engine, the cost of maintaining facilities is greatly reduced. Online trading has effectively replaced the broker and eliminated much of the potential risk.

Some online systems reduce brokerage liability even further by implementing risk management software. This software checks customer account balances and open positions before allowing new trades to be entered. By tracking customer positions on a real-time basis, both the firm and the customers benefit. Customers know the value of their accounts second by second, while firms are better equipped to manage risk and help customers avoid margin calls and debit balances. Unsecured debits have been a source of concern, particularly for futures firms. The combination of online order entry systems and electronic trading engines have nearly eliminated the unpredictable events that have been known to send intermediaries into bankruptcy.

Yet not all exchanges have been quick to make the conversion from floor traded to electronically traded markets. Brokerages continue to be saddled with maintaining trading floor operations, while having to explain to customers why their orders are being filled at glacial speed compared to pure electronic orders. These intermediaries frequently see little choice but to guide their customers away from floor-traded markets for their own protection, as well as to provide a better service to their customer.

The combination of electronic order handling efficiency and the near elimination of broker liability has enabled firms to significantly reduce transaction costs to customers. The personal trader who paid $50 to $75 per round turn futures transaction two decades ago pays less than $20 dollars today, and those costs continue to decline. Stock market trades are being executed for pennies per share. Yet when surveyed, most traders will put speed, reliability, simplicity or user friendliness ahead of transaction costs.

LEVELING THE PLAYING FIELD

Empowered with the ability to control order entry, online customers have discovered new freedoms. No longer do they have to hear the moans of their brokers as they try to cancel or replace an order. No longer do they have to hear their broker's pitch on the trade du jour. Customers enjoy immediate trade execution even during unusual conditions like fast markets or extreme market volatility. They can see the current market prices at the exact same time as all other market participants. These are the benefits of bypassing the traditional broker interface with the markets.

Along with empowerment and greater order entry efficiency, online trading gave many traders a view on the market they never expected to see. In addition to making a connection to the computer for trade matching, online systems connect directly to the Market Data Service (MDS) to get price quote information. Other valuable information accessible from MDS is the current bid/ask prices, current bid/ask size and the book (the price and size of orders placed above and below the current market). Seeing the book is analogous to a floor trader knowing the price and size of orders held in his fellow traders.

Customers are gaining greater independence and unexpected benefits while paying even lower commissions. The brokerage firms are passing the cost savings of less expensive facilities and the cost of unpredictable risks (errors, and legal costs) on to their customers.

Initially, electronic order entry simply replaced the account executive by replicating, electronically, what the account executive would have done physically. Traditionally, futures (and stocks and options) orders were placed through an account executive who acted as an intermediary between the customer and market makers on the trading floor. The account executive placed the order, received the fill, and notified the customer.

Today, from the comfort of their own homes, customers can either connect to an electronic trading platform and at the very least, have their orders routed much more quickly than was possible just a decade ago.

There are reasons for this shift. When online systems hook the customer directly to an exchange's electronic trading engine, a customer can place an order, have the order transmitted directly to the trade-matching engine and, at the end of the loop, have the fill reported directly back to the customer. In many instances, this electronic communication is completed in a fraction of second. Further, as order-entry systems became more sophisticated, a broader array of order types become available to the customer, along with more detailed information. Because the order-entry system is directly connected to the electronic trading engine, a a real-time price can be transmitted back to the customer.

Giving the customer access to real-time prices, a view of the book, and the immediate response to the order placed all have dramatically leveled the playing field for electronic traders.

OUTLOOK OPTIMISTIC

Both market intermediaries and customers are reaping benefits from online systems, but where will they go from here? Some evolutions and innovations are quite obvious, while some stretch the imagination.

A couple side benefits gained by brokerage firms may make the most dramatic immediate impact. These benefits have to do with the technologies that must be implemented to accomplish online trading connections. Firms that have integrated online systems suddenly found that one of their biggest inefficiencies was eliminated. The laborious and time consuming task of posting customer orders became much easier as firms made great strides toward straight-through processing.

One of the greatest expenses incurred by intermediaries is the expense of the back office systems. The back office system creates reports for the firm and statements for customers. As online technologies are improved, the need for independent back office systems is being eliminated, resulting in a substantial cost savings for the firm and ultimately the customer.

Online systems may also reduce another major expense for brokerage firms—the cost of price quotes. The history of market price quotes has put intermediaries behind the eight ball. Firms pay a vendor for the connection to receive the market quotes as well as pay the respective exchange a fee for access to real-time price quotes. Customers must have their own access to price quotes if they are to independently track market price action, and they must also pay vendor and exchange fees.

Since an online system connects directly to MDS, it can access real-time price quotes. Getting quotes directly from the exchange and delivering them directly to the customer eliminates the middleman, thereby reducing the cost to only the exchange fee.

Over the past twenty years market price quotes have evolved from a screen with columns of prices to a system complete with chart, graphs, and analytical studies. Traders expect quote systems to do much more than give them the current market price; they expect a customizable analysis of the price. The online trading system is likely to take a similar tack, but it will develop much more quickly.

A natural outgrowth of the advanced technologies of online trading is an expansion of features. But here's the rub, most online customers are trading over the Internet and have limited bandwidth. The development of online technologies is being restrained by the amount of information that can be shoved down narrow bandwidth pipelines.

In the past, online systems have tried to follow the one-size-fits-all model—or more precisely one system serves all. It has become clear that the system that serves one customer will not necessarily satisfy another. This problem is likely to be solved one of two ways.

Online system designers may create a variety of systems—a stripped down version for those customers with limited bandwidths and/or limited needs, scaling up to an advanced, multifaceted system for the bandwidth-privileged. Another approach is a scaleable online system that the customers can add or remove features to fit his or her needs and to fit his or her bandwidth.

Regardless how the bandwidth issues are solved, it is clear that bells and whistles will continue to be added to online systems. Ultimately the customer will want everything on one screen—where the customer defines what everything means. Given the powerful efficiencies of online trading it is not difficult to imagine how varied this could be.

Solving the technological questions may be the easy part of implementing advancements in online trading. The regulatory issues will be more complex. In recent years we have suffered though difficult negotiations between the Security Exchange Commission (SEC) and the Commodity Futures Trading Commission (CFTC), as they tried to create a body of regulations that bridged their jurisdictions with Commodity Futures Modernization Act.

Wrangling with government regulators in the U.S. and abroad to integrate all of the worlds markets into a single environment may be a bit off into the future. An early test will occur as the NYSE merges with Euronext.liffe.

What is abundantly clear is that online trading will continue to grow, systems designers will continue to find new ways to give customers what they need, and traders will reap the rewards.

By Russell R. Wasendorf, Sr., CEO of Peregrine Financial Group, Inc., publisher of *SFO* and author of *The Complete Guide to Single Stock Futures* and *All About Futures*.

SECTION ONE
Behind the Scenes of Online Trading

Online trading has leveled the playing field for traders, as well as increased flexibility, reduced fees and improved access to markets. The edge that pit traders had from being able to personally sense movement on the floor has been transferred to the skilled electronic trader who understands order entry and flow. That doesn't mean it's as simple as hitting a key to execute an order. Trading is a discipline that requires hard work, determination and self-control. But along with expertise and the right attitude, today you also need the right tools and a plan to get in the game.

In this section, we'll look at the tools you need—both physical and mental—to successfully trade. First, the way you execute trades can affect your bottom line. If you understand the technology behind electronic order execution you can improve your timing and trade execution and make it work for you.

We'll also look at technology—what you need to build your own trading room and how to effectively keep your equipment running smoothly. Most individual traders have no information technology department to call upon when a computer problem emerges. Learn how to keep your computer in tip-top shape, so you can concentrate on trading, not on whether your machinery will do the job it's supposed to do.

Of course, in addition to the right equipment, you have to think about a business plan, including developing a winning strategy, managing risk, writing a comprehensive trading plan, and beefing up your market knowledge. We'll give you pointers on finding the right broker for you. And we'll discuss the tax implications and advantages of setting up an active trading business.

Once you master the basics you can truly take advantage of the untethered freedom that online trading can provide.

1

MAKING ONLINE TRADING WORK FOR YOU

BY LINDA BRADFORD RASCHKE

Electronic trading has fulfilled its promise of leveling the playing field for traders. Everyone now has identical access; the floor traders no longer have the edge from watching order flow in the pit; cost structures have come way down; and computing power, functionality of trade execution platforms and improvements in connectivity continue to increase.

Despite the way technology has changed the landscape, few traders understand the order process and the ways it can affect their bottom line. There is a lot of information on technical analysis, but very little attention is given to trade execution skills. I challenge you to add up the number of trades that you made last year and then calculate the impact to your bottom line had you been able to get just one tick better in price 25 percent of the time. Imagine that extra money in your pocket now. It might be worth focusing a bit more attention on the trade execution side of the equation. But first, let's take a look at the technology behind electronic order execution and how an order travels.

The Technology Path

Let's follow the steps that an order goes through when it is placed. The execution platform from which you place an order is called the front end. This is the software program that resides on your CPU and transmits your orders. Every software program has an application program interface, or API. Black box programs write directly to the API while a discretionary trader enters orders manually. The more sophisticated traders or larger firms write their trade management and execution strategies directly to the API. Black box trading strategies now account for up to between 35 and 40 percent of the total S&P E-mini volume.

The API sends the order to the back end, which includes the hardware involved in processing the order. If you do not have direct exchange access, the order first goes to an Internet server maintained by your clearing firm. Routers and switches direct the orders through blades (part of the networking equipment) that then pass the order to another server. This server routes the order to the proper exchange. Exchange servers, also known as matching engines, pair up the orders and route the fills back to the proper clearing firm.

Five hundred milliseconds (a half-second) is considered a respectable speed at which you should be executing without a direct connection to an exchange. It takes 50 milliseconds for my order to go over the T1 line (direct access would reduce this between five and twenty milliseconds), then another twenty milliseconds for my order to get routed properly, and two to four milliseconds for the backend software to get the order to the exchange (at least in the case of the Chicago Mercantile Exchange). Every time one software application has to talk to another software application it takes time. The less layering in the entire process, the faster the execution and the fewer links to break down along the way.

How often is it, though, that this type of speed really makes a difference? To give you an idea, fast market conditions in the S&P E-minis can occur after morning economic numbers, after Federal Open Market Committee (FOMC) meetings, at key support or resistance levels, or any time there is a disruptive news event. In a fast market, there can be up to 250 price changes per minute. This means that the market can move four ticks in one second. When you consider that eight ticks in two seconds = $100 per contract, you may want to investigate how your particular orders are being handled. Another potential problem is that when clearing firms have too many clients on one server, the server usage may spike too high when markets are most active. This causes delays in quotes at critical times.

One more variable as to why price may seem to have slight delays is that not all execution platforms use a direct feed from the exchange for quotes (also called streaming data). Direct feeds from the exchanges are expensive, so some applications use a secondary data feed to supply price quotes. Unfortunately, traders often get what they pay for—most platforms that use the direct feed also have a small fee to help cover the cost. If you are not an active trader, it should not make much of a difference if you do not have a direct feed. However, if you are trading for a living on a daily basis, you are giving up a significant edge if you are not looking at a direct feed transmitting quotes from the exchange when you are executing an order.

Execution speed makes a difference in another way as well. There is an edge to being first in the queue. The sooner a trader places an order, the more likely the order will be filled when the market touches that level. The importance of understanding location in the queue is most significant in markets like the E-minis or ten-year notes where there can often be 3,000 contracts on the bid or offer.

You should also ask, are your stop orders being held on the exchange's servers or are they synthetic stops? A synthetic stop means that the order is either held on your own computer or an intermediary computer, and when price touches that level, the trade is then fired off to the exchange's server for execution. Active traders will want their stops to be held at the exchange level. That way, if there is any compromise to your own Internet connection, your order is already resting on the exchange's server and thus its execution, as well as its place in the queue, is protected.

Some traders like to use complex trade management strategies such as trailing stop techniques. Applications such as Ninja Trader, Trade Maven, Strategy Runner and TradeStation offer additional functionality. Newer traders have found these extra features to be worth the additional cost and added layer of connections. Keep in mind that each additional layer takes more processing time and adds one more link to the entire order execution process. Know where your orders will be resting if there are Internet connectivity problems. Some of these add-on applications keep the trade management orders on your own PC, which is a problem if you have computer or Internet issues. Keep your firm's order desk number handy so they can check on the status of your order if there is a breach of integrity in any of the links. They can also execute trades for you.

But Are The Trades Real?

Now that some of the technology behind the scenes has been exposed, let's get back to the real challenge of improving trade execution. Unfortunately, the ability to execute at the click of a mouse is the downfall of many traders experiencing challenges in their bottom line. The ease of execution leads to overtrading as well as a tendency to overreact to market noise.

Electronic trading allows all players to see the book, or size of the market bids and offers. What many traders do not understand is that often bids or offers may not be real. For example, a black box system, which works the spread between the bid and offer, might be bidding for 1,000 contracts. But if 200 are filled, the other 800 on the bid are instantly cancelled. Some programs monitor the speed with which bids or offers are filled, and this allows them to cancel or adjust the size they are working on the bid or offer. In the case of auto-spreaders, which work bids and offers on correlated markets simultaneously, orders are constantly being adjusted as one side in the other market is filled. Lastly, there are firms that use automated entry algorithms that send orders to buy or sell 300 contracts every few seconds. Thus it is impossible to tell the real size or offer being worked.

About five years ago, a number of traders made a living scalping off the bid and offer. Proprietary trading shops sprang up, which trained young, aggressive traders to take advantage of short-term market inefficiencies. With the increase in black box systems, which execute trades faster than any human can, this game has all but disappeared.

Jeff Quinto, who was president of Rand Financial (Monroe Trout's firm), has been in the business for more than 30 years. He too started up a proprietary trading firm or prop shop. These have dwindled in number and have been replaced by trading arcades. Quinto now manages the Photon Trading Room, a state-of-the-art arcade. The difference between a prop shop and an arcade is that at a prop shop, a trader uses the firm's capital and receives a percentage of the profits. At an arcade, traders put up their own money and keep 100 percent of their profits, but pay a monthly fee to have access to sophisticated technology and ultra-fast connections. A trader can start up at an arcade with as little as $15,000. In Quinto's opinion, arcade traders are far more consistent and profitable nowadays than prop shop traders because they tend to be more careful, as they are trading their own money.

Quinto also noted that upstairs professional traders must trade on a longer time frame, due to the increased presence of automated trading systems. Quinto's traders have an average holding time per trade of about three to seven minutes. These traders have fast execution platforms and top connectivity. The point is, there are very few traders who make a consistently profitable living trading on a shorter time frame than this. Many upstairs traders do best by stepping out to the 5- and 15-minute time frames (always keeping the longer time frames in mind as well!). If a trader steps out on too long a time frame, he often finds out that he cannot ride out the noise—the inevitable retracements or reactions that will occur in a trend.

Quinto commented on the importance of a professional trader's ability to evolve as electronic trading changes. Traders frequently find one strategy that works for two to three years but are unable to adapt when the game changes. For example, a few years ago, many professional traders were able to trade interest rate market spreads. Traders were making a lucrative living scalping tens and bonds against the cash market as well. This game has now disappeared. One thing remains true in this business: as soon as you find the key to the lock, they change the lock!

Avoid Being Reactive

Here's some advice for traders new to using electronic platforms: Do not stare at the book. It encourages you to be reactive or exit your trades too soon if they are winners. Keep your eyes on the chart and think about why you made the trade in the first place. If the markets are slow, watching the book will encourage you to take mediocre trades. Have you ever known someone who has gone to an auction, gotten caught up in the bidding process, and ended up coming home with something he did not intend to buy? Watching the book too closely has the same effect on traders as going to an auction and getting caught up in the excitement of the moment.

If you stare at the book when you are uncertain in a trade, you are more likely to exit in a reactive manner. Instead, place an order to exit a long trade a few ticks above where the market is trading, while placing a resting stop order just underneath support. You are more likely to exit your trade at a better price on a jiggle up in the noise, and worst-case scenario, the stop takes you out.

If I am looking to enter a long position, I try working a bid first. If the market comes down and trades at my price, but I am not filled, I click the execute button on my platform and my order is executed at the market. If I am looking to exit, in the case of a long trade, I place a resting order to exit. If the price falls short of my level, I hit the execute button, which immediately fills my offer at the market. Each time I enter at the market, it costs me an extra $12.50 in the case of the E-minis. Think of this analogy: the market pays you to provide liquidity (placing bids and offers), but you pay the market when you want it to provide the liquidity.

Most traders underestimate their reflex time. Most traders will have a level at which they know their trade will be wrong. They tell themselves that they will exit their trade when the price gets to that level. However, by the time they place their order, the price has moved beyond their initial mental stop price by a good amount.

It is best to place an initial stop resting in the market, but well outside of the noise (meaning, not so tight that it is likely to get tagged on jiggles). Once a safety net resting stop order is placed, you can tighten the stop as the market moves in your favor or the price action stalls out. You can change the stop price with just one mouse click. You can also take a resting stop order to the market with just one mouse click. You can see how important functionality is in a platform.

The Bells and Whistles You Need

Functionality features that traders need on their execution platforms include the ability to modify orders with one mouse click, to join the bid or offer with one mouse click, to customize their own trade modules, to easily place stop orders, to change the price of a stop order with one mouse click, and to see multiple resting orders simultaneously. Some traders like executing off a ladder, while others like a simple trade module that allows them to join the bid or join the offer. All platforms have developed their specialty niches. Traders should investigate which platforms offer the features they like best, keeping in mind that in addition to functionality and ease of use, reliability is critical. And traders should make sure they do business with a firm that has a 24-hour number where the phone will be answered in two to three rings.

Because most markets now trade 24 hours a day, a market will often test a price high or low that was made in the night session during the U.S. trading day. Just as the S&P E-minis tend to test the Globex high or low, watch the night session highs and lows for bonds, currencies, gold and crude. There is better liquidity in these markets then ever before.

I like to use equitick bars for most of the 24-hour traded markets. This means that each bar on the chart might be composed of between 20 and 500 transactions. This is preferable to a 5-minute bar chart when looking at a market like bonds, which might not have much trading activity around midnight.

Experience Is The Best Teacher

Timing and trade execution skills improve with practice. Traders who are new to the game should always start out trading the smallest size, and learn first to fight for every tick.

Electronic trading has indeed leveled the playing field for upstairs traders. Traders who take advantage of the technology in their own trading can achieve greater profitability. And, as always, how well traders manage their own conduct and emotional states will always have the greatest impact on their trading.

Linda Bradford Raschke has been a full-time, professional trader since 1981. She began as a floor trader and later started LBR Group, a professional money management firm. In addition to running successful programs as a CTA, she has been principal trader for several hedge funds and has run commercial hedging programs. Raschke was recognized in Jack Schwager's book, *The New Market Wizards* (Wiley, 1995), and is well known for her book, *Street Smarts* (M. Gordon Publishing Group, 1996). She is a frequent contributor to *SFO* and other publications. Numerous educational articles are available at her website at www.lbrgroup.com. This article first appeared in *SFO* in April 2006.

TRADING ELECTRONICALLY FROM A TO Z

BY JIM KHAROUF

The combination of electronic access to markets, high-speed Internet connections and computer technology has leveled the playing field for individual traders who want to compete in the markets with the likes of Merrill Lynch or hedge fund giants like John Henry & Co. These days don't fear Goliath. Trading technology has allowed David to mix it up with the guy that could buy and sell the value of his home one thousand times over in a single trade.

David Silverman, a 16-year CME pit trader and author of *Direct Access Futures: A Complete Guide to Trading Electronically*, said today's technology is the great equalizer among market participants and quite a switch from the days when guys in the pits got to see price movements long before anyone else. "For the first time in the history of the markets, you've extracted the inherent edges the system gave to privileged parties on the floor and made it all about trading rather than the edge," says Silverman.

The tools needed to build a trading room can be as simple as a reasonably priced, reliable Pentium computer and a DSL Internet connection. Add a good broker and customer service, some data feeds, useful order entry software, and you're ready to make some trades. What committed professional traders need, however, involves far more than that. Traders and trading system experts say traders need a business plan, trading strategy, and market knowledge that fits them.

Computer Shopping

Traders may as well start with the tool that will take them to the markets, a personal computer. Choices of computers among traders vary widely. Much of that is a reflection of two things—the size of their portfolios and the type of trading they do. For many traders, a Pentium IV processor will do the trick. For others, nothing short of a computer that can pump out nuclear submarine blueprints will do. Andy Reierson, a London-based trader who has traded the FTSE-100 futures contract on the Euronext.liffe futures exchange, said he uses an AMD brand computer with a 1.2 GHZ processor and just one monitor. It's not ideal, he admits, because he's forced to chop his single trading screen into too many smaller windows to keep up with his trades, market prices, analytics and news.

"It's not the top-of-the-line computer, but the processor is perfectly adequate for what I need," Reierson said, adding that he plans to add another monitor soon.

In his Chicago condominium, Ed Spear watches three separate monitors and uses a mid-range Dell with a Pentium IV processor to trade E-mini S&P futures on the Chicago Mercantile Exchange.

"Because of the types of programs you need to run, you need a pretty powerful computer, not an off-the-shelf system you'd buy for $1,200," says Spear, who has been trading since 2002. "The amount of memory in most standard computers really doesn't have the amount of memory you need for multi-tasking. So, one of the first tools you need is a computer that can drive several programs simultaneously."

Jack Hall, a trading equipment expert with Rightway in Duarte, California, says traders should buy a computer with two identical hard drives. One hard drive is used for back-up purposes and storing data, while the other is running the programs for trading. Hall also recommends using four monitors. "Build some redundancy into it, because things do fail," Hall says. "Typically, every system I build has two hard drives in it with System Guardian, which makes an image of your hard drive onto the second hard drive, on whatever schedule you select. And, you can set it so that if your hard drive fails, you can reboot with the other hard drive and you're back up running."

Hall has been custom-building trading workstations for the past six years and creates a complete Pentium IV-based system with a dual hard drive, four monitors with a television tuner for a monitor, and an uninterrupted power supply which will keep a PC running for up to 30 minutes if power is lost. Also, says Hall, "if you're using a computer for trading, for goodness sake, use it just for that. It shouldn't be used by anyone else in the family for computer games, downloads, e-mails; save that for another computer."

If you're serious about putting in the time to trade and, hopefully, profit in the markets, buying an extra hard drive or an additional PC is simply an investment in the tools you need, says Silverman. More than that, buying the best technology enhances your competitiveness in the markets.

"If technology is the level playing field, then what are your edges?" Silverman asks. "Did you set up your technology efficiently? Did you buy the right stuff? Are you maintaining it properly? The truth of the matter is, if someone is willing pay for some speed and technology, that person can be as fast as Deutsche Bank, Morgan Stanley or any institution. But part of getting the edge is knowing what you need, because you probably don't need to be as fast as Deutsche Bank."

Silverman says many traders don't want to become technology experts. In such cases, they can check out a trading arcade that features the best technology available with the best software and fastest Internet connection. Arcades, trading rooms set up for individual traders, have grown in number over the past decade—especially during the equity boom in the late 1990s. Participation in an arcade starts at $1,500 per month. So, why would you want to spend in a month what you could spend in a year on technology? Silverman says it's a matter of getting everything you need, including software, charts, and pencils, not to mention trading tips from pros and better commissions on trades. Trading arcades can also offer top-of-the-line connectivity to the markets, usually with a T1 line which, by itself, costs about $1,000 a month.

Stay-at-home traders can get solid performance out of a high-speed DSL connection. Hall adds that traders should back up their connection with a cheap dial-up Internet service that may come in handy in case the DSL or cable connection fails.

"With a modem on your system, at least you can still be up and trading," says Hall. With all the redundancy talk, Hall may sound like an insurance salesman who has seen the worst, and he has.

"Anyone who has used computers for more than a few years has had a hard drive failure," Hall says. "If they haven't, they've been darned lucky. Back-up tape drives are slow and expensive, and you have to make sure your tapes are there and working. I had two customers in the past three weeks who lost all of their data on a failed hard drive thinking they had a back-up on tape drives. They didn't, and that's no coincidence."

The Right Trading Tools

Finding the right computer to suit your trading style is one thing, but sifting through all the software a trader needs is another. Reierson says he pays for an Internet-based chart and realtime quotes package from RealTick. He first tried FutureSource but wanted a bit more data, such as intraday volatility. On the other hand, with his Real-Tick package, he can only see price data for the markets he pays for, whereas FutureSource provided prices on all exchanges.

Spear uses a complete package offered by his broker. It also includes a charting software package from Q-Charts, and provides the basic analytics he needs to track price trends in the S&P index. "It has the basics such as moving averages and so on," he says. "It has what I need for my level of trading. And I try to focus on just one commodity, so I concentrate on the E-mini S&P. I think by focusing on one thing, you can become better at it."

Other traders recommend Equis' Metastock software for its robust analytics package.

Reierson and Spear both use basic market news channels to keep abreast of the latest developments. Reierson has his television set to Bloomberg, and Spear uses CNBC. Other traders would rather not have the constant yanging of the business news as they consider most of it noise and nonsense, rather than an essential element to their trading. At best, they'd use it for background noise.

Finding the software tools that fit your trading needs can be the most difficult task for traders. For one thing, it's almost impossible to determine the quality of a charting or technical trading program until you try it out for some time.

And, there are dozens of can't miss technical trading systems trying to lure traders. But finding the Holy Grail of trading systems is usually a futile search. That doesn't stop new guaranteed millionaire trading systems from being rolled out each month. But experienced traders advise not to waste your money.

"I don't think the people producing these trading systems for the most part want to produce garbage," Silverman says. "Most are honorable people who have worked really hard on these things. But the reason they are of little value is, if they were really great trading systems then everyone would trade them. I just don't think you're going to get a great trading system for $99 or $999. People don't sell the ones that work." The problem, he says, is that these packages are designed and built during a certain market timeframe that may no longer be applicable.

"It's not a black box," Silverman says. "When you buy a model, you're getting a model that is created until X period in time. Well, time keeps going, and models don't work in perpetuity, if they work at all."

Robert Deel, CEO of Tradingschool.com and author of *The Strategic Electronic Day Trader*, agrees that trading systems are usually a waste of time and money. "What people think they need but don't is trading systems," Deel says. "The fact is that most trading systems don't work and are only as good as the trader trading it. It's essentially laziness. People want to believe there is a magic system out there and they are going to push a button and get an answer. Nothing can be further from the truth."

Another aspect of finding the right trading tools is working closely with a broker.

Spear says he frequently contacts his broker for advice on different trades. He's available through e-mail, but doesn't mind a phone call as well. "I don't think I can realistically trade without the availability of a broker when I need him," Spear says. "One thing I found when looking around for a broker, whether it's a discount or full-service broker, is that the commissions are about the same. So you may as well look for a full-service broker."

Others would disagree and are more concerned with affiliating with a discount firm that has a great online system, where they have a broker at hand when and if they need him or her. Otherwise they just want direct access to the exchange on which they are trading and plenty of fast and responsive customer service should something go wrong electronically or if they just need to know how to maneuver the system.

Jim Spencer, who has been trading the market for 43 years, says a broker with access to all the major markets is important. While electronic trading efficiency is relatively even from one broker to another, Spencer feels more comfortable with a broker with a direct link to the trading floor or electronic trading platform. "Find a good mid-range broker who is not the biggest but is a member of the exchange," says Spencer, who runs J.M. Spencer & Co. in Harbor Springs, Mich.

The Business of Trading

For most traders, the move from part-time investor to active trader is a graduation of sorts, from company man to entrepreneur. Traders should approach the move as if it's a business—because it is. Robert Green, a certified public accountant and CEO of Greentradertax. com which produces trading account software, says traders should be aware of all the tax advantages and pitfalls of trading professionally. One of the first moves is to establish a home business. Traders get the benefit of deductions from the square footage of their actual office space. And, being an active trading business, as opposed to a casual investor, Green says such traders also can receive further advantageous tax benefits.

"A home office can be a great tax deduction," he says. "If you take the care to qualify for the home office deduction, it can put a lot of savings in your pocket and really significantly reduce the cost of starting up a trading business."

Green estimates that traders can save anywhere from $5,000 to $15,000 in home office tax deductions. In addition, active traders established as a business can also write off 100 percent of fixed assets such as that hot new computer with the dual hard drives and back-up data storage under a tax code called 179 depreciation. With the 179 depreciation, individuals can write off approximately $100,000 worth of assets per year, which also includes desks, chairs and other trading equipment. There are a variety of caveats, twists and turns to creating a home-based trading business from a tax standpoint, so it is important to check with an accountant that specializes in them.

Tracking your trades is a matter of debate among traders. Green developed his own software that automatically files every trade so accountants can easily decipher what can and cannot be deducted.

Such software also provides detailed trade information that many broker trade account reports do not. Spear, on the other hand, says his broker provides him with a report daily of all the trades he's made. And, he can request past reports from his broker as he needs. Other traders say Microsoft Money and Quicken personal bookkeeping software is adequate.

Silverman is one of several traders interviewed who strongly advocates drawing up a comprehensive plan to manage a one-man trading company. Knowing the tax benefits and how to set up a company is part of it. Nailing down your trading strategy from a risk management standpoint is another essential aspect.

"Before you click the mouse for the first time, you really need a business plan for how you are going to do this," Silverman says. "I'm not referring to your trading methodology. Those are a dime a dozen. More importantly is, how am I going manage my risk in employing this methodology? Successful traders always understand that you cannot overextend yourself."

Your First Clicks

Volumes have been written about trading methodology and trading strategies that work on this market move or on that contract. Ask any trader who has tried to beat the odds for a long time, and he or she will tell you to find a system or method that works for you and helps you maintain discipline. Trading is enormously challenging, and it's often overwhelming. Doubts creep in when things don't go your way. Pulling the trigger on a trade becomes frustrating when your head and trade signal say go, but your heart is still hurting from the last trade that went south. Reierson says the biggest challenge he's faced during his first seven months of trading was trying to filter the flow of information from the multitude of sources pouring in.

"Early on, I overloaded myself by trying to read everything and chase down everything," Reierson says. "You can get bogged down in too many conflicting views, and that's also why I try to steer clear of chat rooms."

Chat rooms indeed. Not a single trader interviewed had a good thing to say about trading chat rooms. The simple reason is that people in such chat rooms aren't doing what they are supposed to do, which is trading. Long-time traders like Deel, Silverman and Spencer say such cyber places are a waste of time and usually filled with people intentionally or unintentionally passing along misinformation.

The key to staying in the game and winning, veteran traders say, is to keep the odds in your favor. And how do you do that? Silverman says it's a matter of identifying the trades that have a solid risk/reward ratio. In other words, rolling the dice on a trade that could make or break you will more often than not break you and your trading account.

"In an electronic environment, it's important for people, as they move up the learning curve, to get as many trades as they can under their belt," Silverman says. "The way to do that is to trade a four-to-one potential risk/reward ratio, not one-to-four. You're only going to get better as you make more trades."

Traders also should know how the gears of the world's financial and commodities markets turn, Spencer says. By learning how currencies interact with bonds, stocks and physical commodities, traders can identify true trends that will make money. Spencer is the type of trader who will watch the Brazilian real, that country's soybean production and its debt levels with the World Bank. Why? Each can create an event that will move bond markets, world currencies or grain prices—perhaps simultaneously. Such nuances, set in a larger macro-economic picture, will help identify a long-term trend early in the market. To spot a long-term trend, Spencer advises getting a chart as far back as possible.

"Get the longest-term chart you can get your hands on," Spencer says. "Look at charts that go back to the South Seas Trading Company, the bubbles, cotton going to $100 during the Civil War blockade. Most people look at things too short term. A long-term trend will dominate a short-term trend."

Spencer calls it "plain Jane money management."

"Traders don't need a bunch of people whispering in their ear about what's going to happen," Spencer says. "If it's not in the charts and it's not in the fundamental data, it's not there."

Inner Battle

Trading can be an extremely rewarding job. But, for many, it can also be a tough and lonely existence. Reierson says trading by himself has taken time to get used to, especially when the losing trades outnumber the winners.

"It's a lot of hard work," Reierson admits. "I've worked harder on this than on anything I've ever done in life. It's a real test of your nerves. It's like putting your psyche through an autopsy." That thought aside, Reierson says he's happy to be trading from home and believes he is learning the keys to success through winning and losing trades.

Traders often cite a street fighter's determination, coupled with a sharply honed mind as keys to a profitable career. Silverman recalls a trader who sat at his trading desk all day without leaving for lunch or even a bathroom break. "I wouldn't tell traders not to take a bathroom break or to go for a walk," he says. "But he'd be ready to eat the glass on his monitor. That's why he was good."

Deel tells his students that he tries to meet with other traders periodically to talk about new ideas and trends. He speaks and attends various trade shows to discuss his ideas, which helps him escape from his trading office enough. But on a day-to-day basis, trading is simply a tough job.

"How do you get around the loneliness?" Deel says. "You can't."

Jim Kharouf is a financial reporter with 16 years experience. He is based in Chicago and has covered stock, options and futures markets worldwide. A version of this article first appeared in *SFO* in May 2003.

TAMING THE TECHNICAL BEAST: How to Deal Proactively with Computer-Age Challenges

BY JOHN CARTER

Trading in and of itself can be one of the most stressful occupations on the planet. One day's worth of market activity can determine whether a trader's kids are going to study at Oxford all expenses paid or are stuck at the local community college delivering pizza to pay for their books.

Traders who are stuck behind the technology curve are at a disadvantage. From outdated software to spyware getting dumped onto the user's computer, a trader who chooses technological ignorance is setting himself up for disaster. Having a trade go wrong because of technological issues is inexcusable for the serious trader who is trying to make a living at this profession.

Although it's not as exciting as throwing out an order for a hundred lot, the trader who wants to maintain a competitive edge in this business must first be aware of the technological hazards facing him in today's world. In this electronic age, the PC is the trader's most important trading tool, but he can't take its powers for granted. Instead, he needs to be aware of the hurdles he faces and take a proactive approach to attack these issues head on.

That said, there are three main technological problems that can arise for the trader:

1. **Computer Invaders.** Being connected to the Internet, the trader's computer can be abused without his knowledge. This causes most malfunctions on computers today, and he must be aware of how to first remove the crud and then block it so it won't happen again.
2. **Process Cloggers.** Steps need to be taken to maximize computer effectiveness and prevent crashing.
3. **General Technology Problems.** What to do when the technology around the trader fails to deliver…because it will.

Ignoring these preventable issues is like trading without a stop loss. Take the time to take care of this right now, and get on the path to smooth trading.

Get Rid of the Crud

A trader can have the best software available, but if his computer isn't properly cared for, protected and maintained, the greatest trading software in the world is worthless. Each day, the trader's computer is invaded with hidden crud, and it is truly shocking how dangerous some of this stuff is to the trader's PC. For the trader who is serious about making this business a full-time job, neglecting these next steps is akin to McDonald's failing to wipe down their counters or clean their restrooms.

The biggest technical challenge facing traders today is one of which most are completely unaware: staying spyware free. This is one of the most important steps to keeping a PC running smoothly and safely. Why, you ask? Simply, spyware will crash the trader's computer, ruin his Internet connection and make Internet surfing unsafe. Spyware is not a cookie, which we'll discuss shortly in more detail. In a nutshell, spyware is software that companies place on the user's PC without their permission. (Sometimes, though, it is unknowingly with the user's permission, if the user doesn't read the fine print in the agreement he accepts prior to downloading a software program.) Spyware software takes over the trader's Internet browser, collects data on his surfing habits, generates pop-up ads when the trader visits certain websites and, generally, slows down his or her computer. In addition, much spyware is poorly written and can cause incompatibility issues, corrupt important system functions, and threaten the stability of the trader's computer. Those who want to assure that their computers run smoothly, i.e., keep them from freezing up and crashing, must get all spyware off their computers…and then prevent it from coming back.

The first time I learned how to do a search for this malicious software, I found more than fifty spyware programs on my computer. After they were removed, my computer operated faster and stopped freezing up on me. This stuff is downloaded behind the scenes, so it is invisible to the computer user. Incidentally, when I did this, I was certain I didn't have any spyware on my computer. Needless to say, I was wrong.

Yes, You Can Be James Bond

The two best applications for removing spyware are SpyBot Search & Destroy and Ad Aware. They are both dowloadable and free, so there is no reason not to use them regularly. It is important that the trader uses both of these applications, because one finds what the other misses and vice versa. SpywareBlaster is another highly recommended application for spyware prevention. This application sets certain registry entries that prevent spyware from ever installing. It does not run in the background using any resources; the user just sets it and forgets it.

Once these three must-have applications are installed, a trader then needs to update them and keep them current by checking for updates weekly. Similar to antivirus software, the trader needs to be protected on a continuous basis.

To update SpyBot, just open the application from the start menu (use the advanced mode option) and select "search for updates." It then will show what updates are available for download. Always install all the updates. Another SpyBot feature is called "immunize." Select this icon and under "permanent Internet Explorer immunity" select "immunize." This works in the same way as SpywareBlaster in blocking new spyware. It also gives the trader the option of locking the trader hosts file against hijackers, a feature I highly recommend using. To update Ad Aware, just open it and select "check for updates now." SpywareBlaster is pretty much the same. Open it, and select "check for updates." Once this is updated, click "select all" and then "protect against checked items" so these updates take effect. Anything these applications find is spyware and should be removed.

Another device companies use to track information on the trader's PC is called a cookie. This is a small text file that can be good or bad. It's good for visiting a favorite website, such as amazon.com. With a cookie installed, Amazon will remember the user, so he doesn't have to always log in each time he visits the site. However, there also are bad cookies that track site usage, coordinate pop-up ads and, generally, invade the trader's privacy. The best thing to do is to start from scratch and delete all of the cookies on the computer. To do this, go to start, settings, control panel and, then, Internet options. Under temporary Internet files, there is a button that says, "delete cookies." Click this. After they are deleted, go to privacy, advanced. Once here, check the box titled "override automatic cookie handling." Below that I check "prompt" for first-party cookies and "block" for third-party cookies. In this way, when the trader goes to Amazon, a message pops up asking if he wants to accept the cookie. I say yes because it's a site I visit often. Any third-party cookies will automatically be blocked. This prevents pop-up ads and keeps the trader's computer running in top form. If I am asked to accept a cookie from a site I rarely visit, I will say no, and the cookie will not be planted on my computer.

Maximizing System Resources

There are three things a trader should do on a weekly basis to ensure that his computer is running at maximum efficiency. The first two of these involve deleting unnecessary files on the computer. First, identify any unnecessary files, right-click on the icon and choose "delete." Every file the computer user deletes is not really deleted—it is moved to the recycle bin. To really get it off the computer and free up memory, the trader needs to empty the recycle bin as well.

To do this, go to the recycle bin, an icon located on the desktop of the PC. Right click, select "empty recycle bin," and delete the files.

The second place memory is gobbled up is in what is called the cache. This catches all the websites the trader visits to more quickly download the site next time it is visited. With the advent of broadband, this is an unnecessary feature. To clean the cache, go to start, settings, control panel and, then, Internet options. Under temporary Internet files, click "delete files." A pop-up box will appear and ask if the user wants to delete all offline content. This is important to do, so the trader should click the box to indicate yes. Hit "OK" and sit back. If the computer user has never done this, it can take a few minutes to delete all of the garbage on the computer. The serious trader should do this at least once a week.

Finally, once these two things are completed, the serious trader will want to defrag his or her hard drive. Disk fragmentation slows down the computer and often is the cause of a variety of other problems such as hangs, crashes, and errors. Fragmentation accumulates rapidly through normal computer use, and program access time continues to increase, problems worsen and the productive life of a computer will shorten by years. Defragging the hard drive puts all of the pieces back together again, making the computer run much more efficiently. Traders should do this weekly, if not daily. Go to start, programs, accessories, system tools, disk defragmenter. Make sure the hard drive is highlighted (usually this is drive C) and click "defragment." This can take 20-30 minutes if this has never been done before. There also is a program called Diskeeper that eliminates fragmentation automatically, so it is never an issue.

Once a trader's computer is in top working form, technical problems can still occur. In my experience, there are four main problems for which all traders should be prepared:

1. Blackouts or brownouts that cut off all electricity
2. Cable or DSL goes down
3. Difficulty in contacting a broker
4. Data feed/trading platform goes down

These are problems that can happen at any time. Serious traders should prepare themselves for all of these eventualities.

A blackout or a brownout can occur at any time. I've personally experienced half a dozen of these over the last two years for a variety of reasons. They can be caused by weather, a power grid failure, or a car accident involving a telephone pole. They seemingly can happen out of nowhere, and the trader suddenly will find himself without power, losing the ability to see the market and execute trades. To combat this situation, here's what needs to be in place to dull the pain of this type of event:

1. **Battery backups on the computer.** These are available at any major office supply shop. In the event of a loss of electricity, a backup gives the trader about 30 minutes of power, which is plenty of time to close out positions or reset parameters in case the power is going to be down for a long time. This also gives the trader time to manually shut down his computer, which is much safer than having it go out suddenly due to a power loss.
2. **Non-cordless phone.** These are the old-fashioned phones that have a cord attached to the handset. When the electricity goes out, so does the cordless phone. With the old fashioned corded phones, a trader will still be able to make a phone call to a broker. These phones can be purchased for less than $30. Obviously, a cell phone would work in this situation—but those things run out of juice at the worst possible moments.
3. **Cable or DSL can go out even when the electricity is still on.** This usually happens at the absolute worst time, so the astute trader will want to be prepared. The best way to combat this is to have a fully charged laptop connected to a phone line. This way the trader has Internet connectivity if the DSL or cable goes down, and the trader also will have a backup in case the electricity goes out. Having a laptop that is fully charged and ready to go attached to a phone line can save several hours of valuable time.

Use IM

Another technological trend in the industry is for brokers to let computers do all of the work. Although this provides for efficiencies and cuts costs, the bottom line is that if I have a problem, I better be able to get hold of my broker right away. If I call my broker and can't get hold of him, I start foaming at the mouth—a signal that it is time for me to switch brokers. If I want to be on hold, I will call my credit card company, not my broker.

My suggestion here is to take advantage of technology and get the broker hooked up on an instant messaging program such as Yahoo or MSN. This is an incredibly efficient way to stay in touch throughout the day. If my data feed goes down, I can IM (instant message) my broker for a quote. The expectation for my broker is that I can contact him or her via phone or instant message right away. If the broker is not available, I have the number and instant message as a back up. In trading, there is no excuse not to be able to get a live person to help out with an order or question right away. Why else would we pay all of those commissions?

If the trader's data feed goes down, much of what already has been discussed will help. Being able to contact a broker to get a quote or place a trade in this situation is imperative. Yahoo Finance also is a great site to get free quotes on stocks, options and futures.

There are other areas of the trader's computer of which to be aware, including how to block pop-up ads, the best and easiest ways to back up the trader's hard drives, the best software for blocking viruses and blocking hackers, fending off junk mail, battery backups and so forth.

Trading successfully requires an edge. The trader who chooses to remain ignorant about what is really going on with his personal computer or is outta luck when the power goes out, is leaving himself at a decided disadvantage against those traders who are prepared. By staying up to date on the technological front, the trader has an advantage over those who don't. And, having an advantage over others is one of the main things that will make the trader a winner in this business.

John F. Carter grew up the son of a Morgan Stanley stockbroker and was introduced to trading as a sophomore in high school. He has been actively trading for the past 19 years. Carter studied international finance at the University of Cambridge in England before graduating from the University of Texas at Austin. He has been a full time trader since 1996. In 1999, he launched tradethemarkets.com to post his trading ideas for the futures, equities and options markets. In 2005 he launched www.razorforex.com to focus on the forex markets. Today Carter has a following of over 10,000 people. He's a Commodity Trading Advisor with Razor Trading, manages a futures and a forex fund, and recent author of *Mastering the Trade*, released in December, 2005. To keep his sanity, Carter relies on physical activity after the close to deal with the financial swings he and his subscribers encounter. He clears his head running, water skiing, and practicing Tae Kwon Do. This article first appeared in *SFO* in May 2004.

HOW MY WORST TRADE EVER TURNED ME INTO A BETTER TRADER

BY JOHN CARTER

Dear Diary: Why is it that individual traders routinely get the shaft?

This is a question I wrote in my trading journal nearly fifteen years ago. Although a diary is typically associated with a teenage girl who has just discovered her true love in third-period French, it is actually an important tool of self-discovery for the trader. This is especially important for individual traders.

Like hungry cats turned loose on a rat farm, individual traders, unlike fund managers, are unsupervised and have the freedom to act unchecked in any way that they choose. Unfortunately, this kind of freedom reinforces bad habits. The biggest mistake these traders make is a common, yet fatal affliction that plagues nearly all traders: trading to make money. Trading to make money? Isn't that what we as traders are supposed to be doing? You would think so. However, look at it this way; traders certainly place their orders with the idea of making money. But what are most traders doing? They are losing some serious cash. So if trading to make money doesn't work, what perspective should we be trading from? What mental shift is required to stop us from nibbling like sparrows and defecating like elephants?

The Set-Up

It is with these thoughts in mind that I recall my worst trade ever— the trade that beat me upside the head with a two-by-four, snapping me awake to the realities of trading. It was this trade that made me realize that I had to adjust my mental perspective so I could do this for a living. In the early 90s my wife and I were recent transplants to Minnesota. We moved there from Austin, Texas, in September. To say that we were unprepared for the coming brutal winter is like saying China seems to have a slight appetite for copper and cement. Of course we should have known we were in trouble when we saw a sign at Target advertising a sale on fleece underwear. Ah, hindsight.

We started that winter in an apartment where we had to park our cars outside. By the time February rolled around it took us about thirty minutes to get psyched up enough to venture outside in weather sporting wind chills of 70 degrees below zero. And that was just to find out whether our cars would start—most of the time they did not. About the time we had exhausted the rental supply at Blockbuster, we decided it was time to take action. We needed a house with a garage— and we needed it now. We found one quickly and put in an offer at full price. It was accepted just as quickly and our dream of thawing out began to unfold before us.

A Stroke of Genius?

At the time I had been trading for a few years part-time and had built up a trading account to just over $150,000 by trading options. My plan was to take $30,000 out of the account to use as a down payment on the house. As the closing date approached, I was struck with a brilliant idea. Why not just make a few extra trades and create the $30,000 needed for the down payment out of trading profits? That way I could keep my $150,000 trading account intact! Truly a stroke of genius.

I put on the coffee and reviewed my charts for hours that night. I looked at multiple time frames and countless indicators. The hours of study drew me to the same conclusion time and time again—the major stock market averages were approaching solid resistance levels. I therefore made the one deduction that was abundantly clear to me: to buy OEX puts aggressively the next trading day.

The next morning, primed and ready to go, I placed my order and then went to my day job. I was able to get quotes at the office, so I would periodically check to see where the markets were trading and whether or not I had been filled. Around lunch, the markets had drifted up to resistance and I was filled for 100 OEX puts at $8.00, or $80,000. The markets consolidated for a while and edged up just a little higher, driving down the price of the puts to $7.00. Unable to resist this bargain, I went ahead and bought another 100 puts, putting my entire account into this one trade. I calculated that a move of just two points in the option price would get me my house money. Needless to say, Einstein would be impressed.

The next day the markets did an odd thing. They opened higher. Even more unusual, they continue to move higher through mid-morning and into lunch. And strangest of all, the markets closed at their dead highs on the day. I was a bit perplexed, but at the same time I had confidence that the trade would work out. After all, I just needed to make the $30,000 and I would be done. If the market went against me a little, then it just meant that it would take a few more days than I expected for the trade to work out.

The Pain of Loss

At this point, we all know that this story will not have a Hollywood ending, so let's cut to the epilogue. The markets screamed higher for the next four trading days in a row. Unable to take the pain any longer, I finally called my broker and begged him to close me out. I got an unimposing 75 cents for my puts, leaving me with $15,000. In just four days I had caused $135,000 to vanish into thin air. It took a few moments for this to sink in. I had just blown out my trading account. Worse, I wasn't going to have enough money to meet the down payment on the house. I tried to console myself with thoughts like, "At least I'm not part of the first landing wave on Omaha Beach." Or, "At least I'm only 22 and have the rest of my life ahead of me." It didn't work. Omaha Beach actually sounded more appealing. Of course, I did what any rational person would do in this situation—I got cash advances on my credit cards so I could buy the house, and I sure as hell never said a word to my darling wife. (I'm obviously playing the odds here that she won't read this.) I didn't trade again for six months. Let's fast-forward to today.

A Different Time

I'm looking at the markets this morning to scc how everything is setting up. It's one of those interesting trading days as the Federal Reserve's FOMC announcement is at 1:15 p.m. (CST), just three hours away. I know

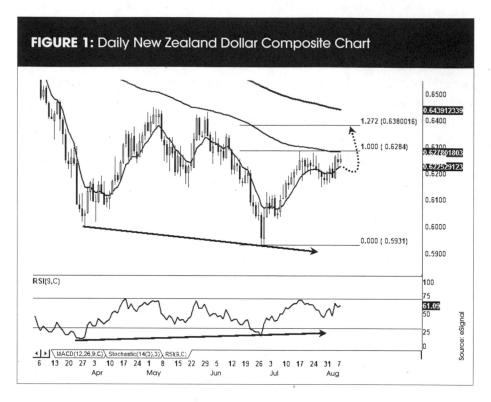

FIGURE 1: Daily New Zealand Dollar Composite Chart

Source: eSignal

most of the markets will be quiet up until that time. The night before I viewed my daily charts in various markets. I generally look at about thirty charts each evening: the stock index futures, metals, energies, grains and currencies. There were a few things that stood out to me the night before. First, the currency pair New Zealand/U.S. dollar (NZD/USD) is trading just under its 100-period exponential moving average (EMA). It's tested this level four times now, and this time I'm looking for a break out up and through that 100-EMA. The main reason for this has to do with a bullish divergence in the 14-period RSI (see *Figure 1*).

Before I went to bed I placed a bid just above the 8-period EMA (about 15 pips) at 0.6238. I placed a stop at 0.6196, which is mostly a money management-related stop. My target is the 1.272-percent extension of this move higher, which is 0.6380. I always like to get in front of my targets, so I place an order to sell at 10 pips below at 0.6370.

Going Through The Ropes

I wake up to find that I'm filled, and it's currently trading at 0.6254, up about 16 pips from my entry. I'm aware that the FOMC meeting is to-

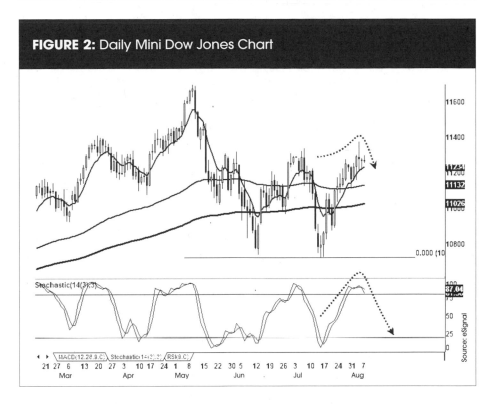

FIGURE 2: Daily Mini Dow Jones Chart

day so the markets could get very volatile. I move up my stop to 0.6222 and leave my target. Although I don't trade heavily during FOMC day, I don't mind having a few smaller positions on as long as the chart setup is clear. I find that many times prices will move up to and pause at a logical technical level on a chart just before a major economic announcement, and then the news will cause the chart to continue along its technical course.

The next chart that caught my attention in my nightly review was a daily chart of the CBOT's mini-sized Dow contract (YM). In looking at the chart (see *Figure 2*), I can see a very clear triple test of the 11,330 area. Last Friday, the employment numbers came out softer than expected, and the markets exploded higher on the anticipation of a pause in the interest rate cycle. However, that strength was short lived, and the markets sold off hard later in the day. Now we are hovering right under that key 11,330 level. The slow stochastic is rolling over, and it's looking like a sell-off is setting up.

For the YM trade I don't place an overnight order as I did with NZD/USD. I want to wait until the next morning to see where the market opens and use the pivot levels to get into a short trade. For this I will wait until after the cash market opens at 9:30 a.m. (CST). Once the market opens, I go short on an early rally to the daily resistance one (R1) pivot level at 11,295. I place a stop at 11,315, which is my standard 20-point stop when using pivots. However, in this case I actually want to hold through the FOMC announcement, so I don't place a target. Because of the chart set-up I viewed the night before, I like the prospects of a downside move after the rate hike. I might be right. I might be wrong. Like pulling the handle on a slot machine, I acknowledge that I don't know what the market is going to do next. My stops are in and there is nothing to do but wait.

The Waiting Game

It's now 1:11 p.m. (CST) and the announcement is coming in four minutes. Both positions are currently moving against me. The YM is rallying into the number release—it's up about 20 points here in the last few minutes, up to 11,275. NZD/USD is falling and is down nearly 20 pips in the last ten minutes.

On a side note, I have been on a water kick, drinking 100 ounces of water each day with no caffeine. No coffee, tea, sodas, etc. I've been doing this for about three weeks now. It was tough to do initially and I felt tired frequently, but for the last week I have felt a lot more consistently energetic and I sleep better. I say this because I'm getting up from my desk just before the number is released to pee.

Okay, I'm back. The rates were left unchanged. After 17 consecutive rate hikes the Fed has finally decided to step back and see what exactly it is they have done to the economy. In looking at the charts, NZD/USD is rallying hard as the dollar collapses, and I'm now up over 50 pips on the position. The YM, however, is also rallying. Before the announcement I was up about 20 points, and now we are at 11,305 and I'm down 10 points. My stop is still in place at 11,315. There is nothing to do here but wait.

A few minutes have gone by and the markets are now reversing. The dollar was collapsing and now it is firming and back to its highs of the day. NZD/USD is off now, trading at .6270, still decently higher from my entry. The YM is collapsing and is now down over 80 points. Ticks are reaching -1,000 levels now, which is an extreme reading, so it's time to cover. I get out at 11,204 for +101 points. (This is something I always do on my day trades. If I'm long and I get a +1,000 tick reading, then I use that as an exit signal, and vice versa.) The dollar continues to strengthen; however NZD/USD is holding up pretty well. Neither my target nor my stop has been hit, so there isn't much to do now with this trade except sit on it. If it can close higher by the end of the New York session, I will raise my stop to breakeven on the trade. Unlike the stock indexes, there aren't any internal readings I can use in the forex markets, such as ticks, to let me know of any good spots to exit a trade. For the YM, it's consolidating near its lows but there isn't anything I want to do with it here. Once the FOMC announcement hits, it generally takes about thirty minutes for the markets to calm down as traders in various states of panic wind down the trades that they made instinct. I'm calling it a day.

A little later in the day NZD/USD sells off and come down to exactly my stop. I get stopped out for -16 pips. It, of course, then goes on to rally over 100 pips. But since I'm trading from the perspective that I have no clue what is going to happen next, I simply move on to the next trade.

Keeping the Cash

Okay, back to the original question: If we aren't doing this to make money, what are we supposed to being doing this for? After my blow-up trade I didn't do any trades for six months. I spent time with other traders to figure out what screw was loose in my head that would allow me to get myself into the situation that I did. I knew I could make money in the markets, but keeping it seemed to be a problem—and keeping it is certainly a key issue for anyone hoping to do this for a living.

The net result was that I realized I had to change my perspective on what it meant to be a trader. I had already found that trading to make money was just courting disaster, as it automatically jump-started in me all of the bad habits losing traders have. Even if my OEX put option trade had worked out, it would have only been a matter of time before I had a blow up. What finally sank in was that when I focused on the setups and not the money, I actually made money. But when I focused on the money and not the setups, money screamed running from my account. So my change in perspective was this: instead of trading to make money, I was now trading to acquire trading skills. This perspective shift automatically kicked in the habits that most winning traders share: Letting profits run. Looking at trading as a series of trades, instead of placing too much emphasis on each individual trade. Cutting losers off at the knees. Realizing you never know what the market is going to do next, so to position size and use stops accordingly. We've all heard these rules before. We know about them. But if we are trading from the wrong perspective, we will automatically override them and will only realize it after the trade is over.

So in closing, dear diary, I thank you for being there so I could record my state of mind during my disaster trade. Had it not been for you, I would have undoubtedly been plagued with additional disasters, and my relief would have been sought not in a book on trading psychology, but a bottle of Jack Daniels. Without you, I would never have learned to shift my perspective so I could do this for a living.

John F. Carter grew up the son of a Morgan Stanley stockbroker and was introduced to trading as a sophomore in high school. He has been actively trading for the past 19 years. Carter studied international finance at the University of Cambridge in England before graduating from the University of Texas at Austin. He has been a full time trader since 1996. In 1999, he launched tradethemarkets.com to post his trading ideas for the futures, equities and options markets. In 2005 he launched www.razorforex.com to focus on the forex markets. Today Carter has a following of over 10,000 people. He's a Commodity Trading Advisor with Razor Trading, manages a futures and a forex fund, and recent author of *Mastering the Trade*, released in December, 2005. To keep his sanity, Carter relies on physical activity after the close to deal with the financial swings he and his subscribers encounter. He clears his head running, water skiing, and practicing Tae Kwon Do. This article first appeared in *SFO* in October 2006.

SECTION TWO
Evaluating Market Opportunities

There is an endless supply of trading advice out there. The key for the savvy investor is separating the wheat from the chaff. We have assembled a few kernels of trading wisdom from top traders: William O'Neil, founder and chairman of Investor's Business Daily, lets you in on his personal strategy for picking winning stocks. Toni Turner writes about how understanding the relationship between volume and price movement can help you predict future price action. And Jon Najarian reminds us that we can't count our chickens 'til we've closed out of a trade.

Movement in price is based simply on the interaction of supply, demand, and the human behavior quotient. Opportunity arises when this equation is out of balance. Whether trading the S&P, or buying a house, a car or a Michael Jordan rookie card, how we make money buying and selling never changes. There are myriad ways to interpret traditional fundamentals or technical chart patterns to discern signals to get in or out of a trade. Most important, however, is to learn how to use these tools to identify patterns that tell the story of supply and demand.

In this section we'll learn how to identify patterns by reading floor-trading emotions into candlestick charts. We'll learn how recurring fundamental patterns like seasons can apply to stocks and bonds, using the federal fiscal calendar, the real estate calendar and even the school year.

And whether you're a technical analysis proponent or just starting to explore it, there are a few concepts that can enhance the work you're already doing to make your picks. Volume can be a critical tool, as one of the key technical indicators unrelated to price movement. We'll also explore the competing theories of fundamentals and technical analysis—or are they really mutually exclusive?

FACE UP TO RISK: Create a Plan To Avoid Decisive Losses

BY JOHN YACKLEY

Before putting together a plan to manage risk—something that seems like it should be a slam-dunk—let's make one thing clear. It is not optional to manage risk; it is essential and not to be ignored. Certainly every trader goes through periods during which every trade seems to be a winner. However, in the same way that a basketball player who is in the zone will eventually miss a shot, things at some point will not go the trader's way. That's when he or she needs a detailed plan to manage risk.

What Is Risk?

Risk is the quantifiable likelihood of loss or less-than-expected return. Put more simply, risk is the chance that something is going to go wrong. Hardly any trader is inexperienced enough not to acknowledge risk, but many traders stop there or simply say things like "I'm going to risk half of the account," or "Honey, when the margin department tells me that I don't have enough money left...that's when I'll stop trading."

Needless to say, neither is a very sophisticated approach to managing risk. A trader owes it to him or herself to put together a much more detailed plan. Before discussing different ways to measure and manage risks in a trading account, let's focus on mitigating risks that emerge from the specific market being traded.

- **The level of liquidity in the market(s) being traded** (especially when trading options, as each individual strike price in an options market can be very illiquid);
- **The present and past volatility of the markets being traded**;
- **The correlation between given markets if the trader is trading more than one**;
- **The underlying value of what is being traded.** In effect, a trader should know what he is actually speculating on, but too few traders do. Even the purely technical trader should reflect on the magnitude of the contract that he is buying and selling. If the S&P 500 is at 1150, and even if you're just a one-lot E-mini S&P trader, you effectively are long or short $57,500 worth of stock with every click of the mouse. Or did you know that if you trade crude oil, you effectively own or owe 42,000 gallons of oil for every one-lot you trade?
- **Potential events that could lead to big moves in the market.** If you're a stock trader, you had better know when the monthly unemployment report is being released. If you trade coffee, you should know what's happening with the weather in Brazil. A technical trader might not want to base all trading decisions on this kind of fundamental information, but ignoring it completely can make all the hard work done analyzing a chart worthless.

What's the Plan?

Once a trader has a general grasp of the markets he is trading and the event- and liquidity-related risks specific to that market, it's time to focus on ways to avoid errors and measure risks specific to the way he or she trades. Every trader will take one or more of the following things, give each a different degree of emphasis, perhaps supplement them with their other risk controls, and finally, create an approach to risk management. There are as many approaches to risk management as there are traders—no two traders will approach risk in the exact same way. But again, the one thing that all successful traders have in common is that they do have a plan that incorporates actual measurements of risk. Otherwise, a trader is ignoring the quantifiable part of the definition of risk. Risk is not some boogey man that stalks only the unlucky; it lurks over the shoulder of every trader, and only those who measure or quantify it better understand it and can deal with it.

Remember what Peter Drucker, the renowned business management philosopher, said: "What you cannot measure, you cannot manage."

A trader should start by staring the most important issue square in the eye—what dollar amount lost would constitute a decisive loss. A decisive financial loss does not come when the trader's net worth hits zero or the house is lost to the bank; it comes much, much sooner. It's the point at which the money lost in the markets begins to affect the trader's desired quality of life. If you enjoy trading, it then follows that avoiding the decisive loss should be the overriding and central goal of your risk-management strategy. All of the other risk-management tools discussed in the next several paragraphs should serve to meet this overriding goal.

Avoid Trading Errors

This one is a no-brainer, so let's start with it. It sounds simple, but a trader must take all precautions necessary to avoid errors. Read what you see on your computer screen out loud before sending it off to the exchange. If trading over the phone, write down the order before calling it in, and don't simply use a piece of scrap paper; it's much too casual a way to record something so important. Do whatever if takes to avoid errors, no matter how tedious the procedures may seem. One error, especially when you don't catch it right away, can easily wipe out a whole month's worth of profits.

Always Know Your Position in the Market

A trader should constantly be aware of his open positions. This starts with a line-item review of the previous trading session's statement. How can you know where you're going if you don't know for sure where you are? And not a single active trader should be getting their statements via regular mail. Active traders must get their statements via e-mail or fax to be able to reconcile the previous session's trades before the next day begins. Snail mail just won't cut it.

As you trade throughout the day, keep a tabulation of your trades. Many online platforms do this for you, but if you trade over the phone, have pencil and paper at hand to write down all pertinent facts relating to an order—how many lots, what commodity, what month and the corresponding ticket number related to each order.

Finally, if your firm offers you a chance to check out over the phone at night, do it! Most firms offer traders the opportunity to call up after the last market closes to see what trades the firm has placed in their account. This might seem like overkill, especially if you carefully reconcile your statement in the morning, but it will help you identify any problems up to sixteen hours earlier than you will if you rely solely on the statement the firm e-mails or faxes you at night.

Fixed-Dollar or Fixed-Percentage Loss Rules

One simple rule to manage risk is to establish a maximum amount of money or a percentage of an account's value that you are willing to lose per trade or per time interval, i.e., per day, week or month. I, for example, use a fixed maximum percentage loss per month in one of my CTA's two trading strategies. Among other rules, I employ a simple five-percent per month maximum loss rule. If at any point my trading program is down five percent versus where it started that month, all positions are closed as soon as possible, and no more trading takes place for rest of that month.

Margin Requirements and Margin-to-Equity Ratios

Many traders consider margin requirements to be something that brokerage firms use to protect themselves and knock traders out of the market. Be happy they exist. Margin requirements are actually one of the most useful ways to measure the risk that an account is assuming. Based on a one's risk tolerance, traders should establish two maximum margin-to-equity ratios that they will allow their account to reach. One ratio applies to the trading day when a trader is at his post, so to speak, and is ready to react; the second is a lower ratio for overnight positions when he isn't watching the market and can't react immediately.

Delta and Gamma Values

These values are measurements that relate to options trading. Delta is a measure of how much futures-equivalent risk an options position entails at a given moment, and gamma measures the rate of change of delta. Various options trading software packages help traders measure these components and give them a better feel for the sometimes hard-to-quantify risks associated with options positions.

Make Rules That Work for You

We've already covered loss limits per trade or trading session. A trader also can limit the number of total trades—win or lose—in a day, week or month. Or he can limit the number of open positions he can have at any given time.

Here's an interesting story about a trader who limited himself in an unusual way. If he ever made $1,000 in the first hour of trading, which often is the most volatile and difficult part of the day in any market, he'd call it quits for the day. He created this rule after experiencing several days when he would make substantial profitable trades early on and still end up being down for day. When it comes to limits, it's whatever works for you, and keeping it simple often makes sense. Limits based on dollars or percentages made or lost are most popular for a reason: they are great tools, because other limits based on margin-to-equity ratios or cumulative delta or gamma values are moving targets and often hard to calculate in the heat of battle.

Now that we've noted many ways to measure risk, it's time for each individual trader to take charge and implement one or more ways to measure risk...and with the all-important goal of avoiding that decisive loss as the centerpiece of the plan. And finally, here's the last part of the risk-management puzzle—discipline. All of the world's risk-management tools will mean nothing if you ignore them.

John Yackley, president and manager of funds at Be Free Investments, a registered commodity trading advisor, began managing money for investors in 1995. He has two unique investment strategies that focus on and trade stock index and interest rate futures and options. For more information, go to www.BeFreeInvestments.com. This article first appeared in *SFO* in September 2004.

LESSONS FROM THE TRADING FLOOR:
Translating Floor Emotion into Screen-based Trading

BY SAM SEIDEN

I have never read a trading book cover-to-cover. I started my career on the floor of the Chicago Mercantile Exchange (CME), not looking at a screen-based chart for the first year. On top of that, from an early age, I was taught not to accept something as true just because someone says so. What I do is apply simple logic to everything that presents a challenge. Trading presents a challenge second to none.

At the CME, I could have taken a variety of classes and started reading all the books but personally chose another means of gaining knowledge about trading the markets. I had two very good friends on the floor of the exchange. One worked for a firm, and the other traded for himself and was one of the more successful traders on the floor. I was young and ambitious and just wanted to learn how he was doing it and, fortunately, he was willing to give me advice.

As I stood next to him in the pit, he pointed out a trader across the pit and instructed, "See that guy over there? Let me know when he makes a trade." I stood and watched the man across the pit, and when he raised his hands to bid for some contracts, I alerted my friend.

Lessons from the Floor

It was loud in the pit, as prices had been moving higher for some time. My friend pointed out to me how desperately the gentleman in question wanted to buy. He stood on his tiptoes, yelling at high volume to anyone who would sell to him. Seconds after pointing out these human behavior traits to me, my friend gladly filled his order by taking the other side of his trade, and we had a short position open; little did I know that my lesson had just begun. A few minutes later, the market fell, and we had a winning position. Being new at the game, I was impressed. In fact, it seemed too easy and very hard all at the same time. We had just profited from a position in minutes, which made it appear easy. The entry, however, came on the short side when it seemed everyone else wanted to buy in a very bad way, and this didn't make much sense at the time.

My friend explained, "That guy is somewhat new in the trading pits and consistently loses. Turns in the market happen when the novice trader has entered the market; therefore, all I have to do is find the novice trader and take the other side of his trade consistently."

I could not believe that this was how my friend had become so successful. There had to be more to his strategy. But, indeed, this was the essence of his trading approach, and he had little else to tell me. He did, however, give me a knowing smile at the end of the day, which conveyed something much more powerful than I realized at the time.

That novice trader was making his decision to buy based on emotion, not objective information. Had he looked at objective information, he would have seen that he was buying after a period of buying (late and high risk) and at a price level where supply exceeded demand (resistance, low odds). In essence, he was entering a position when the odds were completely stacked against him. A profitable trader would never do that; the laws of supply and demand say you can't consistently profit while buying after a period of buying and at a price level where supply exceeds demand. The objective odds are stacked against you.

For humans in general, it is emotion that drives behavior, not intellect. Traders who make trading decisions based on emotion versus objective information will almost always be invited to enter a position when the objective risk is high and reward is low.

The Two Mistakes

In profiling this type of floor trader, two mistakes come to light. First, they buy after a period of buying and sell after a period of selling, which is high risk and low reward. Second, they buy into areas of resistance (supply) and sell into areas of support (demand), which always is a low-odds trade. The laws of supply and demand and how one makes money buying and selling anything indicate that the odds are completely stacked against this trader. Consistently finding this type of trader and taking the other side of his trade would, therefore, stack the odds in my favor.

The principles of supply and demand, of course, have been around much longer than the markets themselves, and they apply to much more than just trading strategies. I was learning the core concepts of markets and how and why prices move. All that was required was to first understand exactly how money is made trading anything. Additionally, it was about learning how to properly analyze the relationship of supply and demand to human emotion in any market at any time.

Further, it's important to notice that the focus is on the loser—what the majority of losers do wrong over and over again. Approaching something by determining how to do it wrong has some impressive results. It worked for Plato and Aristotle, so why not apply it to trading?

The only way we can make money buying something is if someone buys what we have at a higher price. For shorting, it's the other way around. Sound simple? Think again. When we view a trading floor, a screen-based chart, or the account statements of tens of millions of investors, we quickly see that the actions of the majority of traders and investors are completely backward on this concept.

On a trading floor, the person taking the other side of a trade is right in front of other floor traders. Seeing emotion is a tool that can help stack the odds in favor of those who are physically there and recognize what to look for.

In time, preferring the comforts of my own home and a computer screen, I realized the trading floor was not for me. The only question was, how does one read the markets if it's not possible to actually see and hear the people trading? How can one see emotions on a screen? After all, it seemed that valuable information comes with physicality.

When I first looked at a chart, I knew exactly what I should be looking for: the trader who consistently makes the two mistakes. At first I didn't know quite what this would look like on a chart. I figured out that one need not look past price on a chart in a quest to identify an emotional opportunity in the markets in the form of a supply and demand imbalance.

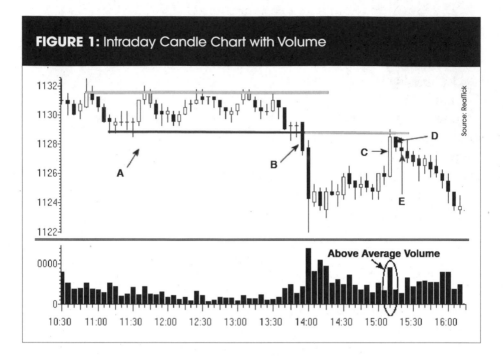

FIGURE 1: Intraday Candle Chart with Volume

Source: RealTick

Price Alone Reveals Buyers and Sellers

It became time for me to begin translating human emotion on the trading floor to the computer screen. I chose Japanese candlesticks, as they make it easy to see which group—buyers or sellers—is controlling the market and, also, which group is about to lose or regain control. Candlesticks (price) represent traders' beliefs and expectations and hold the true objective information traders need when trading.

Let's take an objective look at *Figure 1*. This intraday chart shows a scenario that happens each day. Area A represents what some would call sideways trading. Taking trading to a more professional level through objective simplicity, we will call it a price level at which supply and demand appear to be balanced. At the close of candle B, we can objectively conclude that there is too much supply and not enough demand in price level A, and this is the only reason prices can fall. Some may wish to short this breakdown, but I chose to let prices fall, as entering breakouts and breakdowns is hardly ever low risk and high reward. When candle C forms and closes, one can objectively conclude that the majority of traders who bought on that candle are not consistently profitable. They are buying after an advance in price, though in this case, it is a minor advancement. Most important, they are buying right into a price level where objectively, supply exceeds demand (supply/demand imbalance). Lastly, there are many of them—just look at the increase in volume.

My friend from the trading floor would be glad to sell to this group of buyers as, objectively, the odds are stacked against them each time they take action. The laws of supply and demand tell us that consistently profitable traders can't buy in this situation and profit over the course of a career. When buying after a period of buying and into resistance (supply), the odds a trader will profit on a long position are very low. When we add human behavior into the equation, it is easy to see why the majority of speculators, over and over, is on the wrong side of the market. The short entry for this opportunity comes on candle E, below the low of the candle body of candle D.

The Task:
1. Objective anticipatory analysis: We must enter before others at the right time. In trading, we get paid when others do what we do, but after we do it.
2. Low-risk entries: Low-risk (low-stress) entries are a key to profitable trading and allow us to maximize money management strategies and the largest potential reward.

The Tools:
1. Candlesticks (price);
2. Proper trend analysis;
3. Proper support (demand) and resistance (supply) analysis.

The Analysis:
1. What is the current trend of average prices? Answering this question objectively tells us what side of the market currently carries high odds. In an uptrend (average prices rising), the odds are with the buyers. In a downtrend (average prices falling), the odds are with the sellers. Trading with the prevailing trend always carries the better odds. However, proper trend analysis is about objective anticipation of the next trend, not conventional trend analysis.
2. Where is support (demand) and resistance (supply)? Answering this question objectively will lead us to our low-risk/high-reward entry areas, which are always found at or near support for longs

and at or near resistance for shorts. These areas are where the smart buyers and sellers enter positions. Entries in these areas carry the greatest positive odds.

3. Is there a profit zone (profit margin)? This is the distance from supply to demand, or vice versa, at the time of potential entry. For longs, this simply is calculated by subtracting the support area from the resistance area. The opposite is done for shorting.

What to Look For

Identifying the likely turning points in price comes down to a simple and mechanical set of criteria. Let's perform an objective, anticipatory analysis while looking at a stock.

What is the trend? The data in *Figure 2* illustrate that the trend of average prices is up; this means the longer-term odds are with the buyers. Where is support (demand) and resistance (supply)? Area A represents a price level where objectively, there are many more buyers than sellers. Resistance in this opportunity was significantly higher. We know this because we see that the initial rally in price from price level A is over $6. This rally opens up the initial profit zone as all the significant supply above is absorbed.

FIGURE 2: Gehl Company Stock

During the day candle C forms, it is our job to wait for the novice sellers to sell within the range of our objective demand level. At C, we can say that sellers are selling after a decline in price and at a price level where demand exceeds supply. This is the clear sign of a novice trader who is selling based on pure emotion, not objective rules and logic. Keep it simple and remember, a consistently profitable buyer and seller of anything would never sell after a period of selling and at a price level where demand exceeds supply. The laws of supply and demand ensure this action brings consistent losses, not gains.

It is easy to see this emotion on a trading floor—who is holding a winning position, and who is sitting on a losing trade. But today, many more people trade over a computer screen and have never been nor ever will spend time on a trading floor, so learning what this looks like on a chart is crucial for success.

Many traders' first impressions of trading will come from a book or a seminar, not real person-to-person emotional trading. Your first exposure to markets and trading becomes hard-coded into who you are as a trader. Books teach how to trade based on chart patterns, not generally on human emotional patterns. Trading seminars teach how to use indicators and oscillators on the chart, which can lead to faulty trading, as most indicators and oscillators are very subjective. Most books discuss chart patterns and exactly how to enter them. The problem is that these patterns are based on the premise that traders need a bullish picture to buy and a bearish picture to sell. In fact, an astute trader gets interested in buying well before pretty green candles appear on a chart.

Many trading books tend to drive herd mentality, not lead it. Even conventional technical analysis at its core can be faulty. The key is to base any and all decisions on the pure laws of supply and demand.

The Problem with Head-and-Shoulders

Let's take, for example, the popular head-and-shoulders top pattern. The criteria for entry is to short on a break of the neck line. First of all, if I know that many will be shorting there, and I also know that the only way I can profit is if others enter after I do, it is the last place I want to short.

Furthermore, the most important question when presented with this chart pattern is: why are the shoulders and head forming? That's simple enough; it's called resistance (supply), and that's where the focus should be. This is where the low-risk/high-reward entry is, not much lower which is where the majority of traders are taught to enter (sell).

But, remember, if everyone is taught to enter (sell short) on a break of the neckline and the trader wants to join them, who is left to sell after the trader? So, a trader must strive to be a part of the invitation to enter, as that is low risk and high odds. I use confirmation that the masses use, that is, to confirm a decision that I already have made.

As mentioned earlier, I have never read a trading book cover to cover. Why would I want to learn how to enter and exit positions with others if the only way I can consistently profit is to enter before they do?

Also, the way to make money trading and human nature are inversely related. People, in general, are only comfortable buying if others have bought. They avoid taking risk unless others are willing to share the risk. Traders and investors tend to buy on good news and sell on bad news. Trust me, good news and nice comfortable green candles don't bring prices down to areas of support (demand), which is where the astute traders buy. Unfortunately, it usually is the bad news that tends to offer the low-risk/high-reward buying opportunities.

The Screen Trader's Job

The quest in screen-based trading is to identify human patterns on a chart and then apply simple logic, based on the laws and principles of

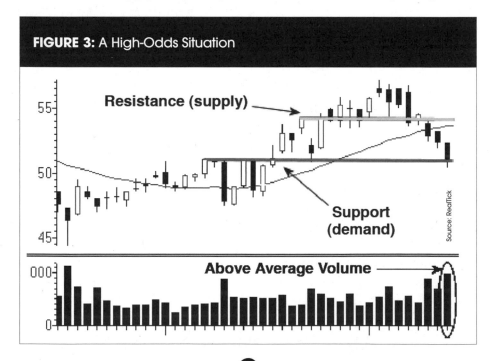

FIGURE 3: A High-Odds Situation

supply and demand. Most traders who fail tend to look at the details of each trade to figure out where they are going wrong. What they instead need to do is step out of the novice box and consider the essence of trading at its core. Instead of reading a trading book per se, a more productive approach may be to read a psychology 101 book on human behavior, followed by an economics 101 book on supply and demand... and then begin their trading careers.

Whether a market participant trades from a trading floor or via a computer platform, how money is made in trading never changes.

Let's review the steps, based on *Figure 3*.
1) What is the prevailing trend? Up
2) Where is resistance? 54 (area)
3) Where is support? 51 (area)
4) Is there a profit zone? Yes, 3 points

The odds are above average as well because of the heavy volume. This illustrates that many traders are entering after a multi-candle decline into an area of support (demand), and all is within the context of a larger time frame uptrend (average prices rising). The time to enter is in this area, not after a green reversal candle. The goal is to be a part of the reversal candle which, again, tends to invite others to buy after we do. Notice how this mechanical set of criteria led to this conclusion before any sign of buying or good news.

In *Figure 4*, it's easy to see that this analysis paid off. Why? We became a part of the invitation to buy. Others entered the next day, and prices met the target for a low-risk/high-odds gain. What is important to understand is that we are a part of that green reversal candle. Most others will look at that and say: "We have a reversal candle at support, let's buy." This is exactly what we want as we have already bought.

Advantage: Online Trader. If this information is as good as it sounds, why write about it? In my years of trading and educating, I've learned that one can spoon-feed the core concepts of trading to people and, yet, most will not be able to apply the simple concepts. Why? The power of human emotions that drive our decisions are too strong. Having been in both floor-trading and screen-trading environments

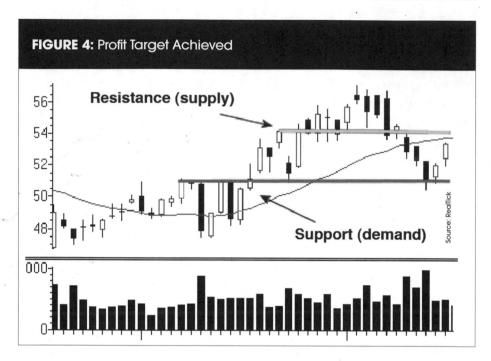

FIGURE 4: Profit Target Achieved

Resistance (supply)

Support (demand)

Source: RealTick

for years, the advantage is now largely with the screen-based trader... as long as they know what information they are looking for on a chart.

All one needs are candles, volume and some electricity for the computer.

Sam Seiden is a trader, research analyst, and instructor with more than ten years of experience, including trading his personal account and fund management. Seiden provides research and guidance to clients through speaking engagements, workshops, magazine articles, and advisory services via www.samseiden.com. He can be reached at sam@samseiden.com. A version of this article first appeared in *SFO* in May 2004.

HOW TO SPOT WINNING STOCKS BEFORE THEY MAKE BIG MOVES

BY WILLIAM O'NEIL

The ideal investing strategy provides a sound defense in bad markets and helps produce the greatest returns in strong markets. Few systems measure up because strategies are often based on opinion rather than fact. A person's investments will improve once he or she accepts that the market works on its own terms, not on any of ours. The stock market doesn't care who we are or what we think. It does exactly what it wants to do, not what an analyst, a pundit or Uncle Joe with a hot tip wants it to do.

It's easy to get caught following someone else's opinion, especially if there is a rave review about a stock. Don't fall for it. Whether a person is new to investing or has been at it a long time, the best way to increase one's profit potential is to study the actual market inside and out. Learning the facts of the market will help an investor block out opinions and tips that only serve to hurt his or her investment potential. Investing can be highly emotional, with our natural impulses getting in the way of our making sound, objective decisions. Learning to only listen to facts—not emotions or opinions—will produce a more successful investing experience.

After studying history's greatest stock winners for five decades, we've learned that great stocks have seven common performance characteristics present before they make their biggest price gains. The seven common traits are now known as CAN SLIM®, a checklist I use before buying any stock, because any purchase I make must have similar potential performance to past great winners.

The American Association of Individual Investors performed independent real-time studies of more than 50 top strategies, and for the past eight years (1998 through 2006), they found that CAN SLIM was the most consistent and best-performing investment system with a 949.9-percent result, versus the S&P's 30.9 for the same period. CAN SLIM outperforms year after year because it's based solely on the facts of how the market works, not on opinions.

C = Current Quarterly Earnings

In Investor's Business Daily's study of the 600 biggest market winners from 1952 to 2001, three out of four posted earnings increases of more than 70 percent in the latest quarter before they launched huge rallies. This is a key fundamental when seeking out great stocks. A company's most recent quarterly earnings report when compared with the same quarter the year before should be at least 18 to 25 percent higher, the more consecutive positive quarters the better.

IBD's stock tables contain an Earnings Per Share (EPS) rating based on a scale from 1 to 99. For example, 80 EPS means that a stock is outperforming 80 percent of all stocks in earnings growth.

A = Annual Earnings Per Share

Any company can report a great quarter of earnings from time to time, especially those engaged in serious cost-cutting measures. That's why annual earnings per share is an important measure to see how consistent the company has been over the long term. A company's annual earnings should be up in each of the last three years by 25 percent or more. A stock also should show positive earnings estimates for the upcoming year and current annual return on equity of at least 17 percent.

N = New Products, New Services, Price Highs

Any company whose stock is worth buying should have an exciting new product or service, or be part of an innovative new industry group. Microsoft, Cisco, Home Depot and eBay were all trailblazers in their heyday. They were part of a revolution in products and services that redefined their respective fields. This kind of new, entrepreneurial leadership is a major defining factor for what constitutes a market-leading stock. It's important to also look for new names to lead the market, not the old laggards. IBD's historical research shows that only one of every eight leaders in a bull market reasserts itself as a leader in the next bull phase. When the market turns and a new bull phase takes hold, it's the new companies and the new names breaking out on huge volume that will make investors the most money.

IBD highlights these in a number of ways, one of which is in *The New America* page each day, where investors can find many of tomorrow's leaders before they become household names. Stocks that appear on this page are included in The New America Index that has consistently performed well above the S&P 500.

S = Supply and Demand

Supply and demand drives stock market prices the same way it determines the price of oil, tomatoes, coffee, beef, etc. That's why the price of a large-capitalization stock with roughly five billion shares outstanding is much harder to move than a smaller growth stock with only 50 million shares outstanding. The larger the total shares, the more shares that have to be bought and sold to affect the price.

Our research has found that these larger-cap performers, which tend to be the Dow or blue chip stocks, usually are lesser performers than the new, exciting growth companies. It pays to watch these trends and invest where you see the smart money, or institutional investors putting their money. It also can be a good sign if companies buy back their own stock. If the top brass are buying back their own company, it's a sign of confidence and faith.

L = Leader or Laggard

The biggest pitfall in the stock market is buying stocks merely because they have a recognizable name. Just having a well-known brand name will not ensure that a stock will be a winner. There are no safe stocks in the stock market—all stocks are bad unless they go up! The best shot an investor has at making big money is by buying a leader just as it breaks out early in a rally. Look for stocks outperforming the market in earnings, sales, return on equity and relative strength.

Even better, is the stock in a leading industry group? A stock is only as good as the company it keeps, so focus on the best stocks in a thriving industry where demand is high for its products or services. History shows stocks in strong and innovative sectors of the economy chalk up the biggest gains. Buying quality leaders is also a great way to build profits. But always check a chart to be sure you aren't too late in the game.

I = Institutional Sponsorship

Institutional investors—mutual funds, pension funds, banks, insurance companies, etc.—account for up to 80 percent of the market's trading. That's why institutional sponsorship (their ownership in a stock) is an important confirming factor prior to buying any stock—because they are the main drivers behind price movement. It takes big demand to move prices up, so a smart investor will search for stocks moving up in price on higher-than-average volume. When a stock jumps in price, it's not because Aunt Mary bought her ten, hundred or even one thousand shares. It takes hundreds of thousands of shares to move prices up or down. So it's crucial that any stock one buys is supported by big money and big players.

Look for an increasing number of mutual funds owning positions in the stock over recent quarters, plus ownership by funds that have out-performed the market over the last few years. Investors also can check *Stocks on the Move*, a page in Investor's Business Daily® and on investors.com, where it's updated continually throughout the day. It tracks unusual volume changes for the last fifty trading days.

M = Market Direction

But owning a stock with the first six CAN SLIM ingredients above won't do any good if the market is unraveling. History confirms that three out of four stocks follow the market's direction. So one can be right on every aspect of a stock pick—earnings, sales, institutional sponsorship, new products and services—but if the market's in a major downturn, chances are that stock is going to break down along with it.

It's crucial to keep up on the market every day—tracking the interplay of price and volume. This is a surefire way to know what it is doing right now. If a decline is confirmed, always be prepared to sell and raise cash. A wise investor will be cautious during a rough market and jump on the big leaders as soon as it turns.

CAN SLIM works precisely because it's the documented way the market has shown to work for a half century. An investor who learns how to analyze and recognize each one of these common characteristics will be on his or her way toward not only spotting great stocks, but also buying them at the right time.

Set Ground Rules

Once a person finds a CAN SLIM stock, it's tempting to think that the next step is to hit the "buy" button and give oneself a pat on the back. But, finding a great stock is only the first half of the challenge. The other half is knowing what to do after buying—there has to be a start to finish plan. Buying a stock without knowing when or why one should sell is like buying a Lexus with no brakes.

That's the lesson millions of investors learned when the bubble burst in 2000. Eighty million people lost $7 trillion, roughly 50 to 80 percent of their portfolios. Few had the right defense strategy to cut and run when stocks began to fall. Think of it this way: who ever heard of a championship basketball team that won with only an offense? You need a strong offense and defense to succeed in the stock market. When buying stocks, ask the following questions:

- What do I do if I'm wrong?
- How do I protect myself?
- What do I do if I'm right?
- How do I turn a paper profit into a real one before it disintegrates?

No investor is going to be right every time. The secret to successful investing is not to be right all the time, but to lose the least amount of money possible. Everyone will make mistakes, so investors have to be able to admit early on that they were wrong, and cut their losses so that they live to invest another day. The following are a few ways to protect capital and maximize profits.

Rule #1: Always Sell a Stock that Drops Seven or Eight Percent Below Your Buy Point.

I know of no better, safer way to defend against huge losses than with this cardinal rule: always sell a stock once it's dropped seven to eight percent below the price paid for it. Period. No exceptions, no excuses. Why? It's simple math. If an investor sells at seven to eight percent on losers and sells when up 25 percent on some winners, he can be right once out of three times and still be ahead.

Not convinced? Just look at the last fifty years of market cycles. The average market leader fell 72 percent after topping, and buying and holding would not have worked. No investor can afford many 72-percent losses. That's why one also never wants to buy stocks on their way down in price—never average down! No one is getting a bargain. It can be more like trying to catch a falling knife. Just ask people who bought Enron, Lucent or Global Crossing as they were getting cheaper because they thought they were getting a bargain.

Rule #2: Identify the Proper Buy and Sell Point to Maximize Return and Minimize Loss.

Learn to read charts. Chart reading is essential to identifying the best possible time for buying and selling stocks, and no investor should buy or sell without consulting a chart. Would someone want his or her doctor to operate without looking at X-rays? And it's not as complicated as some would imagine.

Charts illustrate the price and volume movement of a stock, revealing at a glance the extent of its demand. They show the actual buy-and-sell decisions of thousands of investors, from small fry to massive mutual funds. If a quality stock shoots up on heavy volume, it means the big institutions are piling into it. Likewise, when a stock plummets on heavy volume, it usually means the big institutions are bailing out. A stock rising or falling on little or below-average volume mostly means a lack of commitment either way.

The best way to maximize profit and minimize loss is to buy at the exact moment a surge lifts the stock out of a what we call a sound price consolidation pattern or base on heavy volume. Only a chart can help investors time that entry. At the same time, a chart can help an investor identify when it's time to take profits and run.

While fundamentals tell an investor what to buy, technical analysis tells an investor when to sell. Why? Most of the market's biggest winners break down while their fundamentals are still top notch. Maybe it's because the market is taking a break, or institutional investors get wind of a future profit slump. There could be no reason—it could just be that institutions are simply taking profits. The bottom line is that it doesn't matter. An investor's job is not to know why a stock does what it does, but to recognize what it is doing and react accordingly.

Rule #3: Never Let a Big Profit Turn into a Big Loss.

Stocks have a way of signaling to investors that the good times may be over. There are several indicators any investor can learn to help identify those signals. Relative Price Strength is an excellent indicator for determining a stock's overall strength. An RS line plots a stock's price performance against that of the benchmark S&P 500. It's a quick way to separate the leaders from the laggards.

In Investor's Business Daily, we assign each stock a proprietary Relative Strength (RS) rating from 1 to 99, where 99 means the stock's RS has outperformed 99 percent of the market and a 1 indicates it has outperformed a paltry one percent of the market. If an investor owns a stock with an RS Rating below 70 and falling, it might mean that stock is in trouble.

Excessive stocks splits are another way to identify whether a stock has had its run. Companies tend to split their stock when too many people know about it, and they want to drop the price to entice more investors to jump in. But why might this be a troubling sign? It's typically when everyone knows about a stock, analysts are pounding their desks crying, "Buy, buy, buy," and the company's CEO is on the cover of a magazine that the stock is either overbought, overhyped or both – a warning that its run may be over. Consider excessive stock splits over a short period as a red flag.

Ignore the Noise

Remember that any investing strategy should help one learn how to listen to and understand what the market is saying. Nothing can tell an investor more accurately and honestly what the market is doing than the market itself. That is why it is absolutely critical to block out the opinions of pundits and the hot tips from "experts." It's all noise. Only the market knows what it's going to do next. The best an investor can do is listen closely and follow the market's lead.

William J. O'Neil is the founder and chairman of Investor's Business Daily and developer of the CAN SLIM investing method. He is the author of several books, including his latest books, *How to Make Money Selling Stocks Short* (Wiley Trading, 2004) and *The Successful Investor: What 80 Million People Need to Know to Invest Profitably and Avoid Big Losses* (McGraw-Hill, 2003), which analyzes the 2000-03 bear market. More information on CAN SLIM investing can be found at www. investors.com/canslim. This article first appeared in *SFO* in July 2004.

THE VOICES OF VOLUME

BY TONI TURNER

Ask any trader what two components make a good trade fantastic, and he or she will surely answer, "Volume and volatility." Indeed, as traders, we earn a high percentage of our profits by targeting a stock or other financial instrument, then accurately interpreting price reversals fueled by explosive changes in supply or demand. We measure these changes by evaluating volume.

Volume is the amount of shares or contracts traded in a given time frame. In its simplest form, volume spikes on a chart give the trader an instant message as to the level of enthusiasm — or lack of it — applicable to price movement of a stock or futures contract at any given moment. Taken to a slightly more sophisticated level, and exploding or imploding volume activity can alert us to trend reversals, confirm entry decisions, indicate the health of continuation patterns and act as a potent decision support tool for managing and exiting trades. Combining volume signals with additional signals offered by price action and chart indicators provide us with a strong foundation for entering, exiting and managing trades.

In the discussion that follows, we'll discuss volume as a potent decision-support tool. Next, we'll look at eight voices of volume to interpret the signals they offer on day, swing and position trades.

Volume as a Tool

Most indicators used on charts are a derivative of price. For example, the overbought/oversold oscillators known as stochastics, MACD

(Moving Average Convergence Divergence indicator), and the RSI (Relative Strength Index) all emerge from a statistical manipulation of price action. Volume, however, acts as a variable that is independent of price. This is highly beneficial to us as traders, because it offers important information about the market we are trading that's separate from price action.

On an overall basis, volume signals deliver one of two messages: first, if the momentum and velocity of the volume matches the price action, such as a breakout to the upside on strong volume, it tells us the price move is reliable. We say volume confirms price movement. Second, if volume momentum does not match price movement, it alerts us that implied price action may fail. For instance, a breakout to the upside on weak volume may quickly retrace, or correct.

Most of us use charting packages in which volume is represented as a series of spikes, or a histogram, at the bottom of our charts that relate to the designated time frame of each bar or candle line. Some traders prefer volume to be related in a momentum format. In this discussion, we will present volume in the standard histogram form with a momentum indicator (explained below) applied.

On each chart example, you'll see the simple but powerful indicator, On-Balance Volume (OBV), plotted on the volume scale. You'll also see the 20-, 50-, and 200-day (simple) moving averages and one of two oscillators, the RSI or stochastic (slow). Also note that as the author trades mainly stocks, that is the trading instrument primarily referred to in the following text. The same principles and signals apply to other trading vehicles as well, because volume signals measure human participation, rather than price participation.

The On-Balance Volume Indicator

The On-Balance Volume (OBV) represents one of the simplest and most reliable volume momentum indicators. Readily available on most charting packages, this it also works well with candle charts, oscillators and other charting tools. On-Balance Volume was originally developed by Joe Granville, and it correlates volume to price change. Displayed as a single line, it normally appears over volume spikes. As a running total, it moves up when the coinciding bar or candle closes higher than the previous close and down when the security closes lower than the prior close.

The OBV moves in trends, accompanying price movement as money flows into or out of a stock. Therefore, if your stock is rising in a solid uptrend, the OBV will rise as long as buying comes into the stock. Conversely, a stock sliding in a downtrend will display a falling OBV, as long as selling comes into the stock.

The OBV also precedes price changes or reversals by displaying bullish or bearish divergences (divergence means that the indicator and price move in opposite directions). That gives you a heads up for entries and exits and is particularly meaningful when it coincides with a price oscillator divergence. A full explanation of how the OBV works is beyond the scope of this discussion. For in-depth information on the OBV, read Granville's book, *New Strategy of Daily Stock Market Timing for Maximum Profit* (Prentice-Hall, Englewood Cliffs, NJ, 1976).

The Voices of Volume: What Do They Tell You?

The following guidelines show how relationships between volume and price movement offer predictive signals as to future price action. Please understand that these technical signals are not perfect crystal balls. More times than not though, the confirmations and warnings that price/volume action can display provide valuable information when applied to entry, exit and money management strategies.

1. **Volume precedes and/or accompanies price.** When a stock moves up in the context of an uptrend (higher highs and higher lows), strong to average volume will accompany it on most bars or candles. Keep in mind, however, that while every rising candle may not be fueled by equally strong volume, the volume should maintain solid momentum. As demand absorbs limited supply, a slight decrease in volume may not slow down price momentum.

Figure 1 shows the Microsoft Corp. (MSFT) as it rises into an uptrend in late July and early August 2006. The trend reversal actually took place in mid-June, as bearish volume gave way to bullish support. Note how the OBV also reversed. In mid-August, the bulls' demand pushed "Mr. Softee," (traders' nickname for MSFT) higher in the trend. Additional buyers showed in September, October and No-

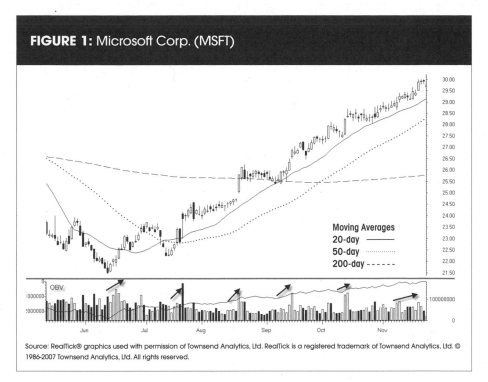

FIGURE 1: Microsoft Corp. (MSFT)

vember, and the healthy volume spurts propelled the giant software stock to within shooting distance of a four-year high. Day, swing and position traders all benefited from this steady uptrend fueled by strong volume.

2. **Low-to-average volume on pullback = bullish.** When a stock in an uptrend retraces in an orderly pullback or consolidates in a horizontal continuation pattern, the volume should contract as well. That shows that the stock is resting in a healthy manner. *Figure 1* shows MSFT's volume contracting on the pullbacks or retracements in the mid-June to November uptrend. This volume expansion on upside moves, coupled with orderly contraction on consolidation or pullbacks, tells us the uptrend is healthy.

3. **High volume on pullback = bearish.** When an uptrend is in progress, if you see increasing volume on the pullback (more than occurred on the prior move up), it indicates market participants are just as willing to sell it now as they were to buy it earlier. That creates strong increased pressure, and the stock may plunge—fast.

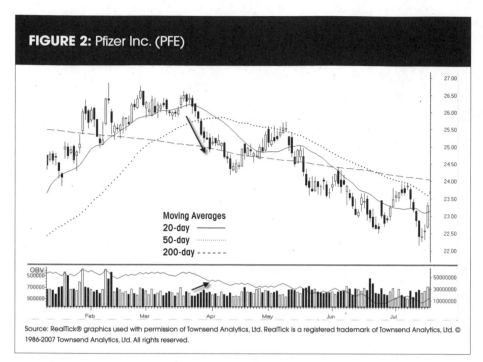

FIGURE 2: Pfizer Inc. (PFE)

Moving Averages
20-day ———
50-day ··········
200-day ------

Figure 2 shows a daily chart of Pfizer Inc. (PFE). Note how the change in volume leads the trend reversal starting in mid-March. In January, February and part of March, the pharmaceutical company had stepped smartly up its 20-day moving average. But strong volume in the mid-March pullback warned traders and investors that the pullback might transform into a reversal. Sure enough, PFE slid into a subsequent downtrend. Note how the OBV rolled over at this time, as selling volume increased. Day traders, swing traders and even position traders would have fared well in PFE during the downtrend, as long as they stayed on the right side of it.

4. **New high on weak volume = bearish.** As previously discussed, when a market continues to achieve new highs in an established uptrend, volume should maintain a healthy pace. So, when a market makes a new high on weak, relatively low volume, it signals that the trend may be ready to shift or reverse. Remember, volume measures levels of excitement and enthusiasm displayed by market participants. Escalating prices accompanied by weak volume suggests a lack of new buyers. This lack of enthusiasm can lead to subsequent panic when it does not confirm a rising price—espe-

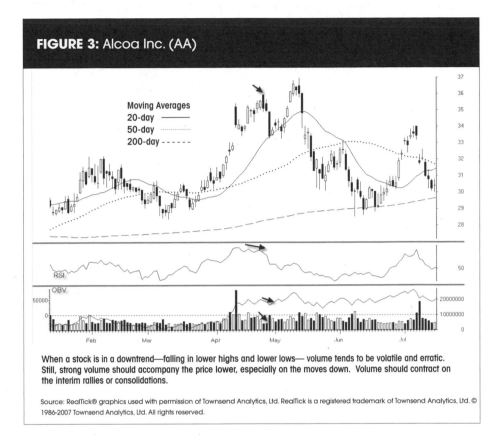

FIGURE 3: Alcoa Inc. (AA)

When a stock is in a downtrend—falling in lower highs and lower lows— volume tends to be volatile and erratic. Still, strong volume should accompany the price lower, especially on the moves down. Volume should contract on the interim rallies or consolidations.

Source: RealTick® graphics used with permission of Townsend Analytics, Ltd. RealTick is a registered trademark of Townsend Analytics, Ltd. © 1986-2007 Townsend Analytics, Ltd. All rights reserved.

cially when it's a new high in an overbought market. As indifference becomes evident, the rally soon becomes suspect. Then fear sets in, and the resulting overwhelming supply from sellers takes the market south.

Figure 3 shows a daily chart of Alcoa Inc. (AA). This giant aluminum manufacturer tech stock climbed nicely to a high of $35.95 on April 25, 2006. However, AA made its new high on low volume. It was also overextended, trading high above its 20-day moving average. Note that I've added a 14-period Relative Strength Index (RSI) to this chart, to indicate how the OBV and a momentum indicator often move in tandem. The correlation of indicators can strengthen your buy or sell signal. (RSI readings below 30 are considered to be oversold and above 70 overbought.)

Besides being overbought in relation to its 20-day moving average, AA soared to 88 on its RSI, an overbought reading for that indicator,

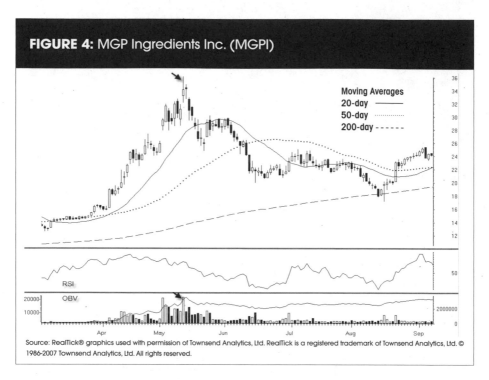

FIGURE 4: MGP Ingredients Inc. (MGPI)

Moving Averages
20-day ———
50-day ·············
200-day - - - - -

RSI

OBV

as well. This false breakout on low volume signaled swing traders on the long side to take profits. Day traders were scanning for subsequent trades to the short side.

5. **Soaring price + explosive volume = impending capitulation (bearish).** In our everyday world, we say, "What goes up must come down." This statement is true for stock prices, as well. Stock rockets or moonshot price moves fueled by rampant, euphoric volume usually find their exhaustion point soon after.

   Figure 4 shows speculative buying that more than doubled the price of MGP Ingredients, Inc. (MGPI), in six weeks. An alternative energy play, MGPI stock shot higher when oil prices soared. The May 11, 2006, high of 36.08 resulted in a candle is known as a "high wave" candle (small real body with extended shadows above and below). Add that to the explosive volume and the four-point intraday range (volume and volatility) and the outcome is extreme confusion. Note that the RSI did not make a new high along with the price move—a bearish warning. The OBV hooked down, as well. Swing traders who

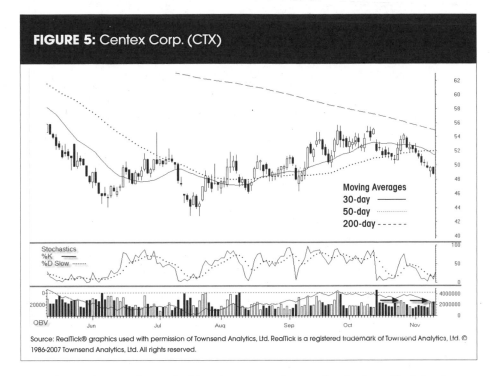

FIGURE 5: Centex Corp. (CTX)

Moving Averages
30-day ———
50-day ············
200-day - - - - -

Stochastics
%K ———
%D Slow ········

OBV

were long the stock probably chose to take profits before that day's closing bell. Active traders who like high risk (despite its problems, the stock is legally in an uptrend, which makes a short position high risk) surely scanned for shorting entries in subsequent days down.

6. **Churning market + rising volume = bearish.** When a market has moved in an uptrend and then churned sideways for a period of time (relative to the time frame displayed), the appearance of steadily rising volume without price breakout may signal that distribution is taking place. That means the stock may soon roll over and head south.

Figure 5 shows a daily chart of Centex Corp. (CTX). Note how the giant homebuilder breaks out of its base and moves higher in September and October of 2006. Then price action gets choppy as if fails to make a new high in mid-October. Strong and steady volume for that pullback under the 20 and 50-day moving averages tells traders that sellers are unloading. CTX made one final lukewarm attempt to run higher again, but just managed to pop over the $54 mark before fall-

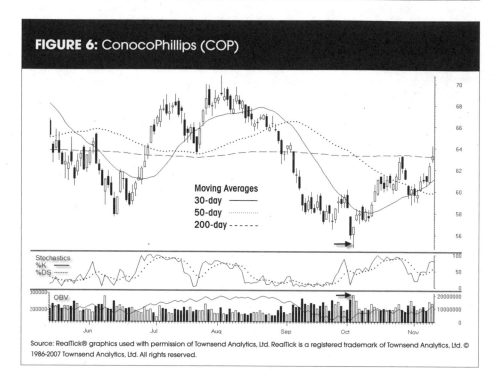

FIGURE 6: ConocoPhillips (COP)

Moving Averages
30-day ——
50-day ········
200-day ------

Stochastics
%K ——
%DS ········

OBV

ing and succumbing to the bears. Note how the Stochastics indicator (middle scale, oversold readings are below 20, overbought readings are above 80) and OBV both topped and rolled over on that high, with Stochastics starting lower just before CTX's price crumbled. Swing traders would have used that high to take profits on long trades or at least exited the next morning when CTX gapped down and closed at the low of the day. Once CTX fell below its 20 and 50-day moving averages, short sellers entering both swing and day trades surely enjoyed the ride lower.

7. **Climactic selling + high volume = impending low or tradable bottom**. When a market is in a downtrend (lower highs and lower lows) and experiences climactic selling on high volume, price may reverse and head higher. The high volume spike indicates that many traders and investors holding long positions are throwing in the towel. This climactic selling, especially if the stock encounters prior price support, is usually followed by a rally to the upside— whether short-lived, or an actual reversal. The signal works well as a warning to short-sellers that it's time to cover their positions.

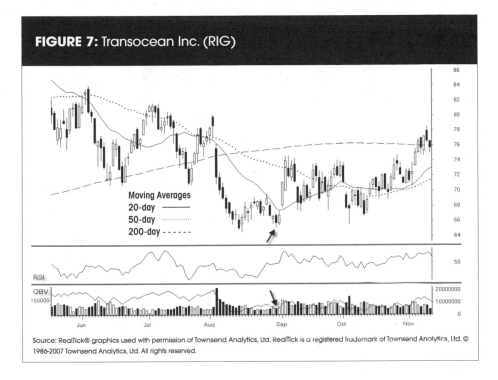

FIGURE 7: Transocean Inc. (RIG)

Moving Averages
20-day ———
50-day ············
200-day ------

RSI

OBV

And, it's best to do so quickly. When a stock bounces off a catastrophic low, short-covering plus new buyers can jettison a stock higher very fast. It's better to cover short positions early than get caught in a short squeeze.

Figure 6 shows a daily chart of Conoco Phillips (COP). The huge integrated oil and gas firm fell from recent highs of $70.75 in August to a climactic low of $54.90 on October 4, 2006. In the weeks just before the October low, heavy volume came into the stock as fearful investors unloaded losing long positions in the wake of lower oil prices. Of course, shorts were covering as well, and new buyers probably started nibbling.

8. **Retest of important low + low volume = bullish**. When a market in a downtrend retests a major low on minimal volume (think double bottom), it indicates a lack of fear and selling pressure. In keeping with the old market proverb, "Don't short a dull market," know that this pattern signals bullishness and implies the downtrend may rapidly reverse to the upside on strong volume.

Figure 7 clearly displays this signal. In the double-bottom formation that formed on the daily chart of Transocean, Inc. (RIG), during August 2006, volume tapered off after the first low. On August 30, the oil services stock dipped to retest the prior low of $64.52 on August 15. On the retest, volume remained low, with selling exhaustion. The retest held on August 31, and volume remained low. The bears found themselves in a short squeeze on September 1, however the price of oil per barrel also held its lows and helped RIG to gap higher. This double bottom pattern (shaped like a W) is common and many times involves a price gap higher when the short sellers realize the stock is headed higher—at least for the short-term. Note how the RSI didn't react to the price drop in the retest—a positive signal. The OBV also created a bullish divergence on August 31.

On the retest, if price support holds from the prior low, short swing traders need to cover early enough to avoid the short squeeze and establish long positions when the reversal takes place. Day traders can play the retest to the long side, but position traders should wait to enter until the uptrend has been established. As you can see, RIG endured three volatile pullbacks after the pop higher. That would have flushed out many position traders who jumped in before RIG broke to the upside in early November.

Bottom Line

As you can see, strong price trends – short- and long-term — are created and maintained when price and volume expand and contract together. When volume diverges from price, price will usually follow volume's lead. Whenever you're not sure exactly what emotion dominates (bullish or bearish, greed or fear) in a volatile situation, bring up a chart of the stock in question on a smaller time frame. This often clears up traders' actual intentions. For example, climactic volume on a single candle on a daily chart can be the result of intense selling in the morning session, a midday price reversal, and then intense buying and short covering in the afternoon session.

These simple, yet compelling, principles give volume its power as an indicator. Add a volume momentum indicator, such as the OBV, candle signals, moving averages, and an oscillator of your choice, and you have a forceful set of combined signals that will furnish high-probability set-ups and entries.

Once in a trade, volume signals can act as a money management tool by alerting you to a possible future trend change or reversal. Whether you are an intraday trader, swing trader, or active investor, let volume, with its many voices, tell you what it prophesies about future price action!

Toni Turner is the best-selling author of *A Beginner's Guide to Day Trading Online* (Adams Media Corporation, 2000), *A Beginner's Guide to Short-Term Trading* (Adams Media Corporation 2002), and *Short-Term Trading in the New Stock Market* (St. Martin's Press, 2005). She is also a popular speaker and educator at financial conferences and forums nationwide. For more information, please go to: www.toniturner.com. A version of this article first appeared in *SFO* in March 2004.

DO SEASONS MATTER IN THE FINANCIAL MARKETS?

BY JERRY TOEPKE

The seasonal approach to markets is designed to anticipate the timing and direction of future price movement. A trader who knows how
a market has normally traded at a given time of year can prepare well
in advance for it to recur. Perhaps a trader armed with knowledge of
history can better understand current price activity and place the endless stream of news in context, helping him or her to act rather than just
react.

Although numerous factors affect markets, some conditions and
events recur at annual intervals. Traders and merchants for centuries
have used a seasonal approach to gain an advantage in markets directly
affected by the annual weather cycle. They know, for example, that—despite changing consumer tastes, economics or even war—nature sustains
an annual cycle in grain supply. They know that cold weather will create
demand for heating fuel. They know that annual cycles in nature create
annual patterns in supply and demand for physical commodities.

But what about financial markets? How can spring possibly affect interest rates? Does the stock market care whether it is hot or cold outside?
Most analysts tend to dismiss seasonal cause and effect as, at best, indi-
rect in financial markets. This discussion is not meant to dispute such
notions, for the seasonal approach is less about interpreting and arguing
than about observing and quantifying. The thrust is simply to introduce
the seasonal approach by discussing what it is, how and why it works,
what it can and cannot do, how traders might benefit from it, and how it
applies, if at all, to financial markets.

Natural Market Rhythms

Seasonality can be easily understood in a market such as heating oil. See *Figure 1*, in which supply and demand are obviously affected by the cycle from hot weather to cold and back again.

As hot weather begins in June or July, for example, demand (and, therefore, price) is at its lowest. As the industry begins to anticipate cooler weather, the market finds increasing demand for future inventory, which exerts upward pressure on price. Rising prices encourage refiners to increase production and distributors to sell inventory. (Refiners also are subject to tax on year-end inventories, providing financial incentive to pump as much product into the pipeline as possible during December. After that supply flush, price rises into peak consumption.) As the market then anticipates the end of cool weather, demand falls—exerting downward pressure on price, which encourages liquidation of supply into warm weather when consumption is again least. Seems simple enough.

Thus, the annual weather cycle creates an annual cycle in supply and demand for heating oil, which then gives rise to seasonal price phenomena—tendencies for price to move in the same direction, with greater or lesser intensity and in more or less a timely manner, with a certain degree of reliability at the same time each year. In other words, an annual pattern of changing conditions (cause) creates an annual pattern of price response (effect). In a market strongly influenced by annual cycles, as heating oil appears to be, seasonal price movement can become more than the simple effect of recurring cause. It can even become self-reinforcing—almost as if the market had a memory of its own. Why? Consumers and producers can fall into their own patterns of behavior. If they rely on seasonality almost to the point of becoming dependent on it, vested interests will maintain it.

The seasonal approach, then, originates from the following premise: each market has fundamental forces peculiar unto itself that act upon it every year. If one can find empirical evidence of a pattern in market reaction to those forces, then one can more broadly define seasonality as a consistent market tendency to repeat similar price movement annually. So defined, the principle is subject to being observed, analyzed and quantified in any market.

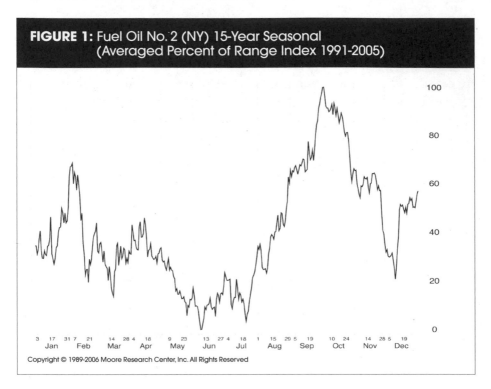

FIGURE 1: Fuel Oil No. 2 (NY) 15-Year Seasonal (Averaged Percent of Range Index 1991-2005)

Seasonal Patterns

Pattern implies some degree of reliability. One primary function of markets is to anticipate the future. To do that, price tends to move when anticipating change (cooler weather) and adjust when that change is realized. When that change is annual in nature, a recurring cycle of anticipation and realization evolves. This phenomenon is intrinsic to the seasonal approach to trading, which is designed to anticipate, enter and capture recurrent trends as they emerge and to exit as they are realized.

The primary focus of seasonal research is to look for recurrent trends within a seasonal price pattern. In the past, analysts constructed crude seasonal patterns from monthly or even weekly high and low prices. But computers can now construct a daily seasonal pattern of price behavior derived from a composite of actual daily price activity over several years. Properly constructed, the pattern reflects where, on any given day of the year, a market has tended to be trading within that market's annual price cycle.

Again, take a look at the seasonal pattern for fuel oil in *Figure 1.* The numerical index on the right-hand vertical scale reflects the

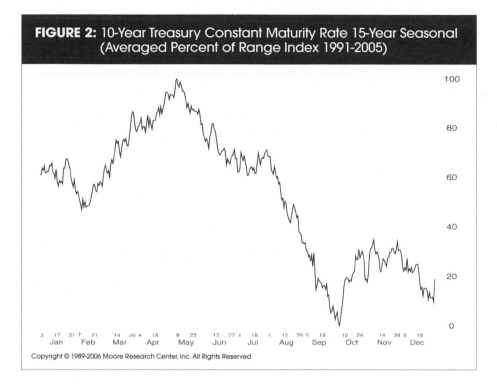

FIGURE 2: 10-Year Treasury Constant Maturity Rate 15-Year Seasonal (Averaged Percent of Range Index 1991-2005)

observed historical tendency for price most consistently to be high, when at 100—the seasonal high, and for price most consistently to be low, when at 0—the seasonal low. So, the pattern plotted illustrates tendencies for that market to reach both its annual peak and its annual bottom and to trend in between—a visual reference from which to better judge current price activity and to anticipate future price movement.

Patterns in Interest Rates?

Financial analysts are correct. Unlike grain or heating oil, interest rates do not depend on the annual cycles of sunlight. Nor does the stock market respond to the annual cycle in temperature. The calendar, however, marks the annual recurrence of important conditions and events. January 1 begins not only a new calendar year but also a new tax year. U.S. income taxes are due April 15. A new federal fiscal year begins October 1. The U.S. Treasury holds a quarterly refunding auction during the second week of the second month of each quarter. The real estate market (mortgage, anyone?) is busiest when school is out. One might suspect that this pattern of annual events affects the

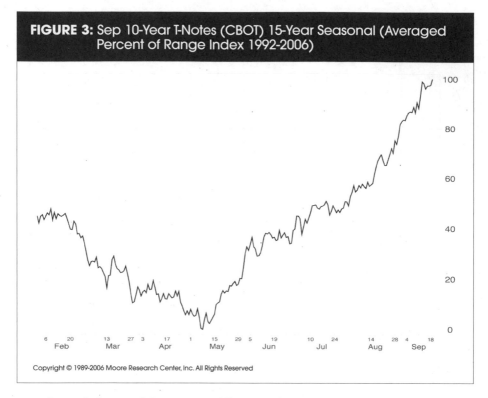

FIGURE 3: Sep 10-Year T-Notes (CBOT) 15-Year Seasonal (Averaged Percent of Range Index 1992-2006)

supply and demand for money. If so, perhaps there is an annual pattern in interest rates.

A wealth of economic data is available from the Federal Reserve Economic Data (FRED) at www.research.stlouisfed.org/fred, including U.S. debt security yields. Extracting data from FRED for the years 1991-2005 to construct a 15-year seasonal pattern in *Figure 2* for the 10-year Treasury Constant Maturity Rate generates a striking image. The interest rate underlying the current Treasury benchmark has exhibited a strong tendency to rise from mid-February into a distinct peak in early May and then to decline persistently into October.

So even someone with little financial background can make certain inferences. If market rates reflect monetary liquidity, then rising rates should reflect liquidity getting tighter. With what do rising rates into May coincide? Could a massive transfer in financial assets from out of the private and into the public sector in the form of income tax payments tighten monetary liquidity? Does re-circulating funds back into the economy loosen liquidity? Does consumer spending then increase through summer and into the holidays? Does the market

FIGURE 4: Financial Market Seasonals

	SEASONAL STRATEGY	ENTRY	EXIT	WIN	WIN YEARS
1	Buy 10-Year T-Notes (CBOT) – September	5/7	8/12	87%	13
2	Buy 10-Year T-Notes (CBOT) – September	5/29	7/14	87	13
3	Buy 10-Year T-Notes (CBOT) – December	8/6	10/4	93	14
4	Buy 10-Year T-Notes (CBOT) – December	8/13	9/15	93	14
5	Buy S&P 500 (CME) – September	6/24	7/3	80	12
6	Sell S&P 500 (CME) – September	7/16	7/23	80	12
7	Sell S&P 500 (CME) – September	7/31	8/8	87	13
8	Buy S&P 500 (CME) – September	8/8	8/25	80	12
9	Sell S&P 500 (CME) – December	9/16	9/24	87	13
10	Buy S&P 500 (CME) – December	10/26	11/16	100	15

Source: Moore Research Center, Inc.

anticipate a flush of new money as the new federal fiscal year begins in October?

Knowing why rates have tended to decline from May into October may be academic. Simply knowing they do, however, may have certain advantages—especially if they have done so frequently and reliably, as confirmed by historical fact.

Seasonal Strategies

To find out, consider the seasonal pattern that has evolved during those same fifteen years in September 10-year Treasury note futures in *Figure 3,* the prices for which have an inverse relationship with their underlying yield. In other words, one should approximate a mirror image of the other. That the seasonal pattern for the futures instrument does so confirms its legitimacy.

But futures also have certain characteristics of their own, such as deliveries and expiration. For example, the sharp decline at the end of February precedes First Notice Day for the March contract. Speculative liquidation to avoid deliveries? On the other hand, after the typical final decline throughout April and, then again after the Treasury's quarterly auction (new supplies of 5- and 10-year notes) in the second week of May, price surges higher into deliveries against June futures. Price appears to then have tended to rise persistently into early

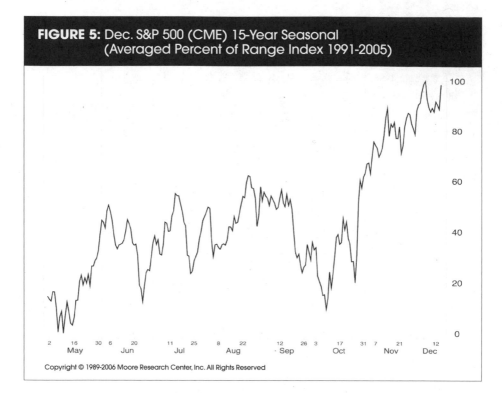

FIGURE 5: Dec. S&P 500 (CME) 15-Year Seasonal
(Averaged Percent of Range Index 1991-2005)

August, to decline modestly into another Treasury auction and, then finally, to spur higher into deliveries and expiration of the contract.

That seasonal trend appears nearly irresistible. But, would one just jump in? Or have certain times been more optimal than others?

Comparing actual daily closing prices for this contract during those fifteen years, computers can simulate all possible combinations of daily entry and exit. By setting standards for such considerations as statistical reliability, duration of time between entry and exit, and for historical profitability, the computer can discover entry and exit days that have tended to generate optimal price movements.

Take a close look at the table of historical strategies in *Figure 4*. Statistics on the first line for 10-year notes simply state the following: "September 10-year Treasury notes have closed higher on about August 12 than on about May 7 in thirteen of the last fifteen years, generating a move equivalent to an average of $2,207 per contract." (MRCI research shortens that trade window when an optimized entry or exit date falls on a weekend or holiday—hence, the word "about.")

Taken together, the table's four strategies for 10-year Treasuries—all historically factual—not only rigorously confirm the pattern illustrated, but also highlight segments of the larger seasonal trend during which recurring price movement has been especially vigorous and reliable.

Is There a Season in Stocks?

What about stocks? We hear about the good six months and the bad six months. We hear about the January Effect. We hear about end-of-month and end-of-quarter window dressing, earnings season and triple-witching—all recurring according to the calendar.

Well, take a look at the fifteen-year seasonal pattern for December S&P 500 futures in *Figure 5*. Tendencies for end-of-month buying surges are readily apparent throughout the chart, albeit muted going into September and October—the season most feared for having hosted some of history's most dramatic declines (1929, 1987, 2002). Why? Perhaps in olden days, wealthy investors returned from summer vacations to take profits and/or sell nonperforming stocks. Nowadays, October punctuates the fiscal year in the enormous mutual funds industry. As such, it has become known as tax-loss selling season, when mutual funds tend to sell poorly performing stocks to offset taxable distributions. Once complete, however, the bad six months usually are over.

Statistics for S&P 500 futures as seen in the table of seasonal strategies tend to confirm a trendless, choppy pattern of trading during much of summer. Despite its typical inability to sustain a trend during July and August, however, the market has oscillated with a great degree of reliability, with brief surges upward regularly reversing into brief declines and back again.

The Devil's in the Details

Such trading patterns do not repeat without fail, of course. Seasonal research is statistical analysis, factual but performed with the benefit of hindsight. Statistics confirm the past but cannot predict the future.

Thus, seasonal research does not generate a black-box trading system to be followed blindly. Like any other approach, it has its own inherent limitations. The research itself cannot be applied in a vacuum because it looks backward only. Think of an optimized date as resting at the peak of a bell curve of distribution— that date may not have been the best in any specific year, but that one date would have generated better results than any other for all years. Going forward then, a trader must consider such practical issues as immediate timing and even the potential for contra-seasonal movement. Fundamentals, both short and long term, inevitably ebb and flow. Some summers, for example, begin sooner and are hotter and drier at more crucial times than others.

Another issue of concern is the size of the statistical sample. Generally, bigger is better. In some instances, however, relying on more recent history may be more useful. Brazil's ascent as a global soybean producer in the 1980s was a major factor in the nearly 180-degree reversal in the seasonal pattern for soybeans from that of the 1970s. Conversely—and perhaps of much greater potential relevance in the immediate future for the financial markets—relying solely on disinflationary patterns prevalent in the last two decades could be detrimental to trading in an inflationary environment. During such historic transitions, patterns evolve.

A related issue is that of projecting into the future with statistics. A while ago, it was popular to project the direction of the stock market for the remainder of the year based on the winner of the Super Bowl. This statistical coincidence had no cause-and-effect relationship, but it raises a valid question: when computers sift raw data, what discoveries are relevant? To rephrase the issue for our purposes, how much does one rely on the simple but isolated fact that a pattern has repeated, for example, in 14 of the last 15 years? If it was the toss of a coin, are the odds any better than 50/50 going forward?

Thus, even trends of exceptional seasonal consistency cannot be taken for granted. The seasonal approach to trading best employs common sense, a simple technical indicator or timing trigger, and/or a basic familiarity with current market fundamentals. Doing so can help one not only decide if the anticipated seasonal price movement is likely to recur this year but also, because dates are not etched in stone, refine entry and exit timing.

But Nevertheless ...

Fundamentals drive markets. Recurring fundamentals drive recurring market responses. Knowing the fundamentals that drive patterns of market response inspires more confidence in their use, but knowing all relevant fundamentals for every market is impractical if not impossible. Properly constructed seasonal patterns can help one find trends that have recurred in the same direction during the same period of time with a high degree of past reliability. Such reliability implies recurring fundamental conditions or events that presumably will exist again in the future and affect the market to one degree or another and in a more or less timely manner. Rather than react with alarm and surprise, a trader who can anticipate a market's response can act boldly and with confidence.

Jerry Toepke is coauthor with Steve Moore and Nick Colley of *The Encyclopedia of Commodity and Financial Spreads* (Wiley, 2006). Toepke has been involved in futures markets since 1977 and is editor of Moore Research Center, Inc.,(MRCI) publications. MRCI provides computerized analysis of historical price movement in the MRCI Monthly Report, a series of historical reports for specific commodity markets; the Weekly Spread Commentary, and at www.mrci.com. Toepke can be reached at jerry@mrci.com. A version of this article first appeared in *SFO* in June 2003.

WHY THE MINIS MAKE SENSE

BY CATHERINE SHALEN

Mini-sized stock index futures (minis) are one of the few trading vehicles that is offered exclusively electronically, with trading hours extending close to twenty-four hours. Mini-versions of all the major U.S. stock index futures are available, the most active of which are based on the most widely followed U.S. indexes, mini-sized Dow futures, E-Mini S&P 500, and E-Mini Nasdaq 100 futures. We examine the factors that make these different minis tick.

The menu of mini-contracts provides a range of choices to traders with diverse capital constraints and appetites for volatility. Most important, it generates efficient opportunities to toggle and spread between the Dow, the S&P 500 and Nasdaq 100, the three key U.S. stock market benchmarks.

Volumes in the minis have exploded. The appeal is size and electronic access. A small contract size allows traders to take on less risky or more tailored positions. Screen trading is synonymous with smooth execution, price transparency and anonymity; it implies fast fills, order book visibility, and simultaneous access to multiple exchanges via front-end systems loaded with trading and risk-management software. These features facilitate arbitrage, spreading and technical strategies. Minis have therefore attracted a new clientele, a mix of individual professional traders, proprietary trading groups, market makers for related options and exchange traded funds, as well as CTAs and hedge funds, all of whom are well versed in these trading techniques.

Mini Trading Menu

Minis are not substitutes for one another; they present different opportunities and complement each other. Hence, it is most effective to trade them as a set. The choice of which contract or contracts to focus on at a particular time hinges on contract specifications but, most importantly, on the technical and fundamental characteristics of the underlying index.

Size - Minis come in several sizes. E-Mini S&P 500 futures and $5 mini-sized Dow currently have approximately the same size, $50,000, and E-Mini Nasdaq futures are both close to $20,000. A number of FCMs have offered reduced brokerage rates, making smaller contract sizes very competitive.

Leverage - Minis also provide different leverage. Margin leverage, the ratio of initial margin to contract size, is approximately 4 percent for mini-sized Dow futures, 7 percent for E-Mini S&P 500 and 9 percent for E-Mini-Nasdaq futures. Another way to look at this is dollar leverage, a bang for the buck measure equal to the ratio of intra-day dollar range and margin. The Dow and S&P 500 indexes have comparable volatilities, but a lower exchange margin rate is applied to Dow futures; hence, average dollar leverage is approximately 35 percent for mini-sized Dow futures and approximately 20 percent for E-Mini S&P 500 futures. The Nasdaq 100 index is two to three times as volatile as the Dow or S&P 500, but its high margin rate decreases dollar leverage to approximately 30 percent.

Underlying Index - The crucial difference between minis is the underlying index. The Dow, the S&P 500 and the Nasdaq 100 have distinctive flavors, different sensitivities to individual stocks, different sensitivities to broad market fluctuations, and different sector exposures. The dissimilarities begin at the construction stage. The Dow is a price-weighted average of 30 megacap stocks, the blue chips, and the S&P 500 and Nasdaq 100 are cap-weighted indexes of 500 and 100 stocks. The effects of price-weighting and a small number of components are to smooth out the distribution of Dow weights.

The upshot of this is:

(a) the Dow is not only very visible, it is also extremely easy to track and to analyze,

(b) the average index stock has a much greater impact on the Dow than the average stock has on the S&P 500 or Nasdaq 100,

(c) mini-sized Dow futures are an effective proxy for Dow stocks. By extension, they will be effective hedges for forthcoming futures on Dow and Nasdaq stocks,

(d) properties of index returns which technical traders follow such as speed of adjustment to market shocks, persistence, and speed of mean reversion differ for the three indexes. In particular, lags between the responses of two indexes to common news create spreading opportunities. Last, index construction has implications for arbitrage between futures and the equivalent basket. The Nasdaq basket and especially the Dow basket[1] are easier to arbitrage. There are fewer stocks and the Dow stocks are very large and liquid.

Since the Dow, Nasdaq 100 and S&P 500 have distinct sector profiles, which minis are most interesting changes over time depending on variations in sector volatility. The Nasdaq 100 is a technology index, even its health component is comprised of biotech stocks. The Dow and S&P 500 are both broad indexes with a diversified exposure to all economic sectors, but the mix is different. The most conspicuous weight imbalances are in four sectors: the industrials and basic materials are overweighted in the Dow, and financials and healthcare are underweighted. The Dow includes more consumer stocks and more old economy stocks. On the other hand, the tech sector weight of the Dow is close to the S&P 500 weight. The Dow used to be relatively tech-lite but this changed when Microsoft, Intel and Hewlett Packard were added in 1999.

An additional way to classify indexes is by style. Studies in asset pricing literature have identified style factors which predict stock performance, probably because they are correlated with fundamental or transaction risks. The main ones are size and the following ratios: book/market, price/earnings and dividend/price. In fact, these ratios have commonly been used by market practitioners to decide whether the style of a stock is growth or value. While stocks in the Dow are decidedly larger than S&P 500 or Nasdaq 100 stocks, all are so large that a measurable size effect is unlikely. The Nasdaq is solidly in the growth camp, and this is confirmed by its high price-to-earnings ratio. However, the signals indicating which of the Dow or S&P 500 is closer to growth or value are mixed. The Dow has a slightly higher dividend yield and lower price-to-earnings ratio than the S&P 500, and this points to value, but its lower book-to-market ratio points to growth. An alternative factor is that the Dow has proved more resilient to downturns, which suggests the market still perceives it as a quality index.

In summary, the conjunction of electronic trading and mini-contracts has opened stock index futures to new categories of traders, retail investors and proprietary trading groups. Unlike funds which traditionally use stock index futures for hedging, equitizing[2] and similar synthetic index strategies, these new traders specialize in technical strategies, in spreading and arbitrage. The minis that have proven most useful are those tied to major benchmarks.

Catherine Shalen, PhD, is a director in the research and product development department of the Chicago Board Options Exchange. This article appeared in *SFO* in July 2002, when she was a senior economist at the Chicago Board of Trade specializing in equity contracts.

1. The Dow basket equivalent to one MiniDow futures consists of N shares of each of the 30 Dow stocks where N = $5/ Dow Divisor for the $5 mini-sized Dow futures.

2. To "equitize" is to create a synthetic investment in the index portfolio by combining a futures position with a money market investment. It is one of the most common uses of stock index futures by funds, particularly S&P 500 futures.

11

IT'S WHERE YOU CASH OUT THAT COUNTS

BY JON NAJARIAN

Back in the 1980s, the Japanese claimed to have eight of the top ten largest banks in the world. It wasn't just their deposits that pumped up those balance sheets, it was an accounting peculiarity that allowed Japanese companies to value assets for the price they were purchased, rather than the fair market value. Simply put, they may have paid $400 million for an office complex two years ago that would fetch just $200 million today, but the bank needn't take that embarrassing $200 million hit, as it could and did still count the purchase price as the value of the property—a strange practice to be sure. But millions of investors do the same thing every day of every year, unwittingly letting profits slip through their fingers.

As a professional trader for the past twenty-five years and as a mentor to many young traders and individual investors, I can tell you that the malady I'm about to describe isn't something with which only individual investors struggle. It's something that everyone from the novice to the seasoned veteran has to deal with: forcing yourself to forget what price you paid for your trade.

Whether I'm sitting in on a morning meeting with floor traders or speaking to a crowd at an investment conference, invariably someone will say, "Stock XYZ was down $5 to $50 yesterday, but that's OK, because I bought it for $40 three days ago, so I'm still up $10."

They usually say this with a sense of pride, rather than embarrassment, perhaps thinking I will congratulate them on their shrewd purchase. Unfortunately for them, I don't applaud this behavior—I abhor it. It points out several weaknesses in their trading, not the least of which is their lack of understanding that every trade (investment) has an entry and an exit. Until you've actually closed the trade, you haven't booked the profit. If you make a timely purchase or sale of a security or futures contract, congratulations. In reality, you're only halfway home. You also need to capture that profit by closing out the trade. It doesn't matter whether you're bullish and your entry is a purchase, or whether you are bearish and your entry is a sale. You can't pop the champagne until you've cashed in your chips.

The other problem with this behavior is that the investor or trader remembers the entry price. That's a mistake because what you paid or where you sold is of little consequence. What matters is where that stock or commodity is right now. An opportune sale is wonderful, but where you cover that short position is eminently more important than where you established the position. When I'm looking at a portfolio, the last thing I care about is at which price the client established a given position. I care about the here and now, where I can buy or sell that asset this minute.

For example, Citigroup may have been an extraordinary buy at $27, but at $50 would I think it still represents a value versus other investment opportunities? If my answer is that I wouldn't buy Citigroup at this level, then frankly, why should I hold onto it? I should take my profit and wait until another long or short opportunity presents itself, but you'd be surprised to see how many people believe that they are playing with the house's money. These are the folks who either take smaller profits than they deserved or, worse yet, turn their winning trades into losers because they remembered where they got in rather than remembering that nobody ever went broke taking a profit!

When I ponder why individual investors have so much trouble with this concept, I have to blame the tax code and the IRS, which doesn't recognize a profit or loss for individuals until they close the trade. This policy has bred the mindless tax-loss selling that shows up every December, as investors scramble to recognize losses and match them against their gains. Professional traders are marked to market every day, meaning the profits and losses are right there in black and red, so it doesn't matter whether we close our trades or not.

Perhaps another reason some of us seem so reluctant to forget our entry price is strictly ego. We want to tell someone else how clever we were. It's more fun at a cocktail party to tell your neighbor that you shorted gold at $720 an ounce when it has retraced the move back to $580. Unfortunately they are missing the point completely—those $140 in profit are not yours to spend until you've closed out the trade. Pros trade in and out so frequently it's nearly impossible to remember every entry or exit price. For example, my brother Pete was a specialist for single stock futures (SSFs) on OneChicago. Pete used to make one hundred to five hundred trades per day in SSFs, hedging with 100,000 to one million shares of the underlying stocks. If he happened to buy the low of the day or sell the top, he may remember it, but not in relation to the corresponding stock or futures trade. The past is just that, history. What matters is where he can get in or out this second, assuming reasonable risk to reap acceptable reward.

Here's a tip for how you can break yourself of the habit of remembering where you got into a trade: sit with a friend and swap portfolios. Let him or her go over your positions and, conversely, you examine his or her portfolio. Invariably, you will find positions that seem to be ripe for harvesting. I think you'll hear conversations that go something like this:

> "Gee Mark, I notice you're still holding onto the IBM 90-95 bull-call spread. It's trading for $4.55, so I don't really think you can justify holding on for two more weeks just to make that last $0.45. If anything, I'm more a seller of that spread at these levels."

> "Well sure, Judy, but I bought that spread back in late November for just $2, so I'm....OK, I get your point. But since you brought it up, what about your butterfly spread in Sears? What are you waiting for?"

Professional traders and money managers go over their positions every day, which is probably too frequent for most individual investors. Daily portfolio assessment is not only impractical; it may also cause undue churning of commissions, which would erode profits.

You need to strike a balance between forgetting the price at which you established your trade and completely letting the market trade you. You should remember that investments in the stock or futures markets are not the same as making a bank deposit and leaving the money there until you need it. A prudent investment with a good risk/ reward ratio can turn into a terrible position, with horribly skewed risk versus reward in a very short period of time. Prudent traders and investors should keep the odds in their favor throughout the life of their trade, keeping their eyes on the prize, but weighing the probabilities and getting out when they've exhausted the edge they originally sought to exploit.

When you conquer the problem of remembering your entry price and, instead, focus on whether you should be in that trade at this level, you will truly be on your way to managing your risk and trading like a pro. If you insist on playing with the house's money, one thing is for sure—it will be the house's money again! Remember the problems with those Japanese banks. It's not what you paid for it. It's where the market is right now that matters.

Jon "Doctor J" Najarian is the editor of ChangeWave's Options Investor and OptionMONSTER.com. After a brief stint as a linebacker with the Chicago Bears in 1981, he came to the trading pits of Chicago, where he has stayed for 25 years. Najarian founded Mercury Trading in 1989, a firm that he sold in 2004 to Citadel, one of the largest hedge funds in the world. Over the past five years, he has developed, trademarked and patented numerous trading applications to find unusual activity in stock, options and futures markets. Najarian's work is widely cited by the financial press, including Reuters, Bloomberg, Dow Jones, Fox News Channel, CBS radio and CNBC. Additionally, he appears daily in more than 200 cities across the country on First Business Television, a business news magazine that commands a daily audience of some 1.8 million viewers. Najarian is also the host of the CBS radio show *Taking Care of Business with Doctor J*, and his market observations are broadcast daily on CBOE TV, a business television program that streams on www.cboe.com. He publishes his market observations, stocks to watch, trades of the day, option trade recommendations and his trading blog on his super-premium subscription web site www.OptionMONSTER.com.

FUNDAMENTALLY SPEAKING, AGAIN

BY PHILLIP GOTTHELF

Those over the age of 50 are fortunate enough to have been exposed to radically opposed schools of thought in the realm of investment market analysis. We know them as technical analysis and fundamental analysis. Before the mid-1970s, technical analysis was considered junk science—a sorry attempt to use past market behavior to determine future events. Everyone knew that the key to prediction was cut from a multifaceted template reflecting supply and demand. Forces that move markets are fundamental. Day-by-day market fluctuations are random and, thus, have no predictability.

With the advent of affordable computing technology, evidence supporting the random walk theory of non-correlated price events was slowly whittled away to the point where technical approaches to market prediction actually usurped traditional fundamental analysis. The battle was hot and heavy through the 1980s, but good old fundamentals finally gave up to the onslaught of cheaper and more powerful personal computers using highly sophisticated statistical analysis.

Today, the majority of trading rooms, dealing in everything from stocks to bonds and currencies to commodities, use technical analysis to determine strategy. Of course, economists still are modestly employed to paint a macro picture for long-term planning, but the bulk of trading is decided from pictures and formulae that seek solutions to technical equations.

Fundamentals vs. Simple Technicals

Yet with the paradigm shift away from fundamentals into technical analysis, one truth remains: all market trends are based upon fundamental changes in supply and demand. This axiom demands a question. Why, then, have so many traders seemed to abandon fundamental approaches to investment decisions? In a word, the answer is simplicity. Using computers, technical analysis is just easier. All that is required are historical price data. If analyzing options

TABLE 1: Some Considerations When Looking at Stocks Fundamentally	
Product or service	Competition
Product or service position	Technology and alternative tech.
Product or service maturity	Balance sheet
Company position	Revenues and expenses
Company reputation	Price-to-earnings ratio (P/E)
Management	Debt structure
Location	Credit rating
Distribution	Distribution of ownership
Insider trading	

TABLE 2: Some Considerations When Looking at Real Estate Fundamentally	
Location	Comparable properties
Size	Comparable recent sales
Design	Demographics
Condition	School system
Taxes	General economy
Mortgage rates	Availability

or commodity futures, one might add volume and/or open interest as statistical adjuncts to price data. But overall, propagating a technical forecast can be as easy as pressing a few buttons on the keypad.

In contrast, consider the most rudimentary fundamental view of a stock issue by looking at just a few superficial considerations in *Table 1*. We've listed seventeen, but the list, of course, goes on and on.

TABLE 3: Some Considerations When Looking at Interest Rates Fundamentally	
Inflation or deflation	Currency values
Money supply	Trade surpluses or deficits
Tax rates and policy	Election politics
Economic growth or contraction	Global conflicts
Relative global interest rates	Trade treaties and tariffs

TABLE 4: Some Considerations When Looking at Commodities Fundamentally	
Land availability	Old crop supplies
Soil conditions	Global competition
Weather	International policies on genetically altered crops
Planting	Hybrid technologies
Seed prices	Insect infestation
Government support programs	Timing for planting
Trade treaties	Timing for harvesting
Fertilizer prices	Economic health
Chemicals including pesticides	Crop insurance premiums
Price relativity to other feed grains	Transportation expenses
Cattle, hog, and poultry on feed	Fuel costs
Other grain suppliers	Irrigation
Global weather conditions	

Furthermore, all of these considerations must be distilled down into two variables used to solve for price: supply and demand. This is true whether we are looking at stocks, bonds or even real estate. What may seem simpler in the real estate arena may be more complex in reality (see *Table 2*). Remember, location, location, location is not the only consideration. Anyone in the real estate business can conjure up dozens of additional factors that would affect real estate values. Subtle aspects might even include Internet availability, water systems, zoning, street access and highway proximity. Actually, the list is quite daunting.

Bond fundamentals might be more condensed because so much depends on Federal Reserve policy relative to economic activity and health. Still, forecasting interest rates involves an enormous amount of data (see *Table 3*). There are more interest rate movers than those on the list, of course, but here again, the point is obvious.

We can even look at what some probably consider the more obvious markets that rely upon supply and demand; but will what might appear simple really be so? In fact, things look all the more complex. For example, one might assume it is easy to measure supply and demand for a commodity like corn. How much was planted? How much are we going to consume? But, as seen in *Table 4*, fundamentals number in the double digits.

These four tables make it clear that detailed fundamental analysis in any investment forum is likely to become extremely complex and cumbersome. However, just as inexpensive computing propelled technical analysis to the forefront of a market-predictive science (or art), so too has cheap computing begun to revive interest in fundamental methodology. Quantitative analysis has reached out to embrace fundamental complexity, and a new generation of market forecasters is adding momentum to a new movement founded in old science.

The one premise shared by fundamental and technical analysis is that supply and demand determine price. The trick is measuring the balance between supply and demand to derive a forecast. The technical approach holds that the number of bids reflects demand whereas supply comes from the offers. The mix of bids and offers produces price patterns that are reflected in charts or through statistical analysis.

In contrast, fundamentals assert that market inputs will generate demand while value creates supply. Thus, if fundamental factors like product line, management and other characteristics engender interest, demand for a stock will increase. As long as the price is perceived as undervalued, demand will lead supply. If a stock becomes overvalued, interest wanes.

Can Fundamentals Be Quantified?

My book, *Techno Fundamental Trading* (Probus), is based on the premise that fundamentals can be quantified and presented like technical analysis to derive patterns of supply and demand behavior. There are two key questions: How do you technically measure supply? How do you technically measure demand?

Beginning with the simplest example, imagine that you have five years of corn production data. By plotting the data, you can derive a chart of corn production with three possible patterns (see *Figure 1*).

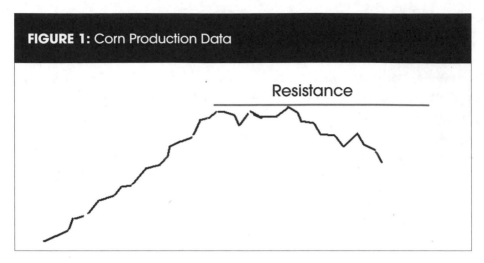

FIGURE 1: Corn Production Data

Resistance

It may show increasing production, decreasing production, or level production. Viewed within the context of technical analysis, we may observe familiar behavior like a trendline, single top, double top, bottoms, consolidations and even the infamous head-and-shoulders formation.

Generally, a supply chart will not look like the typical high/low/close bar chart. Yet we can discern the same formations and patterns with similar explanations. The cycle of production known as boom and bust is predicated upon the tendency of producers like farmers to overproduce with rising prices and underproduce when prices decline. While the government runs interference in agriculture with supports, loan programs and targets, the rules of the game are solid.

The real purpose of the exercise is to extrapolate a pattern and form a conclusion, i.e., farmers tend not to plant more than X amount of corn when prices are Y, or X is the upper limit of farm capacity.

When analyzing equities, fundamentals are reduced to technicals by indexing values. For example, the product may have one competitor or ten or even 1,000. The competition index would be one divided by the number of competitors. A complementary index would be a percentage of market. This produces a rank. These indexes are plotted to see if the company is static or changing position for better or for worse. Each fundamental datum in each category is plotted over time. In this way we see if positive factors are rising, falling, flat, or meeting resistance.

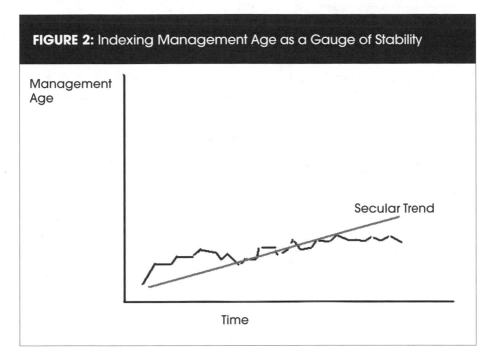

FIGURE 2: Indexing Management Age as a Gauge of Stability

Management Age

Secular Trend

Time

Remarkably, the rules that hold for price charts also seem to hold for data charts. Perhaps this is because chart patterns are inherent in the natural order of markets. There is a practical limit to the number of widgets that can be sold. When this limit is reached, the production line on a graph meets resistance. In a booming economy, this resistance level is likely to be challenged several times. If something changes fundamentally, shifting supply or demand patterns, it will reflect on the specific chart.

Taking Indexing the Next Step

Think about it: indexing is applied to everything from product position to management skills and maturity. While some measurements of management skills can seem subjective, there are objective criteria that include age, experience in years, salary levels, past successes and other criteria. Each is assigned a specific index weight. Then, a composite is summed to provide a comprehensive figure.

In *Figure 2*, we see an upward slope in management age to signify that management is probably stable and aging on a linear basis. If there were a turnover, the line would appear flat at a specific age preference for new hiring. A decline in age means the company is hiring new talent (on average), and we know there is likely to be culture change.

Certainly, a fundamental announcement that a CEO is leaving or upper management is being shaken up has an immediate impact on corporate value and perceived value. One does not need a technical chart of management youth or age to determine whether a change at the helm will be beneficial. We do know that volatile management tends to create price volatility in tandem.

Applying a technical interpretation to a fundamental data series is not the same as simply discerning direction from a chart. We know about momentum, ratios and reversals. The objective is to predict value by forecasting the changing appeal of an investment relative to the supply. With securities, there is a mixed blessing because we ultimately are investing in a fixed pool of shares. Unless a company splits stock or issues additional shares, we know there is a finite supply. This makes the equation somewhat one-sided.

Alas, the simplicity of the supply side is offset by the complexity of factors that comprise the demand potential. As listed earlier, companies encompass a multitude of facets, each reflecting a different response from would-be investors.

In comparison, one might conclude that agricultural commodity contracts represent ultimate simplicity. How much have farmers planted? How much are we going to eat? However, unlike equities, the number of bushels varies from year to year. There are no fixed numbers of bushels as there are fixed numbers of shares. This is further reflected in the additional technical component of open interest, the number of contracts existing between buyers and sellers. With every new contract, the open interest begins at zero and builds. The supply reflected by open interest can rise or fall.

By the same logic, debt tends to be variable. Companies issue more when needed and retire some when advantageous. The supply of U.S. Treasury bills, notes and bonds fluctuates in accordance with federal financing requirements. In this forum, fundamentals such as trade deficits, money supply, personal debt, estimated Gross Domestic Product and price indexes like the Producer Price Index (PPI) and Consumer Price Index (CPI) all form technical patterns of accumulation, distribution and consolidation. Consider our 10-year T-note continuation chart (*Figure 3*).

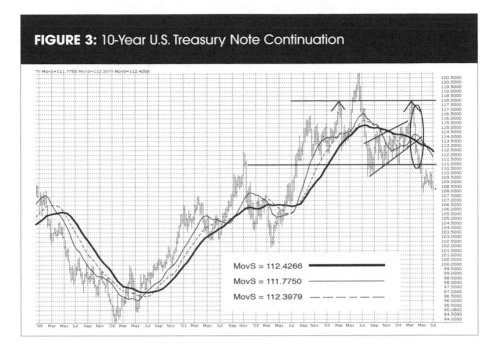

FIGURE 3: 10-Year U.S. Treasury Note Continuation

We see a top made late in the first quarter of 2003 and again in March of 2004. Both met resistance at 118-00 to suggest a trading range high. Notice the upward channel from August 2003 through April 2004. Fundamentals were telling the market that the economy was not improving sufficiently to motivate the Federal Reserve toward raising interest rates. What happened to suddenly plunge principal values below the 111-00 support in the circled reversal? We know that employment finally showed marked improvement. The reaction was sudden and violent.

In 2003, unemployment hit resistance at 6 percent. It was not the ten-year high (as seen in *Figure 4*), but it was cause for draconian measures by the Fed as interest rates touched their lowest levels in more than four decades. Employment, of course, is known as the last of the indicators to reflect economic change, i.e. improvement or deterioration. Business has become more nimble in laying workers off and slightly more resistant to hiring. The trends in employment tend to be smooth and consistent. The bounce off the 2000 low of 4 percent represented a practical limit to the unemployment level. Present theory holds that up to approximately 3.8 percent represents transient employment, which cannot be eliminated.

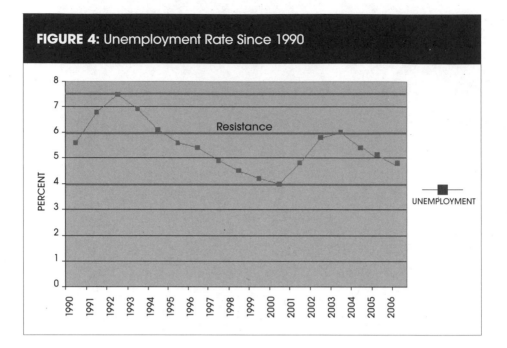

FIGURE 4: Unemployment Rate Since 1990

From a fundamental perspective, we could have assumed a bottom near 4 percent, but not necessarily predicted the turn. We know in hindsight that the stock market reversal in March 2000 acted as a catalyst for the recession that followed. Is there a predictive tool available by studying the chart pattern? We cannot see a definitive pattern in the sample size presented, but we see the formation of a top at 7.5 percent and bottom at 4 percent. We know that the turning points are critical for identifying interest rate trends.

If one is willing to abandon interim movement in favor of secular trends, the correlation is sufficient to derive a trading strategy. Simply put, buy ten-year notes when unemployment is rising and sell when unemployment is falling. This discounts all other factors. The astute reader will, of course, go the extra step in seeking those fundamental components likely to lead rising and falling employment.

A complete explanation of the fundamental revival would take a book—I know this because my first attempt barely scratched the surface at just more than two hundred pages. With new quantitative tools, fundamentals are likely to explode into a more sophisticated science. The debate over fundamental and technical analysis will heat up and perhaps rage onward. In my opinion, there is no cause for fighting. If it works, use it!

Philip Gotthelf is publisher of the COMMODEX, the longest-running daily futures trading system published anywhere, and president of EQUIDEX Inc. and EQUIDEX Brokerage Group. Known for his extensive work in the futures industry, Gotthelf's works have appeared in major industry and business publications. He is quoted regularly in Barron's, the Wall Street Journal, New York Times, Fortune, and Forbes, among others. Gotthelf also has written several books, including *The New Precious Metals Market* (McGraw-Hill, 1998) and *Techno Fundamental Trading* (Probus Press/McGraw-Hill, 1994). This article first appeared in *SFO* in September 2004.

TIME FOR A TRADING TUNE UP?
Maybe It's Time to Incorporate Charts

BY MICHAEL KAHN

Keep your fundamentals. No, really, keep them and use them, if that is your thing. This article is not going to try to convince you to come over to the dark side, nor is it going to attempt to convince you that the deliciously jargon-laced world of technical analysis is right for you.

What it is going to do is show you how employing a few of its tools can enhance, not replace, your investment decision-making process and get you better results with less risk. No, this is not snake oil. And while not a free lunch, it truly is a way to increase your success and decrease risk in the process. As with any methodology, there will be losses, but the ability to avoid more bad or marginal trades and to determine which winning trades should be pushed for all they are worth will immediately tip the scales in your favor. Think of it as try-ing to build a house with a hammer and saw. Wouldn't the addition of a simple cutting guide and nail gun make the work more efficient, more precise and less dangerous? It sure would, and that is the anal-ogy we can take to the bank here. Technical analysis provides tools, not magic.

There is a mantra I use in many of my presentations to budding chart watchers who are looking to buy stocks now and sell them at higher prices later. "Up is good, down is bad."

Is that a trite and condescending statement or a powerful tool that is elegant in its simplicity? That one phrase will differentiate between a stock (or any financial instrument) that is in a rising trend and one that is in a declining trend. It will tell us if something is at a certain price level because people are demanding it or because they are supplying it, whether it is cheap and a bargain or cheap and getting cheaper.

Benefits of Technical Analysis

In the words of Bruno DiGiorgi, CMT, there is one extreme benefit that technical analysis has over any other investment decision-making discipline: "You never restate a chart." In other words, whatever the traded price was will always be that traded price. There are no revisions. There are no restatements. There are no subjective measures. The price is the price, and there is nothing more reassuring as far as data are concerned. What it means is that the market—not an analyst—is telling us where supply and demand were in equilibrium. The chart pattern we saw for Intel in June 1992 is going to be the identical chart pattern if viewed today, tomorrow and ten years from now. There is no subjectivity.

Another benefit of technical analysis is that it can respond instantly to the changing perceptions of the market. This is just as important for long-term investors as it is for active traders because the fundamentals rarely change from day to day. However, in the markets, perception is reality, and what people think something is worth is more important than any analyst's model of its worth. Monitoring that is where a price chart is incredibly valuable—no matter what your time horizon. Blowout earnings and the stock falls? The fundamentals got better, yet the market thought otherwise.

There are as many ways to slice and dice market action as there are analysts, but there are a few basic concepts that everyone needs to know. As chart-watching skills develop, more of them can be employed. But in this discussion, we are just trying to demonstrate how a few concepts can enhance the work we are doing to pick stocks already.

Information in the markets does not flow instantly to all participants, is not absorbed by everyone in the same way and clearly does not elicit the same actions from everyone. If it were, then there would be no market action except between the steady bid/ask spread and no true movement until the fundamentals change. Price would jump in quantum fashion from one level to the next where it would settle into a new bid/ask spread.

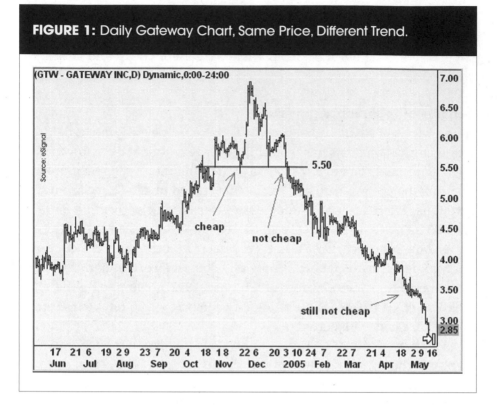

FIGURE 1: Daily Gateway Chart, Same Price, Different Trend.

Obviously, there are trends, and as the old saw goes, "the trend is your friend." We touched on this fact above, as a stock priced at $60 would be cheap in a rising trend on its way to $90 or expensive in a falling trend on its way to $30. The ultimate target may not be known, but as in physics, a stock in motion tends to stay in motion unless acted upon by an outside force (like news or a major change in the fundamentals). Determining the trend is the most important part of the analysis. Even a poor entry price in a strongly rising trend will eventually be overwhelmed by the gains made in that trend. Commissions, slippage, incomplete fills – you name it – are but annoyances in a strong trend.

Figure 1 shows the stock of Gateway, the maker of personal computers, as it rallied in late 2004 and fell in early 2005. For argument's sake, an investor was interested in buying this stock for fundamental reasons in November 2004. Price had pulled back to 5.50, and at this slightly lower price the stock was thought to be cheap. The trend was up and, sure enough, the stock rallied to 6.92 for a 25-percent gain.

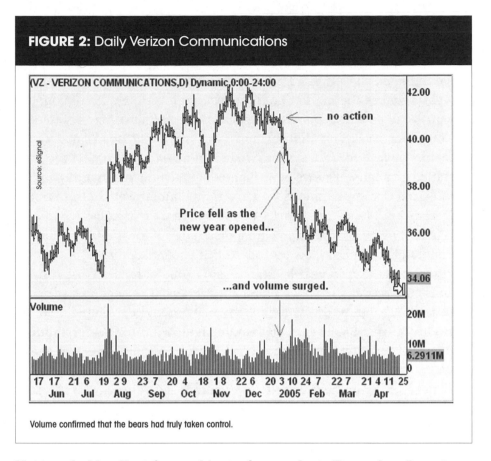

FIGURE 2: Daily Verizon Communications

(VZ - VERIZON COMMUNICATIONS,D) Dynamic,0:00-24:00

Source: eSignal

← no action

Price fell as the
new year opened...

...and volume surged.

Volume

Volume confirmed that the bears had truly taken control.

Not too shabby. Fast-forward just a few weeks to December. Investors were kicking themselves for missing the boat for the year-end rally and saw prices pull back once again to 5.50, the level that was cheap in November. They bought some shares, and again the investor had a nice little profit almost immediately. But the rally ended before it really got started, and price broke down hard, cracking the 5.50 level and never looking back again.

What happened? Did the company change that drastically in just two month's time? Did the overall market collapse? The truth is that there was a profit warning shortly after the peak price was reached, but as a chart watcher, it does not matter what the news was. What matters only is that the trend had changed from up to down, and what once was cheap at 5.50 was not even cheap at 4.00. The trend was down, and that occurred after the stock got an analyst upgrade at the end of November.

Volume as the Fuel

If price tells us where the market found value, then volume tells us how much conviction was behind it. Volume is the fuel behind any move in the market. Why? The more volume traded as the market moves, the more the market believes in what it is doing. For example, if a stock rallies a half-point on 500,000 shares and average volume is 600,000, then it is likely that the move was merely noise. Armed with that simple piece of information, we can more easily question the importance of whatever news or announcement came out that day.

Verizon Communications was in a rising, albeit weakening, trend in December 2004 when its price action suddenly froze (see *Figure 2*). Volatility evaporated and volume disappeared for the traditional Christmas-New Year's slow period. Nothing exciting there.

But when the new year began, the stock opened with a loss on volume that was easily above its recent average. The second day of the year saw an important breakdown on even higher volume, and the trend for the rest of the year was established. Wouldn't understanding this market reaction allow us to act with confidence as sellers of the stock?

There are even more ways to use volume, with the most important being confirmation of price action with volume. When price action goes in one direction and volume, or any indicator goes in the other, they are said to be diverging from one another. This divergence is a key concept in technical analysis, and price usually corrects in the direction of the indicator.

For volume, that means if a stock is rising and volume is falling, the fuel powering the move is drying up, and as the bulls exhaust themselves there will be nothing left to propel the stock higher. It works for stocks, and it works for the stock market as a whole. It works in the futures markets, and it works in bookshops, food stores and lawn care services. If demand from buyers goes away, the sellers of products and services will be competing for fewer customers. Prices must fall.

Everyone Wants to Play

Momentum was the buzzword for the late 1990s in the stock market. Stock prices defied the fundamentals as they continued to rise simply because everyone wanted to play. And nowhere in the world do people want to buy more of something at higher prices than in the markets. This is another area of technical analysis rich with indicators, concepts and techniques. However, it also requires further understanding of the action to employ properly. Consequently, we'll have to leave it at the basic concept, which says that as prices rise, they need to maintain the pace of rising highs and lows. When each rally within the rally starts to get weaker—and we can tell this without the actual indicators—then we'll get the idea that the bulls are getting tired. Wouldn't knowing this help us avoid some questionable purchases before the bad news appeared in the fundamentals? The converse is true in declining markets to uncover tiring bears. Wouldn't knowing this allow us to act with confidence as buyers of the stock if the fundamentals were turning higher?

We've already discussed that perceptions are reality in the markets. What people think something is worth is more important than any model of value. When we step back to ponder that thought, we realize that it is the only way for the price of any stock, house or botox treatment to deviate from the underlying fundamentals. There would be no such thing as overvalued or undervalued without sentiment

The final aspect of technical analysis is time, but for beginning chart watchers it becomes just a subjective measure. We'll leave this for another discussion, preferably one directed at those already using the technicals.

Technical Tool Box

There are tools available to measure each area of technical analysis. For now, though, the best strategy is to keep it simple and choose one, maybe two, to try at this time. Forget the jargon. Think about the concepts:

- What is the major direction of price movement? (trend)
- Is the public participating in the move? (volume)

Then add some of the more advanced concepts:

- Is the trend seemingly normal, or is it moving at an unusually accelerated pace? (momentum at an extreme reading)
- Is momentum waning, whether up or down? (momentum)
- What is the general mood of the public? (sentiment)

All of this can be done (with the possible exception of extreme momentum readings) with a simple chart, a pair of eyeballs and a set of ears. Nothing fancy is required for the basics of assessing whether the market is favorable or unfavorable for the investment purchase or sale.

Because there is only one outcome for any market analysis—the decision to buy, sell or hold—there is no need for whiz-bang studies and Nostradamus-like prognostications of the future. We cannot control that; neither can we know what the future will bring. All we can do is control our actions today, and that means finding likely buy or sell candidates, running your fundamental, quantitative or economic analyses on them, and then turning to the charts to see what the market is saying. The market is always right. Doesn't it make sense to ask what it is thinking?

Michael Kahn is a well respected technical analyst. He writes the *Getting Technical* column for Barron's Online (www.barrons.com), the daily *Quick Takes Pro* technical newsletter (www.QuickTakesPro.net) and is a regular contributor to *SFO*. Kahn is the author of two books on technical analysis, most recently *Technical Analysis: Plain and Simple: Charting the Markets in Your Language* (Financial Times Prentice Hall, 2006), and was chief technical analyst for BridgeNews. He also is on the board of directors of the Market Technicians Association (www.mta.org). This article first appeared in *SFO* in January 2006.

SECTION THREE
Online Trading and the New Edge

Online trading, now well out of its infancy, is constantly evolving to better meet the needs of the electronic trader and even give him or her a competitive edge. Technological sophistication has increased access, provided strategic advantages and reduced brokerage costs.

What does this mean for the online trader? Electronic order execution has become faster, virtually seamless and more transparent. And choices—for everything from electronic interfaces to order routing and stops—-have increased significantly. An order-entry system is your portal to Internet-based trading. We'll give you some pointers on finding the one that works best for you. This section will also outline the new basics on order routing and help you determine the best order type for your trading practice.

Stops, the most common method of risk management, are a critical part of trading. We'll tell you why electronic stops are better today and more important than ever. And we'll discuss the different types of stop orders and how you can benefit from understanding and using electronic order execution tools right.

This section also explores challenges specific to electronic trading—finding a broker who's really available when you need him or her; stopping yourself from trading simply because it's so easy to trade online; and getting caught up in the world of too many bells and whistles.

And lastly, everyone wants to know when to buy, but equally as important is figuring out when to sell. We've collected a dozen quick and handy rules that will help you determine when to get out.

PLACING ELECTRONIC ORDERS: Get Up to Speed

BY TONI HANSEN

The world of online trading is constantly evolving. As you read this, new methods of order execution are being developed, all in the name of establishing a transparent and competitive marketplace.

In the early '70s, placing an order could be quite a guessing game. Stocks were traded on a number of exchanges throughout the country, and the prices from one exchange to the next could differ by degrees that current market participants would find utterly unacceptable. This all began to change in the mid-'70s. The National Market System (NMS) was designed in 1975 to break down the barriers to market competition and the fragmentation of the market. The NMS posted security prices simultaneously on regional exchanges, which ensured that trading activity met specific standards. The goal was to create a strong central market, providing universal access with fair and accurate sales reporting.

A strong backlash against wide spreads between the bid and ask prices during the late '80s led the Securities and Exchange Commission's (SEC) to develop the order-handling rules that dealt with the trading of NASDAQ stocks. These went into effect in January 1997. The most remarkable aspect of these new rules was that they allowed for the creation of alternate means of accessing the market. This opened the door for the development of the Electronic Communication Network (ECN), which in turn opened a whole new world for the individual trader, full of endless execution possibilities. This discussion will outline some of the major electronic execution options that an individual trader has today.

Equity Trading: Level I and Level II

When it comes to trading and investing, my mantra is to keep things as simple as possible, so let's start with the basics. Most independent online traders access the equity markets through either Level I or the increasingly popular Level II accounts. The difference is that Level II access lets traders see more clearly the levels of trading activity already on the books. While Level II still does not show the entire picture, due to specialized order types that may contain hidden liquidity, it can give the individual trader a better picture of the overall market than the simple bid versus ask prices shown on Level I. While Level I access is adequate for many smaller investors, a difference of several cents can be significant to a short-term trader or one who is trading large amounts.

Basic Order Types

In the world of today's online or direct access trading, a slew of possibilities exists for order routing. The two most widely known are the market order and limit order. These can be used by both commodity and equity traders. A market order is used to get into a position at the current market price, no matter what that price is. It will nearly guarantee that one will be buying on the ask or selling on the bid. In a worst-case scenario, a trader can be subjected to a significant amount of slippage. It is, however, the best way to try to ensure a fill.

A trader has more discretion when using a limit order. He has the option of setting his own price at which the trade will be executed. A limit order can only be filled at the specified price or better. Using a limit order presents the trader with the possibility that he may only receive a partial fill or even none at all. Unless a trader is near the first in line for his desired price, several trades may go by without his trade being executed, if there is not enough liquidity to fill all the orders at that price level.

Odd lots, in increments of less than one hundred shares, or orders placed in a rapidly moving market, are the most difficult to complete using a limit order. Light volume also makes execution more problematic. To receive a fill more easily, I try to stick to equities or commodities with higher levels of liquidity and will usually split the spread or buy on the ask when I want a position. When exiting a day-trade position, I often have an order on the books well ahead of the price I target

Terms to know:

Ask: The price a seller is willing to accept for a security. This is also called the offer.

Bid: The price at which a buyer is willing to pay for a security.

Bracket Order: A three-part order, which includes the entry order, stop exit order and target exit order. When one exit order is fulfilled, the other is cancelled.

Conditional Order: An order that is automatically submitted or cancelled only when specified criteria are met.

Electronic Communications Network (ECN): An electronic system designed to allow traders to trade directly with each other when executing orders.

Good 'Til Cancelled (GTC) Order: An order to buy or sell a security at a set price that remains active until the customer cancels it, or it is filled.

HybridMarket: The NYSE's proposal for integrating the electronic and auction markets.

Level I: A trading service consisting of real-time bid/ask quotes.

Level II: A trading service that consists of quotes from individual market participants.

Limit Order: An order to buy or sell at a specified price or better.

Market Order: An order to buy or sell immediately at the prevailing market price.

OCA Order: Orders in a one-cancels-all group will be cancelled when one of the other orders is executed.

Small Order Execution System (SOES): A computer network that was designed to allow small investors (trading under 1000 shares) to execute trades in a fast moving market in the NASDAQ.

Stop Order: An order that becomes a market order to buy or sell once the specified stop price is hit.

Stop Limit: An order that becomes a limit order once the specified price is hit.

SuperMontage: Replaced SuperSOES and SOES as a fully integrated order entry and execution system used by NASDAQ for all securities' transactions.

Tick: The minimum upward or downward movement in the price of a commodity or security.

in an attempt to be one of the first in line to be filled. For instance, if my target on a stock is $50, I will place a limit-sell order at $49.96. The E-mini Nasdaq 100 (NQ) likes to move in increments of five points, so when I am looking to exit into the price resistance at 1680, I will put my order in at 1679.5 to have a better chance of getting a fill. By undercutting the whole number resistance, I avoid fighting with other traders just above me, while still placing myself favorably in my target zone and at higher odds of receiving a fill.

Making the Best Use of Stop Orders

Stop orders are a third type of order that is very popular. These are dormant orders that are triggered and become active only when a stock or commodity hits a price specified by the customer. There are several forms of stop orders. The first is a regular stop order. It is a market order that goes live only if it trades at or beyond the price specified by the trader. If I have to step away from my desk for a few hours and have an open long position in Apple Computer Inc. (AAPL), a sell-stop order would be a great way to protect me from a large adverse move against my position. The order is under the current market price and triggered only if my sell-stop price is hit. Often brokers will let traders set up their trading platform to specify how many ticks must trade at the sell-stop price level before the order goes live. Because this is a market order, the odds tend to be higher that I would end up losing a bit more than the price I specify for my stop. This possibility should be considered when looking at the risk and reward potential on a position.

A stop-limit order, on the other hand, is executed only if it trades at or better than a price specified by the customer. While stop orders are primarily touted as a means of protecting gains or limiting losses, they can also be used to enter a trade. If I want to buy a stock once it breaks $20 but wish to pay no more than $20.20, I can do this using a stop-limit order. I would select $20 as the stop price and $20.20 as the limit price. While I am guaranteed to pay no more than $20.20, which might not be the case had I used a regular stop order to enter, I am not guaranteed execution. If I were using a stop-limit order to exit a position, I would also run the risk of not being able to get out within my limit range.

Another form of a stop offered by some brokers is the trailing stop. This lets a trader set a certain price or percentage at which he can trail out of a position. I am personally not fond of this form of stop simply because it ignores the basic tenets of technical analysis. A trailing stop method that relies on giving back a specified amount regardless of the trade setup itself is rather arbitrary. For instance, if I were to set a trailing stop of $0.10 or one point in a commodity, it would have nothing to do with the support or resistance levels at work in a position, nor does it take into account the time frame of the type of setup involved.

With experience, most traders are more successful when they execute stop-loss orders or trailing stop orders manually. This is an aspect of trading that is difficult for beginners to overcome. It requires a lot of trial and error, as well as patience. Automated stops are important when I cannot monitor a position closely, but typically I prefer to set sound alarms at key levels on my open positions to alert me to ongoing developments. I will keep stop-loss orders on the books only to protect me when I cannot be there to protect myself.

From here on out a trader's options for more precise executions appear virtually limitless. This can often leave new traders quite confounded. The types of orders a trader has at his fingertips depend not only on the exchange but also on the broker with whom he is executing the trade. Within these confines, a trader has to choose not only where to route an order, but also what conditions he wishes to attach to it.

Order Routing

The choices a trader has regarding electronic order execution will expand even more as technology progresses by leaps and bounds. The cutting-edge order-entry options from the late '90s are already obsolete. ECNs and other alternative-trading systems have moved from the NASDAQ to other exchanges, and the lines between them have melded. The New York Stock Exchange (NYSE), for instance, is rolling out its new hybrid market, which combines today's technology with the auction market. The result is greater liquidity and potentially faster order execution.

For simplicity's sake I stick primarily to the smart order routing option when dealing with equities. Smart order routing can be used to trade both equities and options. From the moment a trader enters either a market or limit order, smart orders use a price-sensitive algorithm that searches various market participants and exchanges available at that instant to rapidly locate order flow and match up a trader with his or her parameters. Many of the larger brokers have their own versions designed to improve order routing.

While smart order routing is best for my needs, scalpers and those trading stocks with less than an average daily volume of about 500,000 need to have much better execution skills and finesse to quickly get into and out of a position without slippage. To do this, I would recommend studying the current order options more in depth and consulting a broker to determine the suitability of the routes available.

On the NASDAQ, SuperMontage has replaced SuperSOES and SelectNet, combining the liquidity of both ECNs and OTC market makers with several order types available. On the NYSE, the SuperDot system handles the majority of orders, delivering them directly to the specialist's post. The NYSE recently merged with Archipelago (ARCAEX), one of the very first ECNs to emerge on the scene, whose order routing program handles both listed and NASDAQ stocks and can access the liquidity of multiple ECNs.

While the differences between using a market order versus a limit order or stop order can be rather substantial, dozens of other order conditions also exist. Each has its own place, but there are several that I use with a great degree of frequency when trading both commodities and equities; I will touch upon those dealing with market timing and managing positions here.

When placing an order, one of the choices traders must make is how long they want their orders to remain on the books. A typical order will be cancelled at the end of the trading day. If I am really fond of a setup, however, and am looking at it as a swing trade or longer-term position, I will typically use what is called a good 'til cancelled (GTC) order. This type of order remains active until it is filled or until I personally cancel it. In utilizing this order type, it is important for me to choose to have it executed only during regular trading hours to avoid extreme fills in the after-hours market.

Like many traders I know, getting into a position was always the easy part. Once in a trade, however, it could be tempting not to follow my plan and either jump a stop or take gains too early or too often. While not always ideal, a great way to work on overcoming these issues is to use bracket orders, one-cancels-all (OCA) orders or conditional orders to manage a position and limit emotionally charged, split-second decision-making.

A bracket order is designed to limit losses and lock in profits by bracketing an order with both a stop order and a target exit order attached to the original entry order. When either the stop or target is hit, the opposite side of the order is cancelled. An OCA order is similar. When one of the orders in the group is executed, the remaining orders will be cancelled. If I have an order to take gains on a stock at $49.95 but want out if it goes under $49.50, then I could place an OCA order with a limit sell order at $49.95 and a stop order at $49.44. If the $49.95

order is filled, my stop order at $49.44 will be cancelled. A conditional order is submitted only if the criteria I have chosen are met, so it is also a great option. All three of these order types can be used to help train a trader to stick to their plan and execute it accordingly.

While order conditions are extremely useful under certain circumstances, one disadvantage to using them is that it rules out intuition and discretion, which come with experience. Traders must also watch out for stocks that are gapping past one of their orders, because a stop order will still trigger out of the open even if the price is no longer near where the desired price had been when it was originally placed. I have had this happen to me on occasion when I have not been able to pay close enough attention at the open. The experience was rarely a pleasant one.

A Building Block

As we move toward a global market, the rapid advances that began in the '70s will eventually begin to stabilize. In the meantime it can be easy to become overwhelmed, particularly as a novice market participant. While there are many other options for trading than I have outlined in this article, developing a focus is not as difficult as it may seem when building upon the options described above. Every trader, over time, will develop his or her favorite strategies for trade execution based upon the trader's activity level, preferred trading time frame, and whether he or she trades stocks, futures or options. Just take it slow, starting with the basics. Understanding the different order types and how they can be utilized is just the first step and one of the many building blocks of successful trading.

Toni Hansen is president of The Bastiat Group, Inc., a company founded in 1999 to provide market education to fellow traders. A popular speaker at industry expos, Hansen specializes in trading and investing in stocks, as well as E-mini futures. Her syndicated daily market commentary can be found at www.tonihansen.com. Hansen can be reached at toni@tradingfrommainstreet.com. This article originally appeared in *SFO* in April 2006.

TRADING TOOLS: What You Need to Succeed

BY JIM KHAROUF

Ask a trader about what tools you need today in this fast-evolving electronic trading world, and the answer often is, "It depends."

When looking at electronic trading systems, which include order-entry software, charting and data services, desktop computers, monitors and Internet access, a trader's needs depend largely on the type of trading he or she does. Scalpers and high-volume day traders may use different hardware and software than swing or position traders. And, so, like buying a car, it depends on what kind of driver you are.

But in speaking with almost a dozen traders and instructors, a number of similar ideas emerge when examining the nuts and bolts of electronic trading, especially when it comes to order entry. The most common advice is to find a setup that is fast, reliable and comfortable for your trading needs. That can mean automated functions that allow for many differing types of trades and spreads with one click. It also means that order-entry systems are often just one part of an entire package or trading platform.

There is little debate that electronic trading is becoming easier and more sophisticated. As stock, futures and options exchanges become more electronic, so, too, are the number of contracts available that can be filled in a matter of milliseconds. And as exchanges from Archipelago to the Chicago Mercantile Exchange to the International Securities Exchange introduce new functionality on their trading platforms, order-entry systems are following suit with new spread and multiple order strategies. In other words, if an exchange's electronic platform is offering new functionality, chances are that traders will be getting them on their front-end trading software. Ultimately, using electronic order-entry systems, charting and data are just tools needed to do the job.

Dan Gramza, president of Gramza Capital Management in Evanston, Illinois, and long-time trading instructor, said the entire electronic trading system is an amazing tool, but it still comes down to understanding what a winning or losing trade is.

"What is absolutely wonderful and absolutely terrible about electronic trading is, it is so easy to execute an order," Gramza says. "And so day traders have a tendency to trade just to trade. And that is not the business. The business is identifying clean business decisions. The process to trade should be mechanical. All of the thinking should be done before you ever execute a trade."

Thoughtful consideration should be given when choosing a system. Traders advise sampling a few different front-end trading systems or data and charting vendors to determine the right combination that works for your trading room and trading style. Here are some guidelines to help you make that decision.

Order Up

Talk to enough traders about order-entry systems and eventually you find a common denominator which surprisingly is, they don't think about them much. And that's the point really. An order-entry system should be as comfortable and intuitive to use as the mouse or keyboard in front of you. Some traders advocate a trading screen that has buy and sell buttons at enough distance from one another so a trader is less likely to make a costly mistake. Others say they want a fairly flexible order-entry system that allows a trader to customize the screen and put contracts, prices and so on where they want.

According to many traders, the top element to look for in an order-entry system is stop functionality. While this seems almost a given, traders and gurus say having a variety of stop orders is part and parcel of a day trader's job. Stop orders often serve as the primary risk-management tool day traders use to manage losses in a losing trade. Stop orders also are insurance against technical glitches. If the Internet connection goes down, the computer melts down or the local power company goes dark, you're protected.

Denise Shull, a short-term trader in New York, says her order-entry system automatically installs stops on her trades at her set level. She uses hard stops and trailing stops in trading mini-Dow futures, E-mini S&P futures and E-mini Russell 2000 futures. Shull employs a strategy that breaks down a trade into quarters and adjusts the trade with stops as it goes along.

"You can do just about anything you can imagine with these strategies in terms of initial stops," Shull says. "You can also create specific stop strategies, as opposed to just one hard stop. You can add trailing stops or auto break-evens."

Kate Meyer, a day trader in St. Charles, Illinois, who trades index futures, 30-year bond futures and the euro, says her front-end system allows her to enter multiple orders simultaneously with profit targets, and stops as well as trailing stops.

"For example, if you enter a three-lot, from your entry point your system will automatically sell one at your first target, another at your second target and the last at your third target," Meyer explains. "So if you reached a profit objective, you've automatically moved your stops according to your criteria."

While most of today's order-entry systems offer a long menu of functionality, it is the simple and straightforward instruments that traders use. Complex spreading or multi-legged trades across stocks, futures and options simply are not used often by day traders.

Even experienced traders say the key is to use a front-end that is simple to operate and provides the functions needed.

"I don't need all the fancy gadgets," says Chris Terry, of LBRGroup.com, an online trading service. "I need something that can put a limit in and a stop. That's that. I don't do any of the exotic stuff."

Traders and trading instructors alike want to make the order-entry interface cleaner and simpler, rather than adding or using more bells and whistles. Most just want the basics—buy, sell, stops, limit orders.

Paul Quillen, president of daytradingcourse.com in Atlanta, could be considered a minimalist. He developed his own front end that does not show the account size, profit and loss on a trade—just the market being traded. "We want to be very intuitive when trading and actually want less information than most everyone else," Quillen says. "We want a minimum amount of information on our order-entry interface. We tried using other order-entry front ends, but we couldn't eliminate enough extraneous information, so we developed our own intuitive interface."

Another crucial element of order-entry systems is the broker itself. Finding an online broker is simple enough, but traders advise to make sure the broker is available by phone when something goes wrong. As easy as that may sound when a firm touts its 24-hour help desk, it is essential that your broker have a live person on the other end of the phone in a pinch. More than one trader said some brokers are just as well known for great technology as their reputation of not picking up the phone when a technical glitch occurs. Traders advocate asking others about the phone-service quality before setting up an account.

One feature traders and instructors were unanimous on was on the benefits of simulated trading. Traders say brokers' order-entry systems should allow for real-time simulated trading, although some are tape delays of the market. Serious traders use simulated trading early and often. For one, it gets traders familiar with their order-entry system and charting software. More importantly, it allows traders to understand their mistakes and winners.

"It's critical for traders who have not used that platform to get very comfortable with it," Gramza says. "You don't want to have to pay to learn mistakes made on the system."

He adds that many traders do not want to try out new things with their own money, which can limit a trader's growth and opportunities. Shull, for example, was using simulated trading to experiment with the automatic trailing stop feature on her order-entry system.

"It's a tool that can verify a trade," Gramza says. "So if we assume that if this happens, that happens and I want to do the trade, is that a good strategy? If we've done our research and decided how much risk to take and how much profit—and shame on us if we don't know that before we enter the trade—you can see not only how the system performs but also how the strategy performs."

There are critics who say simulated trading doesn't always work because traders know it isn't real. A losing trade in a simulated environment is sometimes looked at like a car crash in a NASCAR arcade game. You just start over. Gramza, Terry and others disagree completely.

"Some people say there is no emotion attached until they put their money down," Gramza says. "That says something about that person's attachment to money and relationship to having to trade with money. It shouldn't be any different. One of the objectives a trader has is to stay unemotionally involved. Having a simulated environment allows us to say, "Is this a clean trade? If so, I'll take it.'"

Terry advocates using a simulator for several months just so traders can get used to the look and feel of the markets they are trading. "A beginning trader should be real and honest and do simulated trading for six months and not restart every day because yesterday was a bad day," Terry said. "Count your wins, count your losses, and understand how hard markets are."

Clearing Away Clutter

The less-is-more aspect of order entry, data and charting services applies to performance of a trading system as well. This brings up a litany of issues—from a computer's processing power, to the type of Internet connection, to a broker's server configuration. Computer experts say seemingly benign programs such as e-mail or Internet programs can swallow precious memory and slow down order entry or price data coming in. That time lag can wreak havoc on a trader's strategy.

Joe Whitney, technical manager for YJT Solutions (formerly You Just Trade) in Chicago, advocates using a high-end computer for trading and a second computer for Internet usage and e-mails. He recommends at least one GIG of RAM to handle trading, data and software.

And if speed is an issue, he recommends working with the broker's technical staff or the ISV's tech support to help set up the trading desktop for optimum processing. Whitney says many traders do not know how much of their computer's memory is being used in a standard PC configuration.

"A lot of folks order Dell computers, and when you order a PC like that, it comes pre-configured with a lot of bells and whistles running in the background that you wouldn't want stealing your processing power," Whitney says. "ISVs have optimization check lists to get the most out of your PC."

He also advocates checking with your broker to find out how its servers are configured. Many brokers today are dedicating servers to order routing with a completely separate server configuration for its own internal e-mail and non-trade-related traffic.

Keeping an Eye on Things

Finally, there is the visual issue that brings up the number of monitors a trader should use. Not surprising, there isn't a consensus number. Some experts like to have eight or more monitors so they can track a variety of trading opportunities. John Carter, president of Trade the Markets, Inc., in Austin, Texas, says the number of monitors is a balancing act.

"There is a fine line between having enough monitors and having too many," Carter says. "I think two is the absolute minimum. Me, personally, I have eight trading monitors to look at swing-trading setups and day-trading setups."

Others recommend between two and four monitors. Quillen uses just two monitors—one for order entry and the other for a single chart with no extra colors, no grid lines and no trend or support lines. Beyond that, he says, traders should keep their work space as bare as possible, adding that the mind can only handle five to twelve variables that are seen before but are not used.

"Take the twenty Post-it notes off the edges of your monitors," he says. "Doing almost anything well, especially trading, requires intuition. Anything on the screen that puts you into an analytical mode inhibits your intuition."

Jim Kharouf is a financial reporter with 16 years experience. He is based in Chicago and has covered stock, options and futures markets worldwide. This article originally appeared in *SFO* in October 2005.

JOIN THE 21st CENTURY:
Investors Better Served with
Electronic Order Entry

BY DAVID NASSAR

Market myths have survived the years rather well, and while some typically die a very slow death, several of the most classic myths currently are being read their last rites as the result of technology.

One in particular is that brokerage firms are professional traders armed with the skills to forecast the market's future. This is simply not the case. Firms that offer research, analyst ratings, retail brokers, and market making operations make money on commissions and order flow. Therefore, best execution with minimal slippage in price is no more their incentive than casinos offering free drinks. Like the free drinks, brokerage firms use research and analysis to attract trading activity—the more activity, the more revenue. Free drinks intoxicate stupid gamblers—just as free market research yields emotional order flow—profitable activity for either party. As such, the quality of execution and research is immediately called into question.

The self-directed trader and investor must not only take responsibility for decision-making regarding market timing and directional bias, but also avoid sending orders to human sharks that may get paid to eat you. The technological quantum leaps that have occurred in the last several years have destroyed and crumbled myths that have survived for more than two hundred years. And, indeed, those firms that manipulate order flow have found their sustenance from the public far too long.

No Human Sees the Order

We begin our discussion with the proper use of electronic stops through an environment where no human sees your order. Anonymity of order flow is perhaps the greatest contribution to trading since technical analysis. But, just why is that important? Well, traders can actually gain an edge via the use of electronic order entry and stops. The development of new electronic trading platforms has spawned a whole new category of electronic order execution tools that will benefit the screen-based trader (as opposed to those that call in orders to retail brokers). While it may take some time to master the skills of electronic order entry, the value gained will offer esoteric insight in liquidity, supply and demand relationships, and the ability to gain an edge over those using traditional retail brokers (humans).

Stops That Can Be Trusted

In recent years, many traders have ceased using stops via their brokers and simply relied on mental stops, because it was feared (with good reason) that market makers would shoot against their stop orders. We know this as whipsaw risk, which can be caused by market volatility and sloppy trade execution. Due to this reality, we can say that discipline suffered at the hands of poor execution because many trades are stopped out precisely at the point where prices turn.

Technology has provided a trusted alternative by using an order-matching environment of anonymity, equipping the trader with the benefit of using stops once again to protect capital. These are the three most important electronic stops:

- The protective stop
- The technical stop
- The trailing stop

As seasoned market participants know, the stop order simply is an order to exit the trade if a transaction occurs at a certain predetermined price against the position. The very nature of considering where one would exit is the first step toward good discipline. Yet without follow-through to act on the protective stop, it is just good intentions. As stated, electronic stops today can be trusted since no human sees the order; therefore, a protective stop should be placed as soon as a position is taken to defend against extreme loss. Because predetermining risk is a cornerstone to risk and reward analysis, the protective stop should never be moved once placed. If a protective stop were moved, risk naturally elevates while reward targets move farther away—a practice of poor discipline.

The second type of stop order is the technical stop. The technical stop uses technical analysis, i.e., psychology, to help determine the placement of a stop. In most cases, the technical stop will be placed soon after the trade turns profitable. In a long scenario, the trader would place the stop just below levels of potential support. As the stock continues to make higher highs and higher lows, keep raising the stop so it is just under the low in each successive higher low. If the stock breaks its uptrend by making a lower low, the stop will trigger, and the trade will be exited. In the case of short selling, once a profitable level is reached, place the stop just above each lower high, as the trend makes lower lows and lower highs. When the stock breaks its trend by making a higher high, the investor will be stopped out.

There are many investors who buy stocks and become very profitable in their trades, only to watch their profits turn into losses. The technical stop prevents this situation, once again imposing discipline to the trade through electronic systems as a hedge against human subjectivity.

Finally, there is the trailing stop. Often the market moves with high velocity in a short amount of time. Like the technical stop, trailing stops are used when one is on the right side of the trade. Because it can be difficult to know when to take profits, the trailing stop automatically trails the stock tick-by-tick by a specified amount as the market continues to move in your favor. This tactic allows profits to run by setting a discretionary level, which is pegged to each new tick in favor of the trade. Let's review an example.

In the case of a long position, as the stock trades higher (in your favor), the trailing stop automatically will trail the stock higher with each new tick. Let's use $0.15 discretion for the example. Because the trailing stop only moves higher if the stock moves higher, a high water mark is constantly set with each new tick higher. This high water mark will then trigger the exit if penetrated. Therefore, as the stock achieves a new high print or tick, the trailing stop is automatically set $0.15 below (discretionary amount) the new high print in the market. As long as the discretionary amount is set less than the

FIGURE 1: Electronic Trailing Stops

Time	Order Details	Status
9:35	Buy 500 XYZ at 16.30 on ARCA (500 traded @ 16.3000)	Executed
9:35	Bought 100 XYZ at 16.300000 with ARCA3	Completed
9:35	Bought 400 XYZ at 16.300000 with ARCA1	Completed
9:42	Sell 500 XYZ at 16.55 (Stop: 16.62) Deleted	Deleted
9:42	ARCA Order Status: Pending trigger price of 16.62	Completed
12:26	Sell 500 XYZ at Trailing Stop: .15 on ARCA 500 traded	Executed
12:26	ARCA Order Status: Pending trailing stop (trail=.15)	Completed
12:26	ARCA Order Status: New stop 17.04	Completed
12:26	ARCA Order Status: New stop 17.07	Completed
12:26	ARCA Order Status: New stop 17.09	Completed
12:26	ARCA Order Status: New stop 17.10	Completed
12:26	ARCA Order Status: New stop 17.12	Completed
12:26	ARCA Order Status: New stop 17.13	Completed
12:26	ARCA Order Status: New stop 17.14	Completed
12:26	ARCA Order Status: New stop 17.15	Completed
12:26	ARCA Order Status: New stop 17.19	Completed
12:26	ARCA Order Status: New stop 17.20	Completed
12:26	ARCA Order Status: New stop 17.22	Completed
12:26	ARCA Order Status: New stop 17.24	Completed
12:26	ARCA Order Status: New stop 17.25	Completed
12:26	ARCA Order Status: New stop 17.26	Completed
12:32	Sold 100 XYZ at 17.250000 with ARCA3	Completed
12:32	Sold 100 XYZ at 17.260000 with ARCA3	Completed
12:32	Sold 300 XYZ at 17.210000 with ARCA3	Completed

As seen here, we bought 500 shares of UNTD at $16.30. An initial protective stop below $16.30 normally would be placed immediately after the entry, but due to immediate upside price action it was not necessary. After the stock made an upward move, a technical stop limit was placed at $16.62 with a limit down to $16.55. As the stock continued its upside momentum to $17.19, the technical stop was cancelled and replaced with a trailing stop with $0.15 discretion—placing the initial trailing stop at $17.04 ($17.19-$0.15). Ultimately, the stock made a high of $17.41, then pulled back to $17.26, where the stop was triggered and the trade was exited for a $0.96 winner.

Source: RealTick

current profit in the trade, the trailing stop ensures a winner does not turn into a loser—following the age old maxim of "letting profits run while cutting losses short." See *Figure 1* for an example of an electronic trailing stop executed on the NYSE Group, Inc. (NYX) electronic exchange and programmed on the RealTick trading platform.

Adjusting Stops While in the Trade

Another myth is that stops are just for order execution; yet stops are also important to analysis and trade maintenance. In fact, the best traders always consider how much they can lose before they consider how much they can make. In this regard, the winners take care of themselves, while losers need more focused attention. One way to control this balance is to use the psychology of technical analysis, technology and trailing stops together (see *Figure 2*).

Upon close examination of *Figure 2*, notice that the trade was entered at the indicated point; the stock then rallied up to a place where it had found resistance previously. Near this resistance point, the stock moved sideways, then pulled back. At this time, we entered a trailing stop expecting prior resistance to again provide a level of

FIGURE 2: Adjusting Trailing Stops

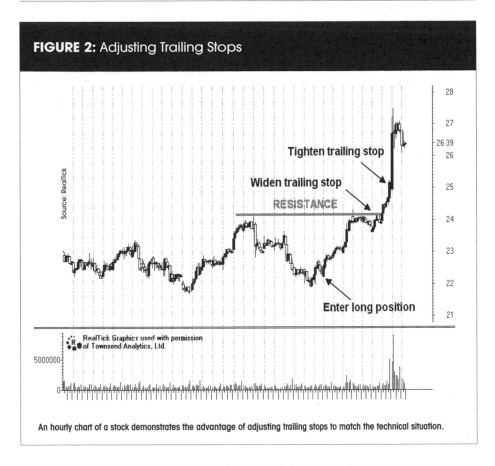

Source: RealTick

Tighten trailing stop

Widen trailing stop

RESISTANCE

Enter long position

RealTick Graphics used with permission of Townsend Analytics, Ltd.

An hourly chart of a stock demonstrates the advantage of adjusting trailing stops to match the technical situation.

sellers. To avoid getting stopped out at this point of resistance too quickly, the trailing stop was widened to allow for the expected pull-back, but also providing an opportunity to participate in the larger move. This method of expanding and contracting the discretionary amount while in the trade allows the trader to navigate the position through support and resistance levels.

Avoiding Market-Impact Costs (MIC)

Electronic limit orders allow the trader to trust that no human will step in and take advantage of the trade limits placed on a trade. For example, if a trader called his broker to buy a stock with a limit of $14 or better, while he can not pay more than $14, one should expect that it is what he will pay—with little chance for price improvement. Using electronic means, this is not necessarily true. Electronic limit orders can be aggressive while buying or selling—all while improv-

FIGURE 3: Electronic Leading Limit Order

	↓	13.94	200	+.54	Net Pos:	500
Bid	13.93	High	14.15	Range	1.05	Avg Price:	13.94
Ask	13.94	Low	13.10	Ratio	3900x63	Closed P/L:
Close	13.40	Open	13.21	Volume	40,406,331	Open P/L:

Name	Bid	Size		Name	Ask	Size
JPHQ	13.93	100		BTRD	13.94	1000
CIBC	13.93	1000		ISLAND	13.94	500
ARCA	13.93	1400		NOCI	13.94	5000
ADFN	13.93	3000		ARCA	13.94	27300
CINN	13.93	6700		BEST	13.94	1000
BRUT	13.92	2300		BRUT	13.94	25600
BRUT	13.92	2300		SIZE	13.94	3800
SIZE	13.92	100		ADFN	13.94	22600
DAIN	13.91	100		CINN	13.94	500
WELS	13.91	100		LEGG	13.95	800

Symbol / Volume 500 / Price 14.00 / LMT / Stop Price 13.96
Route ARCA / Buy / Cancel All / Sell / Sell Short

Buy 500 at 14.00 on ARCA   Executed
Bought 200 at 13.939700   Completed
Bought 100 at 13.940000   Completed
Bought 100 at 13.940000   Completed
Bought 100 at 13.940000   Completed

Source: RealTick

As seen above, the trader placed a limit order through ARCA to buy 500 shares of the stock at $14. The limit order placed was equivalent to saying to a broker, "Buy me 500 shares at $14 or better." Archipelago then searched out the best price and filled the trader at an average price of $13.94. While many shares are available at $13.94 as shown on the Level II (and this fill is no surprise), it is when the markets are moving with high velocity that this technique is most valuable. Regardless, an electronic leading limit order is an order you can trust—because no broker sees the order.

ing the chances for price improvement and, of course, maintaining price protection that limit orders provide.

For example, if a trader wants to buy stock aggressively, he can place an order with a limit price at or above the offer. When a trader places a limit order higher than the inside market, electronic systems such as ARCA, Instinet, Island and others can provide the opportunity for price improvement. Conversely, when traders experience a poor execution through traditional means of calling in orders to brokers, they often pay more than just commission through a market-impact cost, defined as the difference between what they were filled at and what they could have been filled at. For instance, $0.10 difference on a thousand-lot trade is equal to a $100 market-impact cost.

Step in Front of Size

Avoiding unnecessary costs brings up many important opportunities in terms of order-handling rules—in particular, the standing rule that price will take priority over time. If a trader attempts to lift an offer while others are doing the same (at the same price), time will take standing, i.e., first bids buy first. Conversely, the trader who bids the highest price will take standing over all other bids regardless of time. If the market as seen in *Figure 3* shows offers at $13.94 and we bid $14, the $14 bid takes standing over the $13.94, $13.95, $13.96, $13.97, $13.98 and $13.99 bids—regardless whether they are there first. This has important ramifications in high-velocity markets, where shares offered are quickly being taken. As those who are aware of Level II know, often the screen will reflect an offer available at a certain price, only to be absorbed by other traders who are ahead. This can lead to chasing the stock and paying more.

The trader who uses an electronic leading limit order at $14 will do what we call "step in front of size" and take any shares available at the $14 limit and better (meaning lower in this example). Those bidding at $13.94 may find themselves with no shares available, even though the Level II implies shares are available at that price. The leading limit order gives the trader standing over others, even if those orders are placed ahead of them in time. One may be wondering why they would not be filled if it appears shares are available at the current price. The explanation is called "stock ahead," meaning that other orders at the same price took precedence because they were sent in at an earlier time, and no more shares were available.

This condition during high-velocity moves leaves unknowing traders irritated, thinking they got screwed out of the advance by not getting filled. In reality, by bidding higher with a leading limit order, they would step in front of size and still receive the best price available at or under the limit—assuming they are using electronic crossing networks devoid of human interaction.

One might ask, why not use a market order which guarantees a fill at the market? The answer is that high-velocity moments can leave a trader with an execution above his trade parameters based on risk and reward tolerances without limit-order protection. The leading limit order, though, allows him to step in front of the crowd while also maintaining the maximum price he is willing to pay (limit-order protection). The use of this strategy is even more dramatic during a high-velocity sell-off.

Those with long positions will want to ensure liquidity to exit the fastest. The value of this strategy is important because it allows the trader to find true support without finding out the hard way with

FIGURE 4: Handling Discretionary Orders Electronically

	↓	28.08	100	+.83		Net Pos:	0
Bid	28.07	High	28.16	Range	1.44	Avg Price:	0.00
Ask	28.14	Low	26.72	Ratio	100x100	Closed P/L:	
Close	27.25	Open	26.75	Volume	246,786	Open P/L:	

Name	Bid	Size		Name	Ask	Size
ISLAND	28.07	100		ADFN	28.14	100
CIBC	28.07	100		DBAB	28.15	100
CINN	28.07	100		BAMM	28.15	100
ADFN	28.05	1000		DAIN	28.16	100
TRAC	28.02	100		FACT	28.17	100
ARCA	28.00	100		CIBC	28.17	100
BRUT	27.95	200		GSCO	28.18	100
PRUS	27.90	100		BTRD	28.18	700

Volume: 500   Price: 28.00   Discretionary 28.11   Discretionary ☐ Disc. Offset 0

Reserve Amt. ☐ 100   Expiration: Day   ☐ Pref. ARCA   Route: ARCA

Buy | Cancel All | Sell | Sell Short

This figure gives an example of a discretionary order. A trader who wants to go long 500 shares of this stock at $28.11 but does not want to put in a limit order because it could make the stock look strong and reduce the chance of getting filled at the desired price, does have an alternative. He could place a discretionary order to buy 500 shares at $28 with a discretionary price of $28.11. If someone decided to hit the bid or lower their offer to $28.11, the order would be filled. This has value particularly when trading less liquid stocks.

Source: RealTick

a market order. For example, the trader may decide to sell half the position with a leading limit below the bid. If it is filled above the limit, we know there are buyers at that level. This may affect how the trader treats the other half of his position.

Suffice it to say that screen-based trading provides the participant with many specialized order types that are exclusive to electronic trading. These order types can give you an advantage that even most floor traders don't enjoy.

Discretionary Orders

One such specialized order is the discretionary order. This order type gives the trader the ability to passively display one price on the Level II, but in reality, set a range where the trade can be filled. Use this order when trading thinner stocks, where you can influence the market by enabling other participants to see your order (see *Figure 4)*.

Electronic Conditional Orders

Another specialized order is the conditional order. This order is executed if certain conditions are met. There are unlimited conditions that can trigger the order. For example, one could place an order to

FIGURE 5: Customizing Conditional Orders

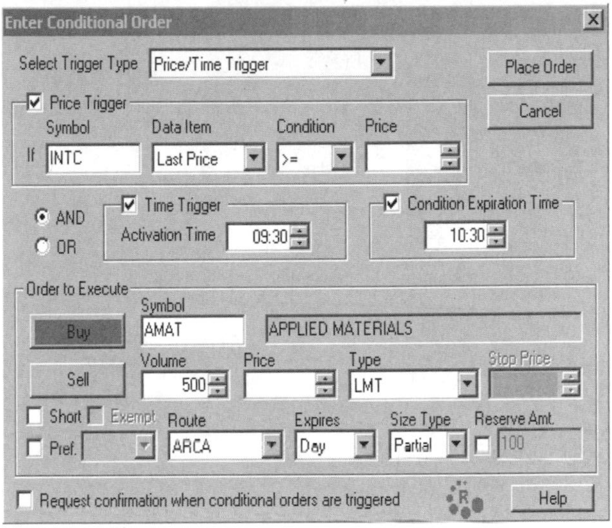

This figure shows the customization that can be done when placing conditional orders. In this example, if INTC trades at a certain price in the first hour of trading, a limit order to buy 500 shares of AMAT would go live. Obviously, the list of alternative conditionals is virtually endless.

Source: RealTick

buy 500 shares of AMAT if INTC breaks a certain price level, only in the first hour of trading (see *Figure 5*).

The conditional order offers a number of alternatives that can be set up pre-market or during the trading day to allow traders to enter or exit positions without constantly monitoring the markets. Again, note that the conditional order is held on a trader's computer; therefore, no broker sees the order. Also, once a trader's computer is shut down, the order also cancels automatically. Many participants who have day jobs enjoy the flexibility of this electronic order tool.

Reserve Book

A direct access tool often used when trading actively is the reserve book. The reserve book allows traders to hide the size of their orders on the Level II. As *Figure 6* indicates, I bought 50,000 shares of JDSU for a quick $2,000 scalp and hid the order size from the market. I showed the market one thousand shares at a time, while actually bidding much more. As trades were executed, one thousand shares remained specified until the reserve amount was transacted. The reserve feature is essential when trading large sizes as well as when trading less liquid securities for the same reasons you would not

FIGURE 6: The Reserve Order

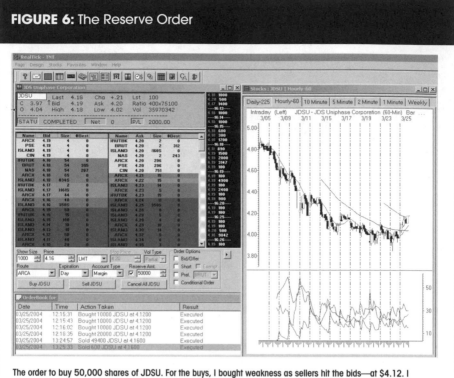

The order to buy 50,000 shares of JDSU. For the buys, I bought weakness as sellers hit the bids—at $4.12. I bought three 10,000 lots and one 20,000 lot all at the same price. Eight minutes later I sold them for a $0.04 winner, yielding a $2,000 profit. With this kind of size, the reserve book allows me to hide my hand from the market—making certain I do not show strength when buying or weakness while selling. This is an invaluable tool when trading big sizes. The trader also can combine the features of the discretionary order with the reserve order to further hide his intentions—I call this the double sneaky order, and it's one of my favorites!

Source: RealTick

yell, "Who has kings?" at a poker game—you don't want to show the market your size. This tool has obvious value to the retail trader and institutional participant alike (see *Figure 6*).

Myriad types of electronic orders let you trade even better than a so-called Wall Street pro. So, not only has the field been leveled in recent years, but today the proficient electronic trader truly owns the edge. While the challenges of mastering the technology may seem demanding at first glance, active traders and investors alike prefer being in control of their orders. Much insight is gained by the way in which an order is filled. Like fishing, when the fish bite fast, it confirms the conditions are right and offers valuable confirmation. Trading is much the same—when orders are taken quickly, the trader learns to interpret this as additional strength or weakness, which is often more telling than the charts. In time, the maturation of sound analysis and electronic execution will provide a razor-sharp edge that most participants do not possess—hence the advantage.

David S. Nassar is one of the founding pioneers of electronic trading. As founder and CEO of one of the nation's first electronic trading firms and a New York Times best selling author, Nassar has been a significant contributor to the industry. He is the author of many books on trading, including most recently, *Ordinary People, Extraordinary Profits: How to Make a Living as an Independent Stock, Options, and Futures Trader* (Wiley Trading, 2005) and *Rules of the Trade* (McGraw-Hill, 2004). Since selling his firm, David spends his time trading and developing real estate. He has formed CrossWinds Capital, LLC to work directly with high net worth investors and institutions. This article originally appeared in *SFO* in June 2004.

HARVEST TIME IS COMING:
Spread the Future

BY PHIL TIGER

There are a variety of opportunities throughout the year when there are profits to be made on seasonable spread trades in the futures market. The basic premise behind seasonal spreading revolves around the timing of planting and harvesting, which occur at approximately the same time each year. For example, in the wheat market virtually 80 percent of the crop is harvested in the spring. On the flip side, almost all of the corn and soybean crops are harvested in the fall. These types of patterns create reliable seasonal factors from which knowledgeable traders can seek to profit. Basically then, annual cycles in nature and weather create supply and demand patterns for physical commodities.

Another basic rule of thumb key to the seasonal spreading concept is that low prices tend to emerge around harvest time, simply because that is when there is the greatest abundance of the new crop. Higher prices generally are seen just ahead of harvest time (the end of the old crop). Based on these patterns, traders can expect wheat to score price lows during the May-June period, while corn tends to make its lows during the November-December period.

What Is a Spread?

While there are several different types of spread positions, let's first take a look at some of the basics of spread trading in the futures market. A spread simply is the purchase and sale of two different futures contracts at the same time. Spread traders analyze the price relation-

136

ships between the contracts, as opposed to looking at individual price levels. So, a spread trader seeks to capitalize on a change in relationship rather than on the absolute value of the commodities...and to look for the buy side to gain on the sell side. There is, of course, a wide array of spreading opportunities, but for this particular piece, we'll drill down primarily into spread opportunities in the agricultural futures markets.

There are two main reasons futures traders historically have looked to spreading as an important strategy in their toolbox. The first is potentially lower risk, and the second involves the fact that spreads usually are subject to more attractive margin rates.

Generally speaking, spreading in the futures market is considered to be less risky than holding outright positions, and the reason is simple—the price of two different futures contract months on the same commodity tends to rise or fall together, not necessarily in perfect lockstep, but at least in the same direction. When a player puts on a spread, less risk is in play as losses from one side of the trade potentially can be offset by gains on the other side of the trade. Because of the generally lower-risk profiles of spreading, it makes sense that lower margins are required. Thus, futures traders can participate more fully in the market with smaller capital outlays.

Price quotes for spreads, too, are different than for individual commodities because they are quoted as the price difference between two related contracts. For example, in May 2004, the Chicago Board of Trade (CBOT) December corn contract was trading at $2.95, versus the July contract at $3.02. To calculate the spread quote, one simply needs to subtract the price of the December contract from the May contract, in this case seven cents.

Basic Spread Types

Now let's take a look at the four basic types of spreads. The first and most common is the interdelivery spread. This involves a trade with the same commodity, usually at the same exchange, but different delivery months. Some examples would be buying July corn while selling December corn or buying July lean hogs while selling October lean hogs.

A second popular type is the intermarket spread, involving a trade with the same commodity such as wheat – hard, soft or white – on

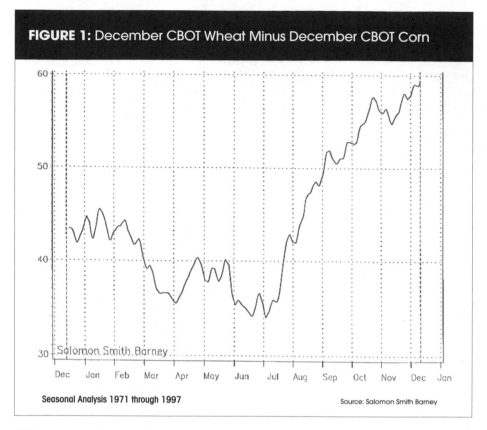

FIGURE 1: December CBOT Wheat Minus December CBOT Corn

Salomon Smith Barney

Dec Jan Feb Mar Apr May Jun Jul Aug Sep Oct Nov Dec Jan

Seasonal Analysis 1971 through 1997   Source: Salomon Smith Barney

different exchanges but generally involving the same delivery month. An example would be CBOT December wheat versus Kansas City December wheat.

A third type of spread is the intercommodity spread. This involves a trade usually with the same delivery months (or close delivery months) and related commodities. Generally these are on the same exchange. Examples would include December wheat versus corn on the Chicago Board of Trade or October cattle versus hogs on the Chicago Merc. Traders should be aware that these relationships often are tenuous and subjective. For example, there were many traders who thought there were significant relationships between silver and soybeans in the mid-1970s. Both commodities had two syllables and began with the letter "s," but beyond that, any similarities seemed creative at best.

A fourth spread variety would be the source/product spread involving a commodity and its products. These would include soybean crush and reverse crush spreads as well as the petroleum crack spreads.

Each of these trading spreads has similar overall trading strategies as outright futures positions. These include predetermined stops and objectives and a money management approach to trade size. Some simple rules of thumb include: do not commit more than 20 percent of trading capital to any one position. Keep 20 percent of capital in reserve at all times. Use multiple positions when possible. Do not add to a losing position. It also is helpful to have charts available for desired positions as well as a seasonal statistics for seasonal trades.

Let's Make Some Spread Trades

The intermarket spread of long December wheat/short December corn (see *Figure 1*) is a popular seasonal trade taking advantage of the difference in the crop years for corn and wheat. A seasonal trade, simply, is one that tends to show specific behavior based on fundamental factors that repeat every year regardless of a given year's anomalies. And the basic concept behind this particular trade idea? – Simply that July is the end of the crop year for corn, while it is the first new crop month for wheat (as mentioned earlier, approximately 80 percent of the U.S. soft wheat crop is harvested at the end of spring).

Another seasonal spread to watch is the long January/short May soybean meal interdelivery spread. This spread historically is viable if it can be established at a May premium in late summer to early autumn. This pair offers a great seasonal factor, as the price of soybean meal tends to be the strongest when the weather is cold. The reason? Simply, meal, which is fed to livestock, spoils during hot weather and is easily stored in cooler weather. Hence, cooler months of the year tend to increase demand for meal.

Another interesting spread to watch is the limited-risk spread of long July/short December coffee (see *Figure 2*). One might consider initiating this spread at 50 percent or more of carrying charges (approximately 180 points month). The South American freeze season runs during May and June, and any adverse weather can impact the spread in favor of the nearby delivery. A stop is not necessary in a limited-risk spread if it is initiated at a sufficiently wide discount. Profit potential is based on perceptions of adverse weather.

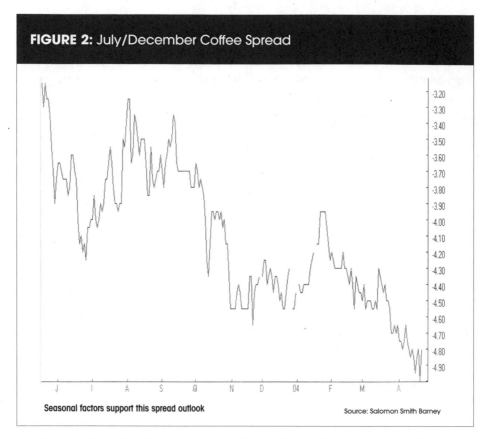

FIGURE 2: July/December Coffee Spread

Seasonal factors support this spread outlook

Source: Salomon Smith Barney

Bottom line for the seasonal rationale? Brazil is a major coffee producer. It gets cold there starting in June, and those cooler conditions may harm the crop and ultimately be a supportive factor for price.

The October/December cotton interdelivery spread could offer some profit possibilities going into the hurricane season if adverse weather develops – if the spread can be initiated at 120 points or more December premium. Given the historical seasonal tendencies of this trade, players could use an arbitrary 70-point stop with the objective of an October premium if adverse weather develops. Bottom line: the hurricane season starts in September, and the cotton crop is harvested in October. If a hurricane damages the crop ahead of harvest, it ultimately can reduce supply.

Think BLT Sandwiches
The livestock markets over the years often have provided a ready source of spread opportunities. There are several relationships in the

meats that might be explored for potential spread trades in the summer. In the hog market, there are the interdelivery spreads of October and July hogs versus December hogs, as well as the intermarket spreads of long July bellies versus short July hogs and long August cattle/short hogs. After all, many Americans eat more bacon, lettuce tomato sandwiches during the summer months. In the livestock pits of the Chicago Mercantile Exchange, it's known as BLT season. Due to that seasonal cuisine tendency, July bellies seasonally tend to outperform hogs.

Check Out Energies

The energy markets provide many potential opportunities as well. However, the costs and volatility are unquestionably high. One should examine the various crack spreads but especially the seasonal intermarket spread of long December heating oil/short December unleaded gasoline. This spread follows the transition from the driving season (May through October) to the home-heating season (November through March). Gasoline is favored during the driving season, and heating oil is favored during the home-heating season.

We have examined some essential futures spreads. Most are seasonals, but all have the potential to generate good returns. Those who have never traded futures spreads before should be aware that it is a completely different type of futures trading, yet offers players great possibilities.

Phil Tiger was involved in the futures industry for 35 years as a commodities futures specialist and the leading authority on spreads and spread trading. He spent ten years with ContiCommodity Services in the '70s and '80s and 17 years with Salomon Smith Barney and its predecessors. Tiger wrote numerous articles and spoke at a variety of seminars and conferences throughout his career. He developed the Seasonal Spread Index in the early 1970s, and it or its variations are used extensively throughout the futures industry today. This article originally appeared in *SFO* in August 2004.

KNOW WHEN TO GET OUT:
12 Rules for Selling Stocks

BY THOMAS BULKOWSKI

"How do I know when to sell?" my brother asked over the phone. This was not the first time he had asked, and I knew he probably ultimately would ignore my answer. Brothers are like that. Here's what I told him.

Rule 1. Use stops.

This is obvious, and most traders know about stop-loss orders, but it's worth repeating: use stops. All traders should determine, before trading, where a stop will go. Once the trade is in place, put in the stop order. The quickest way to a small fortune is to start with a large one, so use stops to limit losses and protect profits.

For example, let's say Joe Trader considers buying the stock shown in *Figure 1* the day after it gaps above the line of support. Where should the stop go? Placing the stop slightly below point A is a good choice because of the massive support line. If price pierces support, then it's a good bet the stock will continue tumbling. The bad news is that the stop is too far away—21 percent below the day's closing price.

If Joe used volatility to place the stop, it would raise the stop price. What does this mean? Compute the average daily-trading range over the prior month, and then triple the result. The value represents the minimum distance a stop should be from the buy price. In other

FIGURE 1: Progressive Stops

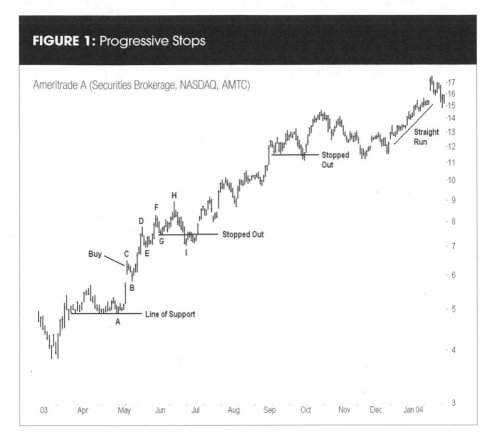

Ameritrade A (Securities Brokerage, NASDAQ, AMTC)

words, subtract the intraday low from the intraday high for each day of the prior month, find the average of those values, and then multiply by three. For AmeriTrade, shown in *Figure 1*, the volatility measures 22 cents. Triple that to 66. Place a stop no closer than 66 cents below the buy price to avoid being stopped out by daily fluctuations. That would place a stop no closer than 5.52, which is below the minor low at point B.

Once the stop is in place, raise it to below the prior minor low each time the stock makes a new high. For example, when price rises above the minor high at point C, which occurs three days before point D, raise the stop to just below point B (10 or 15 cents below B). When price climbs above D, which occurs the day before F, raise the stop to E. Following this method, the stop will execute at G and again near 11.50, assuming another buy along the way.

The beauty of this approach is that the profit potentially can be unlimited. A profit target (like earning $1,000 per trade, or 10 percent,

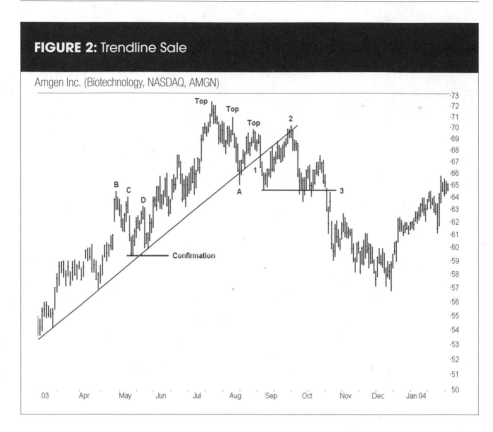

FIGURE 2: Trendline Sale

Amgen Inc. (Biotechnology, NASDAQ, AMGN)

or selling at a fixed price), by contrast, limits the profit. The problem with stops is one of diminished profit. The decline from peak H to stop G is 16 percent, as measured from high to low. That represents a huge chunk of change.

Another problem is that sometimes there are no minor lows in which to place stops. The straight-line run in December to January on *Figure 1* is an example. Where should the stop go? This might be a good place to use the volatility stop discussed earlier.

One corollary to the stop rule is this: if a trader expects the stop to be hit, sell immediately. The stock is going to be sold, so why wait for a lower price? Sell now.

Rule 2. Sell when a stock does not behave as expected.

A trader knows what to expect from a stock. When reality differs from expectation, sell. I use this when I trade chart patterns. If I expect an upward breakout and the stock declines instead, I abandon ship. Fast.

Rule 3. Sell when the trend changes.

What does that mean? *Figure 2* shows an example. An up-sloping trendline blazes a path higher. When price closes below the trendline at point 1, sell. A trader also can sell on a trendline pierce (point A), but a close works better (as in this example).

In *Trader Vic—Methods of a Wall Street Master*, Victor Sperandeo discusses his trend change approach. His strategy reliably signals a trend change based on three tests. Test 1 is a pierce of the trendline (see *Figure 2*). Qualifier 2 is a test of the high (meaning price tries to make a new high, but fails). The final test, 3, is when price closes below the lowest low between the highest high and point 2.

Another approach is to use a chart pattern called "three falling peaks," which signals a trend change. The three peaks (shown as top in *Figure 2*) have intraday high prices below the prior minor high. The pattern confirms and issues a sell signal when price closes below the lowest low between the three tops. In this case, that is a close below point A. Peaks B, C and D look like a three falling peaks chart pattern, but are not. The pattern does not confirm. That example also shows why a trader should not sell prematurely. Wait for confirmation, and then sell.

Rule 4. Sell on a signal.

If a mechanical approach, such as a moving average crossover, Relative Strength Index (RSI) overbought signal or other indicator generates a sell signal, then sell. The sale may be a mistake, but not selling could mean disaster.

Traders who are unable to pull the trigger in a mechanical approach harbor doubts about their system. Additional research about their systems may lead to trust, understanding, and more timely sales, or it may mean a teardown and rebuild of the system. Mechanical systems often need tuning to keep profits coming.

Rule 5. Sell on chart pattern adverse breakout.

For example, if a trader owns stock in a rising price trend and the stock forms a symmetrical triangle, then sell after a downward breakout. Trade with the trend. Because the prevailing price trend is up but the breakout is down, it's a reversal. The trader should be short, not long.

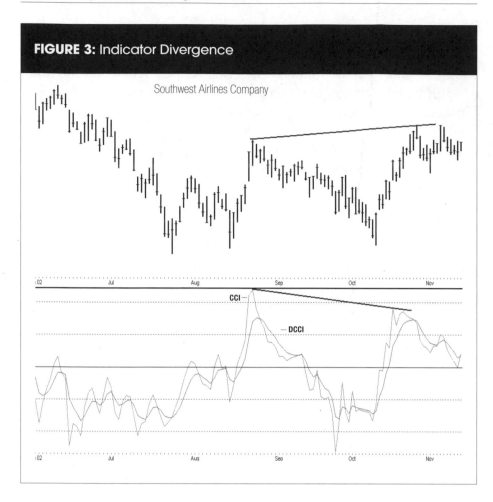

FIGURE 3: Indicator Divergence

Southwest Airlines Company

Rule 6. Sell on divergence.

See an example of a trade I made in *Figure 3*. I owned the stock, and when the Commodity Channel Index (CCI) diverged from the stock price, I sold on the last bar on the right.

Divergence occurs when the price trend diverges from the indicator trend. In other words, CCI made a lower high, but price made a higher high. This bearish divergence suggested lower prices ahead. In my trade, the stock continued climbing for another two weeks, reaching a high of 16.70 before tumbling to a low of 11.72. I sold at 15 and saved a bundle.

I also found, but have not tested for verification, that peaks about a month apart provide the most reliable divergence signals. *Figure 3* shows a peak-to-peak distance of about two months.

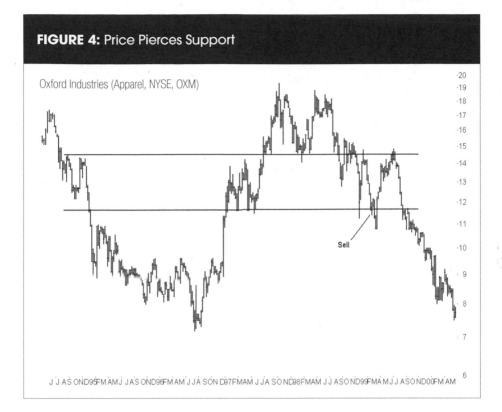

FIGURE 4: Price Pierces Support

Oxford Industries (Apparel, NYSE, OXM)

Sell

J J A S O N D 95 F M A M J J A S O N D 96 F M A M J J A S O N D 97 F M A M J J A S O N D 98 F M A M J J A S O N D 99 F M A M J J A S O N D 00 F M A M

Rule 7. Sell on hitting a profit target.

I often use a measured move up (MMU) chart pattern to determine
how far price will climb. What is an MMU? Look back at *Figure 1*. The
distance from A to C usually equals the climb from B to D. Thus, if
the values of A, B, and C are known, a trader can compute the target
D. When price reaches point D, it often (but not always) declines back
to the support zone between B and C. Set a sell order just below the
computed high at point D to capture the uptrend. This also works on
the larger scale: the move from A to H projected higher from I; just
make sure the legs (A to H then H to I) look proportional. For example, don't expect the measure from A to F then to G projected higher
to be meaningful, because the F to G retrace is not proportional to the
up move A to F.

Sometimes traders want to make a set amount, like $1,000 per
trade, or sell when the gain reaches 10 percent of invested capital. I
have found that profit targets work well for short-term event patterns
(such as earnings surprises), but recognize that setting profit targets

FIGURE 5: Tail

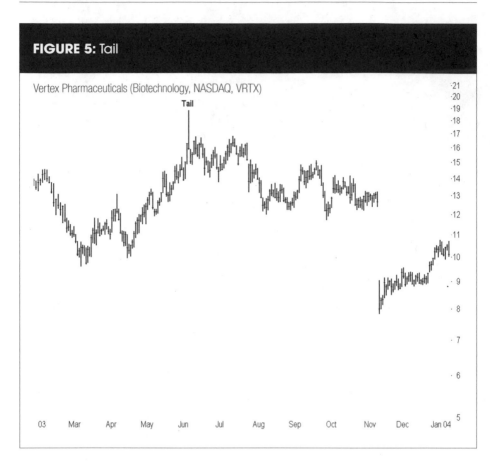

Vertex Pharmaceuticals (Biotechnology, NASDAQ, VRTX)

limits the upside profit potential. After selling the MMU target at point D in *Figure 1*, look at how much money remained on the table during the rise to 17.

Rule 8. Sell when price pierces support.

Figure 4 shows a crude example of this. A support zone exists between the two horizontal lines. The price closing below the lower boundary was the sell signal. A trader selling at the trendline (about 11.63), would have saved his wallet from the decline to 7.50, a profit giveback of 36 percent.

Rule 9. Chart pattern sell signals.

Figure 5 shows what traders call a tail. A tail is a long, one-day price spike with a close near the intraday low. Some call it a one-day reversal or selling climax when heavy volume accompanies the day

I recently sold a utility that made a tail. Leading to the tail, price climbed two or three points in just a few days, and I owned 1,000 shares. Since a quick decline often follows a quick rise, I decided to sell the next day and kept $7,000 plus $1,300 in dividends. Since that time, price has trended lower.

Tails represent short-term turning points, so do not be fooled by the severe decline shown in *Figure 5*.

Rule 10. Check on others in the same industry.

I do not buy or sell shares without first looking at others in the same industry. If other stocks are having problems (prices are trending down or are showing topping patterns), then it is a sell signal. For example, high oil and natural gas prices will affect air freight and air-travel stocks, oils, and chemicals, among many. A check of those stocks against one another and against oil and natural gas prices will clear the picture.

Rule 11. Don't forget the fundamentals.

If trusted investment newsletters or brokerages downgrade a stock, there's a reason. Sometimes earnings problems are difficult to solve. One bad quarter turns into two or three soft ones in the future. That is the reason I avoid stocks six months to a year after a dead-cat bounce (DCB) chart pattern. A DCB occurs when price drops 30 percent to 70 percent in one session, then bounces upward before the decline resumes. In many cases, bullish chart patterns appearing in the stock turn into duds when the company reports continued troubles.

Rule 12. Pay attention to technical indicators.

Is volume receding even as price rises? Has the stock tried to make a new high but failed? Is the general market turning down? Is the market going up, but the stock isn't moving? The answers to those questions may suggest a sale. Investigate further and, if needed, sell. .

Having reviewed a dozen sell signals, how does one go about pulling the trigger? Imagine mom calls Joe Trader and voices her concern about her retirement nest egg. A portion of it is in XYZ stock, the same stock Joe is afraid to sell. What advice does Joe give her? Chances are he tells her to sell. He should follow his own advice. Trading stocks is a business, and in this business, one has to sell to show a profit.

Thomas N. Bulkowski is a private investor and author of several books: *Getting Started in Chart Patterns* (Wiley 2005), *Encyclopedia of Chart Patterns*, 2nd Edition (Wiley Trading, 2005) and *Trading Classic Chart Patterns* (Wiley, 2002). Before earning enough from his investments to retire at age 36, he was a hardware design engineer at Raytheon and a senior software engineer for Tandy Corporation. Bulkowski's website is www.thepatternsite.com and he can be reached at tbut@hotmail.com. This article originally appeared in *SFO* in May 2004.

SECTION FOUR
Trading with a System

A good system can provide a solid foundation for successful trading, but a poorly designed system can start you down the road to ruin. Before you begin trading a system, you must evaluate it carefully. If you continue to trade, you'll likely spend a lot of time assessing the strengths and weaknesses of various systems. Not everything in mechanical system trading is automatic. We'll provide you with the tools to develop a process for judging a system for yourself.

It's tempting to grab a singular trading program that's earned big money recently, but it is difficult to make money consistently trading a single system. Over time, diversification may be a wiser and more profitable course. This section will explore the ins and outs of combining systems in a portfolio to maximize returns.

We'll also give you the basic tools to start to develop your own trading system. A properly designed personal system should reflect the trader's individual needs and expectations. Technical indicators, chart patterns and seasonal patterns are valuable tools to use in developing your system. We'll also look at an example of a simple, price-based system that uses five-minute pivot levels as its foundation—an actual system one of our authors trades each day. John Carter shares the rules and calculations behind his five-minute multi-pivot play, giving you a chance to work it out for yourself.

19

MAKING THE MOST OF MECHANICAL SYSTEM TRADING

BY NIGEL BAHADUR

On May 6, 2106, Rebecca Adams woke up at 6:30 a.m. and started preparing for her day. She showered, dressed, gathered her beach equipment and then went downstairs for breakfast. At 7:45 a.m. she stepped into her office. Displayed on the industry standard, OLED, wall-sized monitor were the results of her overnight trading. Her profits from trading the Shanghai 1000 E-mini futures contracts were offset by her losses from the Bombay 50 options. But overall she had booked a nice profit while she was sleeping. The computer informed her that there had been a communications glitch, but that the backup lines had kicked in so her positions were never in jeopardy. Had there been a problem that couldn't be rectified, the computer would have woken her up with a phone call or sounded a shrill alarm guaranteed to wake the dead. She smiled with satisfaction, turned around and went to spend her day on the beach, where she would kick her friends' butts in beach volleyball. The computer would continue trading while she was out...

Many beginning system traders have been seduced by this fantasy, and as technology races ahead, portions of this fantasy edge tantalizingly closer to reality. However, a self-correcting, self-adjusting, automated-trading cash machine that will fulfill traders' fantasies remains as far off in the future as the stories of Isaac Asimov. For now, system traders will have to develop (or purchase) one or more trading systems and create an infrastructure and routine for implementing the trading signals. So given the time-consuming tasks system traders must undertake, this article will focus on developing and evaluating a trading system – either one that is being written by the end user or one that is being considered for purchase or lease.

Reality Check

Every day thousands of extremely intelligent folks (think PhD-types) try to find new ways to wring money out of market inefficiencies but have yet to develop a system that consistently makes money over the long term. Experienced system traders know this. Instead, they will trade a basket of systems on a basket of commodities on multiple time frames. Over the long run, this is the only way to consistently make money with mechanical systems—at least until we can program a machine to do the bulk of the work for us.

Of course many readers may disagree, but that depends on how a system is defined. After all, many traders have a single system that they use day in and day out, and they make a good living trading it. However, these systems allow some wiggle room for the trader. For the purposes of this article, the term "trading system" or "system" will mean a mechanical trading system that has strict entry and exit rules with no room for discretion.

It is extremely hard, if not almost impossible, to consistently make money over a long period trading a single mechanical system. A single robust system generally has only a small edge, which will dull over time, and returns only a small profit on a risk-adjusted basis. Systems must be combined into a portfolio in order to maximize returns and reduce risk.

Take a Good, Long Look at a System

There are hundreds of statistical measures that any trading system can generate. Regardless of what numerical attributes of a trading system are used for evaluation, all of those factors are based on historical data. Without the luxury of peeking into the future, the best you can do is monitor the system and compare the performance to historical norms. When the system starts to deviate—and it will—the trader will have to evaluate the reasons for the deviation and determine if the underlying assumptions on which the system is based still hold water.

Over time I have arrived at my own favorite measures for evaluating systems. Out of the hundreds (maybe thousands) of measures, I've narrowed mine down to the sixteen listed here. Although this list may not necessarily be the best set of factors for everyone, they work for me and can be a good starting point for newer traders.

1. **Underlying premise.** The first question that you should ask when looking at a system is this: "What's the underlying assumption or driver of the system?" Then you should ask if that underlying assumption makes sense. Every system has an underlying driver that should make intuitive sense. In my experience, most robust trading systems are usually based on very simple underlying drivers.

2. **Profitability.** Many of you reading this will say, "Duh! Of course I'll look at profitability." But what I mean by this is to look at whether the system is profitable on a single contract. Many systems use money management that changes the number of contracts on each trade. But remove that and the profitability on a single contract is not so enticing – in some cases the system may even be a losing system. Varying the number of contracts is used to control risk and leverage the system; it should not be used to turn a losing system into a winning one.

3. **Profit factor.** This is just another way of looking at profitability. It is calculated by dividing the gross wins by the gross losses. A profit factor of more than 1.0 is a winning system. Short-term trading systems tend to have profit factors of less than 2.0 with a large number of trades.

4. **Drawdown.** What is the maximum drawdown as a percentage of the profits made? A drawdown of $100,000 in order to make an equal amount over five years is not attractive. Where did the max drawdown occur? Was it at the start, end, or middle of the equity curve? If it's at the end (i.e., recently), it's a warning sign that the system is starting to fail — unless it's due to unusual circumstances like 9/11.

5. **Percent winners and average profit per trade.** What is the percentage of winning trades? A high percentage of winning trades will be accompanied by a lower profit per trade and a higher average loss per trade. If it's not, you are, more than likely, looking at a system that will not hold up over time. Does the underlying premise correspond with these numbers? For example, breakout trend-following systems tend to have a lower percentage of winning trades, but the average winning trade will be larger than the average losing trade.

6. **Testing period(s).** What was the length of the testing period? What types of markets did that period cover? For systems based on daily charts, there should be, ideally, ten years of data. The market data should show multiple uptrends, multiple downtrends and multiple sideways price action, so you can see how the system handled each type of action. Did the system catch the majority of the action that it was designed to catch? For example, if the system is a trend-following system, it should have caught most of the trends.

Next, look at how the system was developed and tested. Ideally, the developer would have taken the data and broken it into three sets. The middle 60 percent would be the development set (the set on which the initial testing was conducted). The first twenty percent and last twenty percent would be the out-of-sample set. Out-of sample data is data on which the system is tested that was not used in the initial system development. At best, testing on this data set is done once and only once—it either works or it doesn't. Some development shops will only allow their developers access to the development set. They aren't even allowed to see the out-of-sample data. Instead, the system is handed off to others for the out-of-sample data testing—this goes a long way toward preventing curve-fitting.

7. **Sample size.** The biggest and most difficult factor that system developers have to guard against is accidental curve-fitting of data. A large sample size goes a long way toward mitigating that risk. So, the larger the sample size, the better. For short-term swing and day-trading systems I want to see two hundred-plus trades. For long-term trend-following systems I like to see fifty-plus trades. The sample size can be on one market or across multiple markets.

8. **Consecutive losers.** I'm simply looking at one thing here—can I psychologically handle the number of consecutive losers that the system has had in the past? If the system had ten consecutive losers, can I handle that? Will I stop trading it in frustration after losing five times?

9. **Equity curve.** You do not want to see a 45-degree straight line on the equity curve. If there is one, then chances are it is curve-fitted and will not hold up over time. Of course there should be a steady

trend up, but a robust system will be punctuated by drawdowns. Another item to look at here is the length of time it took to recover from the maximum drawdown.

10. **Year-by-year analysis.** Look at some performance measures by year. For example, I want to see a consistent number of trades on a yearly basis and a consistent winning rate year after year. It's important to note here that in some markets a system may produce less absolute profit today than it did ten years ago. A big reason for this can be a reduction in volatility. Look at the underlying premise of the system to determine if reduced volatility will result in reduced profits. If so, then you do not necessarily want to discard a system since profitability can be restored via money management rules that factor in volatility.

In addition, determine the return you would expect next year on a percentage basis. If the system spends a significant amount of time exposed to the market, then you would want this to be much higher than the so-called risk-free return you could earn with T-bills.

11. **Reaction to unusual events.** How did the system respond to unusual events like the market crash of 1987, 9/11 or the Asian currency crisis in 1997? If the system made money, how much was it relative to the overall profitability of the system? What does the system performance look like when those trades were taken out? If the system was unprofitable during those times, how well did the system control risk?

12. **Friction costs.** In trading, as in physics, friction slows things down. Friction refers to slippage, commission and the costs of missed trades, all of which must be considered when looking at a trading system. You should factor in an appropriate slippage cost for each trade – as little as one tick in highly liquid markets to multiple ticks and points in less liquid markets. There have been many systems that went from nicely profitable to break-even or losing simply because of slippage and nothing else. Also, make sure that you analyze the system with reasonable costs in mind. Commission costs ten years ago were very different from costs today. And finally consider how well the system would perform if you missed ten or twenty percent of the trades? It would not be unusual to miss twenty percent of

a system's trades if you were trading the system manually, or if limit orders weren't filled or were only partially filled.

13. **Multiple time frames.** What time frames does the system consider when trading? Systems that use a longer time frame to determine the dominant trend and shorter time frames for entries tend to be more robust than systems that use a single time frame.

14. **Multiple types of data.** What types of data is the system using? Systems that use some fundamental data combined with technical data are more comprehensive.

15. **Multiple markets.** How well does the system work on multiple markets? For example, a system developed on the S&Ps should at least be profitable on other broad market measures such as the Russell and the Dow. How well does the system work on non-correlated markets? Systems that are at least profitable on non-correlated markets may be more reliable.

16. **Monte Carlo simulation.** A Monte Carlo simulation is a relatively simple concept. It takes the trades that a system produces and randomly mixes them up to produce new sequences of trades. This ensures that the system can be tradable even if the trades occurred in a different sequence. Most of the simulations should be profitable, and most of the drawdowns and consecutive winners or losers should be within your tolerance level.

Mix It Up

The last thing on most beginning system traders' minds is diversification. Evaluating a system is complicated enough, yet this has the most potential to keep a system trader out of trouble. Diversification can help to mitigate the two largest stumbling blocks to trading systems: adequate risk control and adequate return on equity.

By diversifying, the distribution of drawdown periods between systems can often offset each other. Diversification can be trading multiple systems or multiple system types (short-term, long-term, trend following, counter-trend, etc.), trading systems on multiple time frames and trading systems in multiple, non-correlated markets.

Ideally, a system trader's portfolio will comprise all three forms of diversification, but even incorporating one can add a much-needed measure of diversity to a portfolio. An entire book could be written about how to ensure that your portfolio diversification choices mitigate risk instead of adding risk, but the point to be made here is that some diversification is usually better than none.

Make the Most of Mechanical System Trading

A disciplined, systematic evaluation process and a properly diversified portfolio of systems are two of the foundations of successful mechanical system trading. Between your own ideas for trading systems and the hundreds of additional systems that are available commercially or in the public domain, you can and will spend a lot of time evaluating systems. In order to make the most of your time, having a fixed process to examine each system is essential.

It also takes a portfolio of systems to be successful in the long run. Markets change and individual systems fail. That's a fact of system trading life. As with any type of trader, system traders have to adapt to these changing conditions. A well-diversified portfolio of systems ensures that a sudden change does not put you out of business before you've had a chance to adapt.

Incorporating diversification and a systematic evaluation of trading systems will boost your chances of success as a mechanical system trader — and may make you almost as efficient as that power computer of the future.

Nigel Bahadur leads the research and development program for LBRGroup. Prior to this, he was the Senior Vice President of Research and Development for EXE Technologies. As one of the principals of the company, he spent ten years helping the company grow from five employees to six hundred employees in thirteen countries, culminating in an IPO in 2000. Bahadur was instrumental in developing cutting-edge programs and technologies that solved complex global enterprise-wide problems for Fortune 1000 companies. Bahadur is a member of the American Association for Professional Technical Analysts. When not involved in the markets, he expends his energies on swing, lindyhop, and salsa dancing and martial arts. Bahadur can be reached at nigel@lbrgroup.com or via the www.lbrgroup.com website. This article originally appeared in *SFO* in September 2006.

BOOST YOUR TRADING RETURNS BY DIVERSIFYING YOUR SYSTEMS

BY JOHN HILL & GEORGE PRUITT

Many of the more popular and successful trading systems that are available at the retail level are long-term trend-followers. These trend-following systems diversify via a wide variety of futures, some of which are likely to be in a trend that will overcome the drawdowns of the ones that are in a choppy range. Sometimes, however, diversification among futures is not enough. It may lead to a smaller loss. Yet, that's still not a profit.

But there is another approach to diversification that may improve a trader's ability to profit: trading multiple systems that are anti-correlated with each other. In other words, when one system is making money, the other one is either making more or at least losing less than the one that is winning. Ideally, the combined equity curve of such an approach will yield a much smoother curve with less heart-wrenching drawdowns. (An equity curve is a chart that plots the ups and downs of the value of an account.)

To put together three systems that fit our criteria of low correlation and, in turn, determine whether a multiple trading system approach has benefits, we explored our data bank of systems being tracked. The easiest way to determine anti-correlation of systems is by examining the frequency and duration of trades for each system. In other words, one wants to find long-, intermediate-, and short-term systems to combine. In addition to the degree of correlation, we wanted to select systems that have been tracked for a number of years and have shown positive results. Though there may be other systems that fit our criteria, here are the three we chose.

TABLE 1: Performance of the Aberration System

	Total $PL	Avg $PL/Yr	Max DrwDn	In Last 12 mn $PL	DrwDn	Trds /Yr	% Wins	% TIM	W:L	%Gain /Mr+DD
US Bonds	30160	1453	26370	4890	3870	5	48.5	58	1.3	5.0
Treasry Note	22560	1087	26830	1180	2960	5	46.8	59	1.3	3.8
Euro Curr-DM	100125	4845	27225	-3788	11538	5	45.5	61	1.6	16.3
Japanese Yen	115213	5552	19113	275	10538	5	48.4	63	2.1	26.1
Swiss Franc	49313	2377	16688	-7288	9113	5	49.5	63	1.4	12.8
Crude Oil	48200	2323	34420	-20380	28450	7	52.8	71	1.4	6.1
Heating Oil	58040	2797	27737	-8513	22151	7	46.4	68	1.4	9.4
Natural Gas	118950	7246	46910	8870	46910	7	47.1	70	1.6	13.7
Soybeans	-3755	-181	45390	-1640	5840	7	34.3	59	1.0	-.4
Cotton	61045	2942	15990	-3080	3890	6	45.6	63	1.6	17.3

	Net $PL	Max DrwDn		Date	# of Trades	% TIM	Avg. Mrgn	$PL/Yr*10 /MaxDD	%Gain /Mr+DD	%Gain /20%DD
Last 6 Months	-15778	69942	on	8/14 2006	35	100	13720		-33.9	
Last 12 Months	-55970	98260	on	8/14 2006	64	100	13709		-46.1	
Average/ Year	28898	33769	Avg. Hi	20	56	100	15134		49.6	
Full Run TOTAL	599631	107140	on	8/14 2006	1159	100	15134	2.7	22.0	5.4

Trend-Following System

Keith Fitschen's Aberration is one of the first systems that comes to mind when considering a well-rounded trend-following methodology. Fitschen is a well-known technician and has done great work in the area of trading system development. This system was released to the public in December 1993. It holds a trade for an average of sixty days. The one word that best describes Aberration is simplicity. The system essentially uses one parameter that is exactly the same for each market; corn and Japanese yen, fundamentally different markets, use the same number to generate buys and sells and liquidations. The performance of Aberration since 1993 should squelch the voices of those who tout optimized parameters (see *Table 1, Figure 1*).

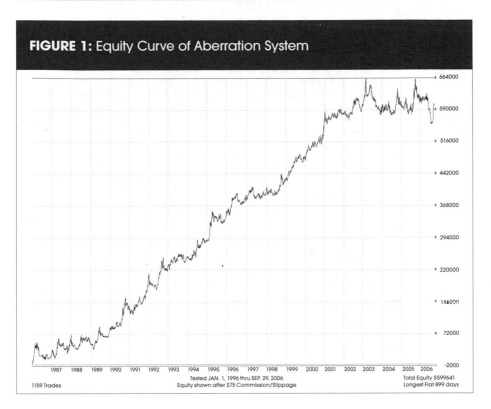

FIGURE 1: Equity Curve of Aberration System

1159 Trades

Tested JAN. 1, 1996 thru SEP. 29, 2006
Equity shown after $75 Commission/Slippage

Total Equity $599641
Longest Flat 899 days

Swing System

Samurai 7, developed by John Hill and released in May 1998, is one of the few short-term systems that has been profitable since its release. Hill developed this system because of the vacuum of the profitable shorter-term systems. The average trade for this system is 4.2 days. Samurai is a pattern-based breakout methodology that looks for short-term swings inside longer-term trends. Like Aberration, Samurai 7 uses one parameter set for all markets. *Table 2* shows the performance of the Samurai 7 system.

Daytrade System

One can't get any further anti-correlation than adding a daytrade system to the mix. Like the aforementioned systems, R-Breaker has a robust methodology that has been profitable over an extended period of time. Richard Saidenberg of SoundView Capital created R-Breaker back in 1992, and Futures Truth has been tracking the system since 1993. The system was the prototype of many daytrade systems that have been and currently are being sold. R-Breaker is a combination of two

TABLE 2: Performance of the Samurai-7 System

	Total $PL	Avg $PL/Yr	Max DrwDn	In Last 12 mn $PL	DrwDn	Trds /Yr	% Wins	% TIM	W:L	%Gain /Mr+DD
US Bonds	87800	4231	18300	10760	2370	36	47.0	43	1.4	20.1
Treasry Note	40590	1956	14800	3810	1420	35	43.2	44	1.2	12.0
Euro Curr-DM	69675	3371	26450	-3238	8425	31	45.9	41	1.2	11.6
Japanese Yen	36700	1769	31763	-250	7125	31	40.8	45	1.1	5.2
Swiss Franc	21775	1049	59350	-12500	15650	33	41.0	43	1.1	1.7
Crude Oil	48690	2347	13690	660	6280	35	43.9	43	1.3	6.1
Heating Oil	84004	4048	19908	11407	9173	34	44.9	42	1.4	18.5
Natural Gas	187360	11413	46510	-1180	46510	32	48.7	46	1.7	21.7
Soybeans	45530	2194	9500	-6180	7080	37	40.8	45	1.3	20.2
Cotton	81140	3910	9975	-3755	5715	38	43.8	47	1.5	35.6

	Net $PL	Max DrwDn		Date	# of Trades	% TIM	Avg. Mrgn	$PL/Yr*10 /MaxDD	%Gain /Mr+DD	%Gain /20%DD
Last 6 Months	-8937	56541	on	8/25 2006	178	100	12016		-22.1	
Last 12 Months	-16156	59038	on	8/25 2006	332	100	11373		-19.3	
Average/ Year	33841	21388	Avg. Hi 20		335	100	12321		73.8	
Full Run TOTAL	702196	62179	on	8/25 2006	6957	100	12321	5.4	39.0	10.9

different methodologies: breakout and counter trend. The bulk of profit in a daytrade system usually comes on those days when the market opens, takes off and continues in the same direction for the entire day. The bulk of losses comes on the days when the market moves just enough to get the trader into a position and then quickly reverses and stops him or her out. R-Breaker tries to take advantage of both types of days. Based on the real-time simulated performance, it seems to have achieved its objective. *Table 3* shows the performance of the R-Breaker S&P day trade system.

The Diversified Program and Hypothetical Trading Criteria

A diversified portfolio of ten liquid and diverse futures was selected for the trend-following and short-term system. They are Treasury bonds, Treasury notes, euros (currency), Japanese yen, Swiss franc, crude, heating oil,

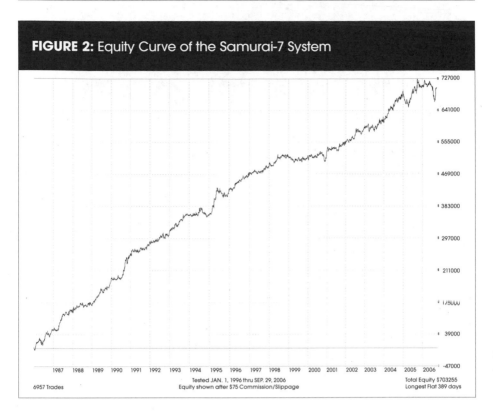

FIGURE 2: Equity Curve of the Samurai-7 System

Tested JAN. 1, 1996 thru SEP. 29, 2006
6957 Trades
Equity shown after $75 Commission/Slippage
Total Equity $703255
Longest Flat 389 days

soybeans and cotton. Remember, we are trying to achieve diversification through systems and markets. The bases of the studies are as follows:

- Test period was from January 1, 1986 to September 2006.
- Commission and slippage used was $75 per round turn. One contract per signal was traded.
- Capital investment of $400,000 was selected. (Everyone looks at capital in a different light; thus, it is hard to select a one-size-fits-all amount. Based on studies and general information in the CTA world, investors are looking for profits of 20 percent-plus, with a drawdown of less than 10 percent. We do know that 50-percent returns will scare more money away than it attracts. Only 10 to 15 percent of the equity is required for margin. The balance of funds could be in an interest-bearing instrument.)

Performance Results

Let's take a look at how the systems stacked up. Now that we have seen the individual equity curves and reports, let's see what happens when

TABLE 3: Performance of the R-Breaker S&P Day Trade System

	Total $PL	Avg $PL/Yr	Max DrwDn	In Last 12 mn $PL	DrwDn	Trds /Yr	% Wins	% TIM	W:L	%Gain /Mr+DD
US Bonds	87800	4231	18300	10760	2370	36	47.0	43	1.4	20.1

	Net $PL	Max DrwDn		Date	# of Trades	% TIM	Avg. Mrgn	$PL/Yr*10 /MaxDD	%Gain /Mr+DD	%Gain /20%DD
Last 6 Months	1450	9475	on	9/22 2006	83	51	2921		19.0	
Last 12 Months	-4075	15625	on	2/7 2006	162	47	2726		-19.1	
Average/ Year	14293	11721	Avg. Hi	20	147	45	2610		81.8	
Full Run TOTAL	296575	44900	on	2/7 2006	3054	45	2610	3.2	28.2	6.4

we combine all three systems together. *Figure 3* shows the combined equity curve.

Reading Between the Lines

So, what does the data show? The average annual return when trading Aberration alone was 7.2 percent on capital, with a maximum drawdown of 26.8 percent. However, combining Aberration and Samurai 7 offered a better annual return on capital at 15.7 percent with a maximum drawdown of 40.1 percent. The kicker is that once one puts all three systems together–Aberration, Samurai 7 and R-Breaker—the annual return on capital is 19.3 percent with a maximum drawdown of 40.1 percent. Thus, with diversification, the three systems together offered a higher annual return to maximum draw down ratio.

The Takeaway

Traders considering using systems to achieve diversification should take note that adding the two additional non-correlated systems does not materially increase the maximum drawdown but does increase the return from 7.1 percent up to more than 19 percent. Traders also must remember that the maximum drawdown is a one-time occurrence over twenty years. Our experience has shown that the average of twenty drawdowns over the test period will be in the area of 50 to 60 percent of the maximum. One should always be aware of the worst case scenario,

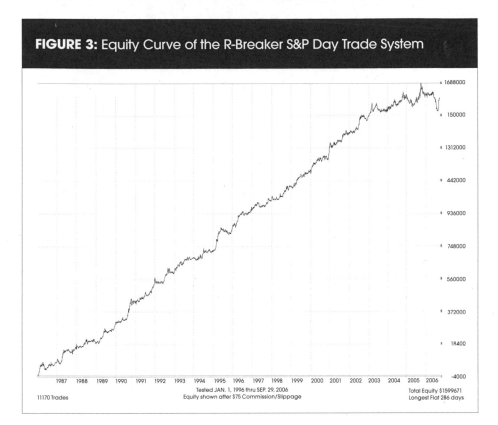

FIGURE 3: Equity Curve of the R-Breaker S&P Day Trade System

11170 Trades

Tested JAN. 1, 1996 thru SEP. 29, 2006
Equity shown after $75 Commission/Slippage

Total Equity $1599671
Longest Flat 286 days

but perhaps think in terms of the average. For instance, the 9/11 attack showed big losses for some systems but was far from the normal. In other words, drawdown should not be the only criteria in selecting a system.

Monte Carlo students will throw rocks at some of these conclusions and rightly so. [In applied mathematics, the name "Monte Carlo" (after the casino in Monaco) is given to the method of solving problems by means of experiments with random numbers.] In the real world, drawdown certainly could be greater than the hypothetical study. This generally holds true for any system. If capital less than $400,000 was used to trade the Aberration, many traders might abandon the system because of the $107,000 drawdown in 2006.

Even still, the data clearly demonstrate the value of trading a mixture of short-term and long-term systems. Basically, the two additional systems get a free ride in relation to return versus drawdown; however, as with all forms of speculation "past performance is not indicative of future results."

FIGURE 4: Combined Equity Curve

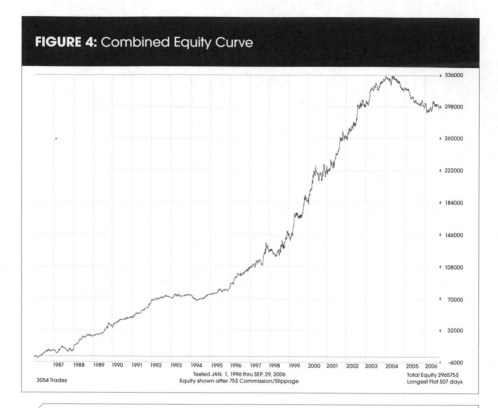

| 1987 1988 1989 1990 1991 1992 1993 1994 1995 1996 1997 1998 1999 2000 2001 2002 2003 2004 2005 2006 |

3054 Trades

Tested JAN. 1, 1996 thru SEP. 29, 2006
Equity shown after 75$ Commission/Slippage

Total Equity 296575$
Longest Flat 507 days

John Hill is founder and president of Futures Truth Company, an organization that has analyzed and rated publicly offered futures trading systems since 1985. A futures trader since 1958, he has been a frequent guest on CNBC and has spoken at numerous investment conferences in the U.S. and abroad. For more information visit www.futurestruth.com.

George Pruitt is director of research at Futures Truth. He is also the co-author of *Building Winning Trading Systems with TradeStation* (Wiley, 2002) and *The Ultimate Trading Guide* (Wiley, 2000). This article first appeared in *SFO* in August 2004.

Authors' note: Since this article was originally published in 2004, most systems, long- and short-term, have suffered through some very difficult market conditions: extreme volatility in the energy sector, market indirection in the financials, and below normal volatility in the stock indices. A 40-percent maximum drawdown would probably get a fund manager fired. However, the concept presented here is still valid as we have shown an increase in the annual return/maximum draw down ratio by adding multiple systems.

MAKE IT A WINNER: Develop Your Own Trading System

BY STEVEN LANDIS & MARK PANKIN

Countless articles have been devoted to developing trading systems, often from a highly technical approach. We have chosen to present the topic in a less-technical format, focusing on the basics of system development. It is safe to say that those who trade for profit and manage money can be categorized as either 1) looking for high profits and tolerant of the accompanying risk or 2) looking to achieve market returns with reduced risk versus buy-and-hold scenarios. Merely as a frame of reference, both authors of this article are in the latter camp.

Traders can choose between black box systems, subscription services or self-created systems. A black box system is a software program for which the inner workings, or algorithms, are unknown, and the variables cannot be modified. A gray box system is similar in that the algorithms are unknown; however, it allows variables to be modified, so the system may trade better or more to the liking of the user. Subscription services provide the subscriber with buy and sell signals via email, telephone hotline, fax or Internet website. But many traders consider neither black/gray box systems nor subscription services as viable alternatives, so for the purposes of this particular article, we will not be reviewing either of them.

Make It Your Own

When formulating a system, the trader inputs his logic, rationale, risk tolerance and expectations for profits—no small task. In the process, the system becomes a reflection of the trader. If the process is conducted properly, the resulting system should fulfill nearly all of the trader's needs and expectations. This extensive work gives the trader the ability to feel how the system will react under various scenarios. Traders can learn to anticipate how a system reacts and can prepare for a trade before it is signaled. Having a sense of an impending trade allows one to mentally prepare for a trade. Obviously, reducing the element of surprise can prove advantageous to the trader who might, otherwise, be unprepared for a trade.

Another benefit of developing one's own system is the ability to analyze problems associated with underperformance, or worse, system failure. Knowledge of what drives a system enables the trader to better determine the underlying causes of a system failure. This insight can help the trader decide if use of a failing system should be continued or abandoned, temporarily or permanently.

For example, a system that trades on short-term indicators might suffer failure in a congested market. Associating the short-term indicators with the presence of congestion can help the trader recognize that the problem likely is temporary, rather than a permanent situation. Scrapping a good system, solely because the system is temporarily out of sync with the market, is rarely a wise decision.

Taking responsibility for one's performance is important to becoming a successful trader. If a trader is always blaming the markets, the Fed or some other convenient culprit for the failure of his system, he'll likely never trade up to his potential. Recognizing the cause of trading failure and taking action to correct those problems is another trait of a successful trader. So, how does one develop his or her own proprietary trading system?

First and foremost, the trader should be confident of a system's ability to signal profitable trades and not be unnerved when losing trades occur. In developing a system, traders must ask themselves the following:

- How much time is required to monitor the system in real-world situations? Does the system require intra-day, close-of-business, market-on-open, weekly or monthly monitoring?
- How frequently are trades signaled? If a system meets all of a trader's requirements but trades daily, will he have time to monitor and execute trades? An extension of high-frequency trading is

trading costs. Will the costs become excessive and eat up all of the profits? Are tax consequences (long- versus short-term gains) an important issue?

- What is the percentage of winning versus losing trades? In a perfect world, one could hope for a system that provides a high percentage of winning trades and high profits. Realistically there is a tradeoff between the two, so which do you prefer: a system with a high rate of winning trades (and possibly, lower per-trade profit) or a lower percentage winning trades (with potentially higher per-trade profit)?

- What is the profitability of the system (average win/average loss)? Many traders want a system to provide a ratio of at least 1.5:1 ($1.50 in gains for every $1.00 in losses).

- What is the longest run of losing trades that might be expected? Will you be able to stick with a system that might experience six to eight consecutive losing trades?

- How large is the system drawdown (equity peak to low)? What is your tolerance for loss of capital before the system resumes its winning ways: -5 percent, -10 percent, -15 percent or more? How quickly do you require that such drawdowns be recovered when the system's winning ways resume?

Create the Right System

A conservative trader will prefer a system that trades less frequently, has a high percentage of winning trades, experiences relatively short runs of losing trades, and has a low (five- to ten- percent) maximum drawdown. The more aggressive trader will be less concerned about these factors so long as the profit objective is met. The right trading system is one that meets the trader's emotional, risk and profit requirements. If a trader lacks confidence in his system, he will never trade it successfully. Such personal insight can be gained only through hands-on, real-time, real-money investing and trading over a period of several years.

Before beginning to develop a system, one first must determine the instruments to be traded. Will the system be used to trade individual securities (stocks or bonds), mutual funds (stock, bond, foreign equities, index-based, junk bonds), ETFs, or other derivatives, such as futures and options? Decide which instruments to choose based on the ease of access to the security or other instrument, cost of trading, trading restrictions (e.g., short-term redemption fees) and capacity—nothing, for example, is worse than having a great mutual fund system, but no funds that will accept your money. We both trade mutual funds that, preferably:

- are available on a no-transaction fee platform;
- accept trades of the size and frequency we trade;
- impose no short-term redemption fees; and
- trade profitably with our systems.

Once a trader has determined which instruments to trade, he must formulate a hypothesis. Will the system be based on classic market timing, sector rotation, swing-trading, tactical or dynamic allocation or some other approach? Depending on one's trading style, the availability of mutual funds can be crucial. For example, if a trader wants to trade index funds that impose no fees and no restrictions on trading frequency, he would not be trading conventional index funds. He can, however, trade his system with fund families such as Direxion (formerly Potomac) Funds, ProFunds or Rydex Funds – companies that are trader-friendly. As such, capacity can be a non-issue.

Developing a trading system involves a great deal of time and countless failed attempts. While this is especially true for the beginner, even seasoned traders experience failure. One can spend years testing, developing and paper-trading candidate systems. It can seem a waste of time and effort, but the time can prove well spent as one discovers how systems work and various classes of securities interact and correlate. A trader learns the systems with which he is comfortable and those that hold promise. Remember, a personal investment of time is an investment in future trading success.

Central to developing a successful system is formulating a logical basis on which to trade. Doing so will yield one or more hypotheses to be tested. For example, one might design a system based on observations of the relationship between multiple securities or asset classes. Does it appear that small stocks rise after large stocks have begun to gain ground and fall after their larger-capitalization brethren? If this were the working hypothesis, one would design a system that detects a change in the trend of large-cap stocks, possibly by analyzing the movement of the S&P 500.

Next, one would observe the future course of small-cap stocks, using the Russell 2000 index. Does the relationship exist to a significant extent, and can the change in direction be forecast with reasonable accuracy? Or does the hypothesis appear to be null and call for a fresh, different approach?

Suppose one has developed a system that has been traded based on the assumptions above. As a result of the time and effort, the trader understands how it works and what might be the cause of its failure (at some time in the future). If the historical relationship between large- and small-cap stocks (the basis of the system) has changed, the trader will know to stop trading the system until the relationship resumes.

Another advantage of formulating a logical working hypothesis is avoidance of data mining. Today's powerful software and abundant data make it too easy to look for and find relationships that may or may not exist. Given enough data and enough searching, a trader almost certainly can find something. It is akin to the old saw that if a million monkeys sit at a million typewriters, after a million years one of them will write the first sentence of a prize winning novel. An example of a spurious relationship, although traders do not usually take it seriously, is the famous Super Bowl Indicator. (A triumphant team from the old American Football League, now the American Football Conference or AFC, foreshadows a down market; and a winner from the old NFL, now the National Football Conference or NFC, means the bulls are coming.) Though it is impossible to do justice to the subject, here are some of the major concepts, their characteristics, and how those features might affect systems.

Trend Following

Many traders find trend-following systems attractive due to high profits and low trading frequency, so it is not surprising that many, possibly a majority of, technical indicators are designed to identify market trends. The concept of a moving average (MA) is among the simplest and most popular trend indicators, and signal generation is very straightforward: buys and sells are generated when the price of the security crosses a moving average of the closing price of the security.

It is also popular to base signals on the relationship of a shorter-period moving average to a longer-period one. For example, buy the S&P 500 index when its 21-day simple moving average moves above its 50-day simple moving average.

Indicators based on a moving average incorporate parameters, usually a number of days, weeks or months that determine how frequently signals are generated. Systems that use a shorter-term MA will generate signals more frequently and try to identify trends earlier. System parameters will result in characteristics that a trader needs to evaluate to determine appropriateness. A good trend-following system with short period parameters likely will generate many short-term trades with small losses, sometimes called whipsaws, and a small number of much longer trades that produce substantial gains

In contrast, a system with longer, slower parameters is more likely to produce a higher percentage of winning trades, but it might not be as profitable as the best trades of the faster system. That is because it normally takes longer to identify a tradable trend, so some of the potential profits will be missed. Also, the slower system likely will suffer higher drawdowns as the system will sell later and lower than the faster system.

Another important difference between slow and fast trend-following systems is risk management, something that is critical to all trading methods. A fast system probably has risk management built in, as it will exit from trades earlier and with smaller losses. In contrast, slower systems are exposed to greater market volatility and may have difficulty exiting quickly if a trend ends abruptly. Consequently, such systems must incorporate separate risk control factors such as stop-losses.

Counter-Trend, Trend Reversals

All trends eventually come to an end, and when they do, it may be time for traders to take action. To some extent, trend-following methods will identify when the trend has ended, resulting in either a reversal or congestion (sideways movement). A system with longer period parameters is likely to signal a genuine reversal, but the trader may want to use more sensitive indicators to make confirmation.

Counter-trend traders will not be so concerned about whether the primary trend is still in place. These traders know that there will be shorter moves counter to the main trend, and quite often those moves are an opportunity for nice profits from relatively short-term trading. With this approach, one normally sets a profit objective and closes the trade when it is reached or when it appears that it resumes its move in the direction of the dominant trend. One advantage of counter-trend trading is that one can set very close stop-losses (exit points) based on resumption of the dominant trend. Thus, risk management is built in, but the trader may have to live with a fairly high percentage of small, losing trades.

Trading Range

A significant percentage of the time markets do not exhibit a trend. During such non-trending periods, the market is moving sideways, and that usually means it is in a trading range. The trading range will be bound above and below by levels determined during relatively recent history. Individual stocks have been known to stay in a trading range for long periods of time. One reason is that the lower level may be where fundamental analysis indicates the stock is attractively priced, while the upper level is that price at which analysis indicates the stock is overvalued. Until there is some significant change in the fundamentals of the stock (for example, earnings are well above or well below consensus expectations), the stock may trade within a well-defined range.

There are many ways to take advantage of an identified trading range. The most obvious is to buy near the bottom and sell near the range high. Additionally, options provide many ways of profiting should the trading range hold. Like counter-trend trading, one can usually set very close stop-losses below the presumed bottom or sell-stops above the presumed top of the trading range. These provide risk control, but the trade-off is possibly living with many small, losing trades. Some options-trading methods will overcome this problem, but the trade-off is reduced profit potential.

Overbought/Oversold Analysis

Oscillators are technical indicators that attempt to identify when prices have gone too far and a security has become over- or under-priced. The two most popular such indicators are stochastics and the RSI indicator. Traders looking for counter-trends may find these quite helpful. However, it is important to realize that in a strong trend, it is common to see overbought or oversold readings persist for quite some time. A more sophisticated use of the oscillators is based on identifying when the oscillators have reversed their trends.

Seasonal Patterns

While these typically are associated more with agricultural commodity futures due to the annual planting- growing-harvesting cycle, they appear with other commodities such as heating oil and gasoline that have repeating seasonal patterns. Stocks, too, exhibit seasonal or cyclical patterns. In fact, there is the widely known technique of owning stocks during the November-April season and being out of the market for the rest of the year: sell in May and go away.

While the system may be reliable over a period of decades, it will not work every year. For example, the S&P 500 index was down 12.6 percent during November 2000-April 2001 and up 14.6 percent from May-October 2003. Consequently, a trader using seasonal patterns, particularly as a stand-alone system, needs to have the discipline to stick with the system for the long haul and/or institute stop-loss orders.

Chart Reading

Many successful traders rely on their interpretation of chart patterns that illustrate variables such as a security's or an index's price (high, low, open and close) and volume. From these data the chartist may add indicators including those developed by Gann (fan and line), Fibonacci (arc, retracement and time zone), and linear regression and standard deviation lines.

For those interested in charting, an excellent starting point is the endless texts and articles that describe charting methodologies and analysis. Effective chart reading, a skill developed through years of application, is not something all traders can do successfully. Nonetheless, skilled chartists have developed a trading method that is right for them and can be highly successful. Chart reading, like all technical indicators, is a valuable tool that is best used in conjunction with other methods.

Fundamental Analysis

Although we are focusing on technical analysis, fundamentals should not necessarily be ignored. Some traders, especially those who trade short term, may never consider fundamentals such as supply and demand, earnings, sales and interest rates. Others may incorporate some fundamental measures into their technically oriented trading systems. A basic method might be to generate signals using technical indicators and then look at the fundamentals for confirmation. If the fundamentals do not support the trade, the trader may decide to pass on it, waiting for a statistically better opportunity. Traders who do this should maintain records of trades not taken, so the value of incorporating fundamentals can be evaluated.

Evaluating the effectiveness of your fundamental analysis is especially important because it tends to be more subjective than technical analysis. Technical indicators more reliably issue signals that are objective in nature. Moreover, technical-based systems can be back-tested and developed using historical data. Back-testing a fundamentals-based system is much more difficult, if not impossible.

Most technical systems are developed by formulating and testing a hypothesis against historical data. The goal is to produce a purely mechanical system that can be run on a computer. There are several popular commercial software programs for system development and testing. Some traders prefer to roll their own by using spreadsheets or programs that they have written. In any event, the goal is to generate objective evaluations using well-defined rules. We suspect that virtually all technical traders, except for avid chart readers, now use computers and historical data to develop, test and refine their trading methods.

It would require another article to provide a good overview of the development and testing process. Once the system's basics have been defined, the major issues to consider are:

- What data periods should be used for system development (in sample) and testing (out of sample)
- Which parameters should be varied, over what ranges and at what intervals;
- System returns (overall profitability, percentage of profitable trades, consistency);
- Risk evaluation and control measures – money management;
- Reward to risk;
- Optimization: to do it or not. If doing it, how, and evaluation criteria.

Keep It Simple, But...
We are reminded of Einstein's advice that things should be as "simple

as possible, but no simpler." In other words, you will want to include as many indicators and techniques as necessary to capture the effects that are the basis of the system, but refrain from tweaking the system in an attempt to make it closer to perfect. Striving for simplicity reduces the possibility of curve fitting and increases the probability that the system will continue to work in the future. Even more importantly, making it simple can give you the understanding you need to determine if the system is really broken when you run into one of those inevitable periods of poor performance.

In the end, most traders likely will perform better by developing their own systems. The process will not be quick. There almost certainly will be some blind alleys and lost effort along the way. However, there are substantial rewards to be garnered by trading an effective system that is right for you.

Steven Landis is the founder of Landis Financial & Investment Services and has been a past president and chairman of the National Association of Active Investment Managers (NAAIM), an organization for professional, active investment managers. A registered investment advisor and Certified Financial Planner®, Landis has, in the past, been ranked among the top group of Select Advisors out of more than 250 traders monitored on the website SelectAdvisors.com money management platform. He can be contacted at steven@stevendlandis.com or at sdlandis@yahoo.com.

Mark Pankin, who has a PhD in mathematics, is the founder and owner of MDP Associates LLC, and has been the secretary and a member of the board of directors of NAAIM. Before becoming a registered investment advisor in 1994, he taught math at the university level and worked as an operations research analyst. In 2000, his Rydex sector fund-trading program ranked in Select Advisors' top five for the year. Pankin can be reached at mdp2@pankin.com. This article first appeared in SFO in August 2004.

FACE THE DAY ARMED WITH A SYSTEM

BY JOHN CARTER

When it comes to trading for a living, investors fall into three categories: those who have a system, those who are developing a system, and those who don't believe in utilizing a system and are still trying to explain to their spouse how they lost all of their trading capital.

The point of this, of course, is to emphasize the importance of facing each trading day with a game plan. A very large part of that game plan involves having a specific system or setup and, more importantly, a trading methodology to apply to each system or setup. Without this combination, a trader is like a wounded antelope in the center of a lion pride, where it is not a question of if the antelope is going to get whacked, but rather when.

My daily trading routine utilizes eight systems. One of the simplest and most effective is one I call the "five-minute multi-pivot play," a setup I use on the electronically traded mini-sized Dow futures contract. There is a similar setup for the E-mini S&P, E-mini Nasdaq and E-mini Russell futures, but for the sake of simplicity, we'll focus on the mini-sized Dow setup in this article.

The main advantage of this system is that it is price-based as opposed to indicator-based. By the time most indicators generate a buy or a sell signal, the move is already well underway. By following this price-based methodology, there are many instances in which I get into a trade before the indicator-based traders, and I usually end up handing off my position just as a buy or sell signal is being generated on a stochastic or other oscillator-type system. I do follow 2-, 4- and 13-period exponential moving averages (MA) as well as a 7-period relative strength index (RSI) on each 5-minute chart, but I don't use these for signals; instead they are used to point out when these lagging indicators are creating buy and sell signals—when the crowd is jumping in. Before detailing how to use the system, let's look at its main components.

Pivots

There is no big mystery to pivots. These are simply support and resistance levels originally calculated by floor traders using a simple mathematical formula. They are readily available and have been around for a long time, but they now are widely known and have moved off the floor.

Though many traders are aware of pivot levels and attempt to use them, many unquestionably are using them incorrectly. To add to the confusion, there are different formulas and time frames used when calculating pivots. Let's look at one of the standard pivot formulas:

R3: R1 + (High - Low)
R2: Pivot + (High - Low)
R1: 2x Pivot - Low
PIVOT: High + Low + Close/3
S1: 2x Pivot - High
S2: Pivot - (High - Low)
S3: S1 - (High - Low)
R = Resistance
S = Support

Once a trader has this formula, he needs to gather the high, low and close of the previous session. I like to consider twenty-four hours worth of data for my own trading, so I use the 24-hour session from 4:15 p.m. (ET) to 4:15 p.m. (ET) the following day. Once the high, low, and close are gathered, they can be plugged into an Excel spreadsheet

FIGURE 1: Chart of a Mini-Sized Dow Contract with Pivot Levels

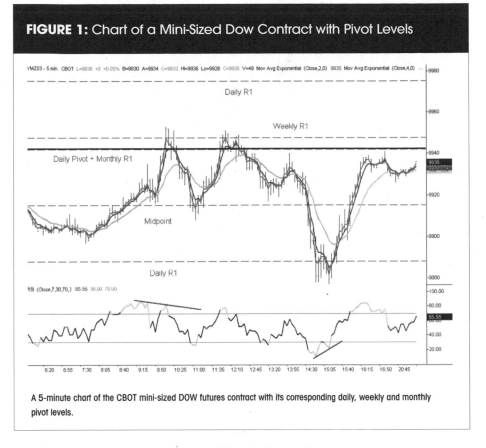

A 5-minute chart of the CBOT mini-sized DOW futures contract with its corresponding daily, weekly and monthly pivot levels.

with the formulas listed above. This information generates seven important levels for the next trading day: a central pivot, three levels above (R1, R2 and R3), and three levels below (S1, S2 and S3). Not surprisingly, the central pivot has the most weight of the seven levels.

In addition to these daily levels, I use weekly levels (calculated using the high, low, and close of the previous week) and monthly levels (using the high, low, and close of the previous month). On days where the action is volatile, creating a trading range of more than 150 points in the mini-sized Dow or 15 points in the E-mini S&P, I also will utilize midpoints. These literally are the halfway point between each of the daily pivot levels. Once the pivots are created and drawn, they will resemble the chart in *Figure 1*.

Remember that it is rare for a stock index to hit its R3 or S3 levels because they are the extremes of the range. This is impor-

FIGURE 2: Chart of Mini-Sized Dow with Labels 1, 2, 3

A 5-minute chart of the CBOT mini-sized Dow contract with system entry and exit levels.

tant to know because if a market rallies to R2 or sells off to S2, that usually ends up being the dead high or the dead low of the day. This knowledge will help temper a trader's emotions and keep him on track to follow this system. That said, let's take a look at my rules for trading the pivots.

I look for trades against the pivots, and my ideal trades are fades against these levels. If we are rallying up to a pivot level, I am either already long and am looking for an exit, or I'm flat and looking to initiate a new short position. For example, the markets rally to a daily level, and I short (sell) the move. Or a market sells off to a daily level, and I buy the move.

I don't wait for the moving averages or the RSI to confirm the action. Instead, I set up the orders based on price action. Ideally, I will get moving average (MA) confirmation at least twenty to thirty minutes after I place the trade, if not sooner. In truth, the trader can trade this system without the MA confirmations—I personally just like to see them turn in my direction after I'm in a trade. This is when most traders are just now getting in the trade—way too late!

On Friday, January 16, the price action on *Figure 2* is showing three trade setups.

1) As the markets rally to the midpoint near 10,565, I set up a short, with my target the daily pivot that is sitting below at 10,529, plus three points (covered in my next trading rule).
2) On a move to the pivot, I close out my short and end up going long, with my target being the midpoint.
3) After hitting the midpoint, I close out my long and reverse and go short, with my target once again at the daily pivot.

Now that we have the basic idea, let's go over entry points and stops. I enter and exit trades by placing limit orders or buying or selling stops + or -3 points from the multi-pivot levels. The orders are +3 or -3 points depending on which side of the pivot the market is trading. The idea is to be first in line. For example, let's say that one of the levels is 10,500, we are rallying up to that level, and I am already long. In that case, I will place a sell order to exit at that level -3 points (10,497). Or, under another scenario, if the market is falling to a pivot at 10,400 and I am short, then my target is the pivot +3 points (10,403). I use this +/-3 points for entries, stops and targets. Again, the idea is to be in front of the pivot and to be first in line to get in or out. On days when I am using the midpoint between the daily levels, I just use the actual midpoint pricing level for buys and sells against the midpoints (instead of + or -3 points).

My initial stop is almost always 20 points, never less than that. If I place a trade and it is near the overnight highs or lows—say 25

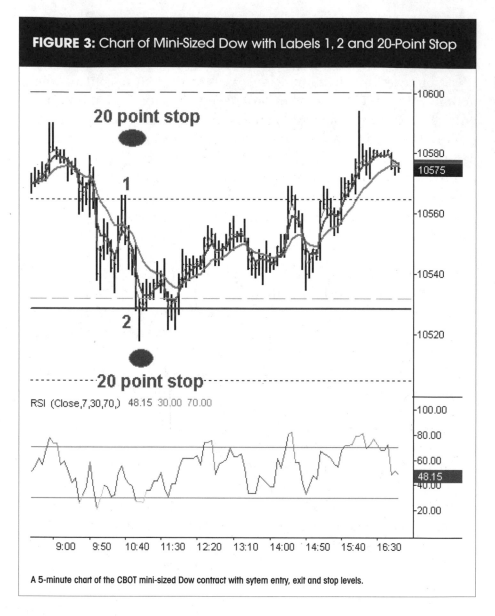

FIGURE 3: Chart of Mini-Sized Dow with Labels 1, 2 and 20-Point Stop

A 5-minute chart of the CBOT mini-sized Dow contract with sytem entry, exit and stop levels.

points away—I will use that level as my stop. However, 95 percent of the time it is just a 20-point stop.

Figure 3 shows entry levels with their corresponding stops in place.

1) When I was filled at my short at the midpoint 10,565, I immediately placed a 20-point stop at 10,585.

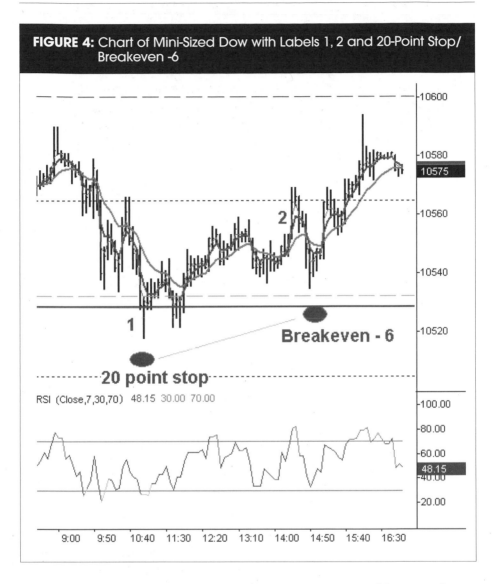

FIGURE 4: Chart of Mini-Sized Dow with Labels 1, 2 and 20-Point Stop/Breakeven -6

2) A long at the weekly level 10,532 + 3 at 10,535 would mean that the trader placed an immediate 20-point stop at 10515. The stop is based on the trader's entry level, not on the pivot level.

I'm not a big fan of aggressively trailing stops. However, if I get close to my target—usually within five points—I will move my stop to the next level + or - 3 points on the far side. This means if I am long, I would bring my stop to the previous pivot - 3 points, which would set up a breakeven -6 play.

Figure 4 shows an example of where to move up a stop.

1) Here we have our original 20-point stop from our long entry on a decline to the weekly pivot + 3 points.

2) When the market gets within five points of my target, I move the stop up to the same pivot I used as my entry level and subtract three points. In this case, the entry pivot was the green dotted line—one of the weekly levels. Thus, the stop is three points below that level, which is six points below my entry (because my entry was weekly pivot + 3 points).

After Two Losers in a Row, I Quit for the Day

This seems like a simple rule, but it is hugely important. The concept of trading is to keep the trader's losses small so he can live to fight another day. With this system, if the trader's first two trades of the day are losers, then he is down 40 points, or $200 per contract traded. This rule is quite reasonable and will prevent a trader from having a killer drawdown day where emotions run rampant, causing overtrading.

Size

With this system, I personally trade one contract for each $12,500 in my account. Technically, of course, the trader could use very aggressive margin rules and trade ten contracts for each $10,000 that he has. The problem with this approach is that if he has two losers in a row, he loses $2,000, or 20 percent of his account in one day. Losing $200 on a $12,500 account equates to a 1.6-percent loss of equity. Losing $200 on a $25,000 account equates to a 0.08- percent loss of equity.

The key to futures trading is managing equity swings. If a trader loses 20 percent, he has to make 25 percent to get back to breakeven. One of the biggest mistakes new traders make is doubling or tripling up from their original plan. A trader can be right five times in a row, but if he continues to pyramid and add contracts, he has to be wrong only once to suffer an enormous loss. Decide how many contracts to trade, and stick to it on each and every trade.

Avoid the Dead Zone

Ignore new trade setups between 12:00 p.m. EST and 2:00 p.m. EST. If I am in a trade, I will stay in it and keep my parameters on.

However, if I am flat heading into this time frame, I will not initiate new trades. Why? This is the dead zone of the day. The institutions are done trading until after 2:00 p.m. EST because there is not enough volume to handle their orders during the afternoon. The resulting price action is choppy, and the only people who benefit from this are brokers, as traders overtrade their accounts, giving back all of their profits they made in the morning. I've found one of the best ways to improve profitability is to not trade during this time of the day.

Those are the rules I follow. What is nice about this system is that the trader doesn't have to watch it very closely once he is in a position. Again, I'm not an aggressive trailer of stops. I like to get in a position, set my parameters and then focus on other things. Depending on the trader's work situation, he could do this at the office, especially on the West Coast. He could set alerts at the key levels, and when the market gets near them, he could place the parameters in his execution platform and proceed to carry out his everyday job. He can go to the next meeting or appointment and let the parameters baby-sit the position. This takes emotion out of the equation.

Just One of Eight...

This is just one of eight systems I follow throughout the day. I also use the pivots in conjunction with volatility readings to catch bigger moves. And, of course, there are additional indicators that can be used to determine whether or not to fade a move to a pivot level or to look for a break of the pivot level.

The key to this system and all of the systems I use is that the trader gets everything set up on his or her charts in advance of the opening. Once it is set up, all the trader has to do is watch, or better yet, set up audio alerts when a pivot is hit. A trader also can place orders in advance, as the exact targets, entries and stops are known before the trade is entered. In this way, the trader can focus on other things if they come up. When the trader hears the alerts going off, he knows that it is time to go back to his charts and explore what is going on. There is no chasing. The orders either will get hit or they will not. This system is constructed in such a way as to naturally enforce the mindset of a professional trader, which is the only consistent way to make money in the financial markets.

John F. Carter grew up the son of a Morgan Stanley stockbroker and was introduced to trading as a sophomore in high school. He has been actively trading for the past 19 years. Carter studied international finance at the University of Cambridge in England before graduating from the University of Texas at Austin. He has been a full time trader since 1996. In 1999, he launched www.tradethemarkets.com to post his trading ideas for the futures, equities and options markets. In 2005 he launched www.razorforex.com to focus on the forex markets. Today Carter has a following of over 10,000 people. He is currently a Commodity Trading Advisor with Razor Trading, he manages a futures and a forex fund, and recent author of *Mastering the Trade*, released in December, 2005. To keep his sanity, Carter relies on physical activity after the close to deal with the financial swings he and his subscribers encounter. He clears his head running, water skiing, and practicing Tae Kwon Do. This article originally appeared in *SFO* in August 2004.

DEVELOPING MY FIRST TRADING SYSTEM: A Cautionary Tale of Hubris, Humility & Hope

BY DAVID SILVERMAN

This year I celebrate my 25th anniversary as a trader.

I am no superstar, but I make a living, which distinguishes me from the vast majority of individuals who, during this period, have tried to make it as professional traders. I take a certain amount of pride in having outlasted many of my competitors, but it hasn't been easy. Like all veteran traders I've had my share of ups, downs, and sideways (often more frustrating than the downs), and even after all these years I struggle each day to understand the vicissitudes of the markets and overcome my fears and inhibitions.

If I have developed any insight after a quarter-century, it is that trading is an evolutionary process. The trader begins life as a weak, defenseless organism. With a puny brain incapable of processing information efficiently, he acts self-destructively, fading the market, adding to losing positions, promising God to never make the same mistake again, if He will just intervene this one time. Predators lurk and entice the novice into their traps. If, somehow, the trader survives, he may earn a place on the food chain, but he cannot rely on past successes to keep him there. With every tick of the market, other traders are on the prowl. So much for intelligent design. Such is the process of natural selection in the marketplace.

187

Playing by the Rules

In that context, I have given a great deal of thought to the question, what do successful traders have in common? While there are a number of answers to this question, above all, successful traders know how to follow rules. By rules, I mean a set of fundamental beliefs so deeply held that it becomes inconceivable to think of deviating from them. It almost doesn't matter what those rules are, only that the trader believes they work and implements them in all instances. As for me, a single rule governs every trade I make. I will never, under any circumstances, put myself in a position where an individual trade or a series of trades will wipe me out. The way I accomplish this is to limit my losses to a maximum of two percent of the equity I am trading. So, for example, if I am trading a $1,000,000 account, I can lose up to $20,000 on a trade and still be in compliance with my rule. More importantly, I would have to make dozens of uninterrupted losing trades of two percent in order to lose all of my money. This is almost inconceivable.

In practice, my losses are almost always less than two percent. While I sometimes experience a number of consecutive losing trades—I don't think it's ever been more than a dozen or so—my winning trades tend to be much larger than my losers. I suppose the two-percent loss threshold is somewhat arbitrary. I could extend it to five percent or more without putting myself in too much peril. But in order to justify doing this, I'd have to believe that I could make at least two-and-a-half times as much. Because I'm not sure this is a reasonable expectation and because the additional risk scares me, my two-percent rule remains the underlying principle upon which all my strategies are based.

The two-percent rule also creates a structure for my trading decisions. For example, assuming a $1 million account value, if I want to buy Google (GOOG) and my stop loss is $5 lower than my entry price, I know that I cannot buy more than 4,000 shares (this is actually an oversimplification, because I rarely execute my entire position at one price, but for the purposes of the example, using round numbers illustrates the principle easily). In other words, if I want to establish a bigger position, I need to choose a stop price closer to my entry price or wait until GOOG trades lower. Moreover, if I am long five different stocks from the same industry, this must be considered a single position with a single two-percent maximum loss (as opposed to five separate positions with a maximum loss of ten percent). Treating the aggregate position any other way is inconsistent with the basic principle. This goes for pairs trading as well. If, for example, I am spread long GOOG versus short Yahoo! Inc. (YHOO), this is a single position with a single two percent maximum loss. It's not very elegant but, as I say, I make a living.

Developing a Trading Model

With these rules in mind, I decided last year to conduct an experiment, in which I would take a single trading idea and develop it into a formal trading model. This, of course, is done all the time by sophisticated trading firms using custom-built technology and by retail traders working with comparatively simple platforms such as TradeStation, MetaStock, Fidelity's Wealth Lab Pro and other off-the-shelf software from brokers or independent vendors. Everyone seems to be searching for the perfect trading system, the elusive Holy Grail of systems.

Not me. I feel fortunate when I can find my keys in the morning, so I have no delusions of grandeur. My more modest goal was simply to discover whether my cherished rules held up when subjected to the model developer's standard techniques of backtesting and optimization. In a way, the prospect intimidated me. For one thing, I was concerned with the potential cost. I know of traders and firms who have spent hundreds of thousands or even millions of dollars developing systems. Because such amounts are far more than two percent of my trading equity, I vowed to enter this project with a stop loss, no different than if I were trading GOOG. Additionally, a part of me feared the outcome for an entirely different reason. What if Burton Malkiel was right when he said, in his classic text *A Random Walk Down Wall Street*, that a blindfolded monkey throwing darts at a newspaper's financial pages could select a portfolio that would do just as well as one carefully selected by the experts. Simply put, what if I found that the principles upon which I have based my career were without substance? It's not like the "Random Walk police" were going to come to my house and lead me away in handcuffs in the middle of the night, but how would I deal with the blow to my psyche? What would this mean for my trading strategies? Could I come to work on the day after and pretend nothing had changed?

Calling the Geek Squad

This would not be my first attempt at system development. About fifteen years ago, I tried to learn how to write code to develop trading models, first using relatively primitive software from a company called Logical Information Machines and then, when that didn't turn out well, using TradeStation. The promotional literature from both companies implied that the software was so simple to use that anyone, except perhaps a village idiot, could be programming in a few short hours. Imagine my humiliation after a hundred hours of unsuccessful attempts. Well, not this time. This time I knew what I needed: I needed a geek. I turned, reflexively, to the University of Chicago, my alma mater. They allowed me to place an ad on their website, and within days, I had thirty-five resumes. I eventually interviewed fourteen impossibly young, impossibly bright graduate students. One of the candidates had a bachelor's degree in mathematics, a master's degree in computer science, and solved a Rubik's Cube in front of me in less than a minute, blindfolded. While this demonstration was as sad as it was impressive—imagine how many Saturday nights this poor boy spent alone playing with his Rubik's Cube—I was awed by his impressive display of right-brain thinking. I had found my geek.

I began spending money immediately. While I believed my new employee—let's call him Rube—had the technical skills I was looking for, I was concerned that teaching him the basics of the market, as well as my particular approach, was going to consume a great deal of my time. I was right about that. It cost me approximately forty hours of one-on-one tutelage, but I viewed this as a necessary tradeoff. Time spent with Rube at the outset would surely produce a dividend when the programming process commenced. There were additional upfront expenses. Two PCs and four monitors cost about $3,500. Two broadband connections added $100 per month. Various pieces of software, books and training manuals added a few hundred dollars more to the tab. His salary cost me $1,200 per week. He also drank a lot of Red Bull and a can of that stuff costs more than a gallon of unleaded gas.

Finding the Right Software

Once we got past the initial learning stage, I instructed Rube to investigate obtaining system-writing software and quote data, to determine the best way for us to conduct our research. While there are many software packages available containing preprogrammed functions and actual black-box systems, I did not believe they met my needs. First, it is very difficult and time consuming to ascertain that the definitions and assumptions the vendor made in creating the software are acceptable. Second, these packages tend to be expensive. Some require that you open a brokerage account. Others are sold for a monthly fee.

So instead, I decided to use a program called Wealth Lab Pro (WLP), available to me through Fidelity's Active Trader Pro (ATP), the front-end trading system I use to execute my transactions. Fidelity provides the software for "free" to its active traders, although, of course, nothing in the financial services world is really free, and were I not paying commissions on ATP, Fidelity would certainly charge a monthly fee for the model-building software. Rube informed me that in WLP he could write programs in C++ and easily export data to and import data from Microsoft Excel, where he could manipulate the database and do additional programming. I had no clue what he was talking about, but it seemed to make him happy, and when my geek is happy, so am I. One of the best features of WLP is that the quote feed from Fidelity comes directly from the exchanges and is fairly reliable. This is extremely important because when it comes to modeling, if the quote data is defective, so too will be the results of the research. In other words, garbage in, garbage out.

Another important consideration is that data, especially historical-intraday and real-time data, can cost thousands of dollars. Using WLP, which includes a huge amount of data at no extra charge, allowed me to keep my costs relatively low. Finally, Fidelity supports its products extremely well. The ATP/WLP help desk is open before, during and after trading hours, and I have found the people who answer the phone to be knowledgeable and patient. Knowing there is someone available to curse at when you get frustrated is an important value-added service. None of this is to suggest that WLP is the only or best way to conduct this sort of research. But after I fully investigated the readily available software, it seemed like WLP was the program that best met my specific needs. Nor am I suggesting that one needs to hire a computer programmer in order to successfully test trading ideas. Unless, of course, you are a village idiot. In that case, it is highly recommended.

By this point, we were ready to begin programming. It would be impossible in this short space to describe everything that went into building my model because we performed thousands of tests using ten years of data for the 500 stocks in the S&P 500 and the 100 stocks in the NASDAQ 100. I will say that the concept is based on a type of trade I have been making for 25 years that somewhat simplistically can be characterized as my "rubber band" strategy. The idea behind it is that as the market moves, it stretches — like a rubber band — and when it can stretch no further, it will snap back. This approach requires one to fade the immediate trend. So, for example, one query we posed goes as follows:

1. Stock XYZ is up at least ten percent between the close of Day 1 and close of Day 2.
2. Sell short 100 shares of XYZ on close of Day 2.
3. Buy back 100 shares of XYZ on close of Day 3
4. Or, on Day 3, buy back 100 shares of XYZ if XYZ moves up more than five percent from close of Day 2.

There are three possible outcomes to this trade on Day 3: cover the short position with a profit on the close, cover on the close with a loss of less than five percent, cover before the close with a stop loss of five percent. And the verdict? The rubber band system is profitable. It generated more than 24,000 trades over ten years, an average of about forty trades per stock, four trades per year per stock and overall, about ten trades every day from the universe of 600 stocks. The system made about $1 million, an average of slightly more than $50 per trade. Fifty-five percent of the trades were from the long side and 45 percent were from the short side. Long trades were far more profitable, generating about $800,000. As I dissected the data, I found that certain stocks seemed to respond well to the system and others lost money every time the signals were present. Illiquid stocks (stocks with less 100,000 shares per day traded) performed especially poorly. I could go on, but I just want to give you a sample of the information one finds in an analysis of this kind.

So you ask, why not just make the daily ten trades in perpetuity and collect the winnings? Well, we haven't looked at the entire picture. Commissions on the completed transaction are $16, which brings the average per trade down to $34. Then, we must factor in slippage. Let's say that amounts to $25. We've now reduced the average to about $10. The margin of error is now so slim that what looked initially like an interesting system now appears to be a breakeven proposition.

But wait! We're just getting started. What if we cherry-pick, acting only on signals for stocks that make money with this system? Or what if we simply buy 200 shares of every stock that responds well and only 100 shares of those that don't? What if we only execute trades on the long side, which produced most of the profits? What if we filter from the system stocks that trade less than 100,000 shares per day because they are a drain on profitability? What if we alter the original query variables? Buy XYZ after a 20-percent move? Get out on Day 10? Sell stop of 15 percent?

I have no idea whether there is any individual change or series of changes we can impose that will salvage the rubber band system. The only way to know for sure is to test. This optimization—the attempt to find the variables that will produce the optimal results—can, theoretically, go on for infinity. At some point, however, one has to decide if the system is worth trading or is a dud?

Even after months of study, I remain unsure. While some of the work Rube and I have done looks promising, I do not believe we have tested our results rigorously enough to justify committing my trading capital to them. But we are getting there. The next step is to take our findings to a professor in the Graduate School of Business at the U of C, an uber-geek, who will use all of the mathematical tricks in his financial engineer's bag to break my model. If he cannot, I may be on to something after all. This exercise will cost big money, but I have discovered that model-building is like raising a child. Shoes, braces, college, weddings — you just keep writing checks and hope to God that one day they will support you in your old age. In the meantime, I continue to trade the old-fashioned way and continue to make a living.

Also, I have become surprisingly good at Rubik's Cube.

Mr. Silverman is a successful trader who spent sixteen years on the trading floor of the Chicago Mercantile Exchange (CME) and made the transition to electronic trading nearly a decade ago. Silverman was elected to the CME Board of Directors four times and served more than eight years as a director of the exchange. From 2000 to 2005, as a principal of Aspire Trading Company LLC, he founded, built, and managed an electronic trading arcade. Silverman currently is an independent electronic trader and a consultant to brokerage firms, exchanges, and fund managers. He has taught a course in electronic trading in the graduate school of business at the University of Illinois at Chicago, lectures regularly about the financial services industry, and writes regularly for *SFO*. Mr. Silverman is the author of *Direct Access Futures: The Complete Guide to Trading Electronically* (Wiley, 2001). This article originally appeared in *SFO* in March 2006.

SECTION FIVE
An Introduction to Options

Options are among the fastest-growing segments of the investment community, yet they also can be intimidating to first-time traders. Bernie Schaeffer, one of the foremost options experts in the country, has written a basic primer on options. He demonstrates how they can and should have a place in many investors' portfolios. With limited risk, a lower purchase price than stocks, and the significant potential for upside leverage, traders should consider options as a way to take advantage of short-term swings to capitalize on market volatility.

Many traders feel they are fairly adept at picking stocks; but when they try to apply their talent into the options market, they lose money. We will give you information on how to choose wisely, including spread strategies that combine options to manage risk and increase profits. We will help you decide which option to buy, when to buy it, and show you how to perform a reasonable risk analysis. We will explain how to find and use an option-pricing model (including information on a good free model).

Volatility, particularly implied volatility, is one of the most important indicators to understand when trading options. George Fontanills and Frederic Ruffy explore strategies to use both low and high volatility to maximize your odds of success. And Lawrence McMillan outlines the common mistakes of the option trader, as well as ways to avoid falling into these all-too-familiar traps.

A PLACE FOR OPTIONS IN YOUR PORTFOLIO

BY BERNIE SCHAEFFER

When you've been intimately involved with options as long as I have (more than twenty-five years), it's easy to lose sight of the perspective of the beginner and some of the basic questions that someone who's never traded options may have. So for those who may be thinking about options but are perhaps a bit apprehensive about sticking a toe into the water, I'm returning to the most fundamental question for those who are just starting to learn the basics: Why Options? I see three main reasons for considering options as a part of nearly any portfolio.

Limited Risk and Exposure

An option buyer benefits from being able to control the movement of a stock at a far lower cost than an outright stock purchase. Plus, he can never lose more than this modest dollar amount. As a result, he can keep the bulk of his investment dollars in the safety of cash, where it is immune to the wild and often scary swings in the market.

Why buy stocks outright when one basically can lease them with options, especially when one's market expectations are likely to change more frequently in today's volatile markets? Buy-and-hold investments still may have a place for long-term investors, but an individual can also set aside a portion of his portfolio to benefit from the more frequent swings that potentially can create even greater profit opportunities for traders positioned to capitalize on market volatility.

For example, if an investor feels a stock is due for a rally, he could buy a call option for a fraction of the cost of the stock itself. This call gives him the right, but not the obligation, to buy the stock at a predetermined price at any time until the option expires. If the stock goes up, his call option gives him the opportunity to purchase the shares below the market price. Thus, he can fully participate in any resultant stock move with far fewer dollars at risk. Alternatively, he can sell his option for a profit without having to incur the cost of owning the stock. This lower capital outlay leads to the second major advantage of options: leverage.

The Magic of Leverage

Leverage, or the percentage gain in an option for a given instantaneous percentage move in the stock, is probably the most attractive and well-known benefit of options. Investors who are pleased to have called a quick ten-percent move in a stock often could have made 100 percent or more buying an option on that stock. Options offer upside leverage, and in addition offer downside risk control if one's market view is incorrect. The key is for an investor to use options when he's confident about the direction of the underlying stock over a certain time period.

Let's look at an example. In April 2004, Amazon.com (AMZN) posted impressive first-quarter earnings numbers of 23 cents per share, beating the Street estimate by four cents per share. But the stock dropped sharply in after-hours trading, making it apparent that investors had even higher expectations that weren't met. Lackluster price action followed as the shares struggled with overhead resistance from their twenty-week and ten-month moving averages.

The key to our analysis, however, was the marked degree of optimism displayed toward AMZN shares on several fronts. One way we gauge such sentiment is through put and call activity for shorter-term options. Our research showed that options players were showing a significant preference for AMZN call options (bullish stance) over put options (bearish stance). This suggested that options players were expecting more upside from the stock. In addition, the number of shorted AMZN shares was resting near a multi-year low, another indication that investors were anticipating more upside from the stock. Combine this optimistic sentiment with the stock's price weak-

TABLE 1: Stock Price Compared to Put Price

	AMZN Price	AMZN May 45 Put Price
April 26	46.25	1.05
May 11	42.80	2.60
Percent gain	7.5%	148%

TABLE 2: Profit Outcomes at Various Prices

Stock Price	$50	$80	$90	$100	$110	$150
Short-sale profit ($10,000 invested)	5,000	2,000	1,000	0	-1,000	-5,000
Put-buying profit ($1,000 invested)	4,000	1,000	0	-1,000	-1,000	-1,000

ness following a strong earnings report, and we believed the downside potential outweighed any upside expected by the market.

One way to play these bearish expectations was to buy a put on AMZN. A put gives the buyer the right to sell the underlying stock for the strike price at any time until the option expires. Therefore, a put buyer benefits if the stock declines because he is able to sell the shares to the put seller at a price above the market. As the stock declines, the put increases in value, giving the buyer the alternative of selling the put for a profit without having to incur the costs associated with buying and selling the stock.

Two trading days after AMZN's first-quarter earnings announcement, we recommended a slightly out-of-the-money (where the put option's strike price is below the underlying stock's current market price) May expiration 45-strike put that had an ask price of 1.05. This put gave the buyer the right to sell 100 AMZN shares at 45 up through the option's expiration on the third Friday in May, no matter how low the share price might fall. Thus, we were looking to take advantage of our bearish outlook by owning the right to sell at a fixed price (45) even though the market price may decline well below the strike price.

As it turned out, AMZN followed that forecast and continued to slide through the first two weeks of May to nearly reach its March low. This share price decline increased the value of the AMZN May 45 put, as shown in *Table 1*.

Readers should note how shorting AMZN would have resulted in a 7.5-percent gain over eleven trading days. However, buying the out-of-the-money put and then selling it on May 11 garnered a profit of

148 percent, nearly twenty times greater than shorting the stock itself. While this certainly doesn't happen every day, leverage of five to ten times is very achievable with winning option trades.

Note also that the capital commitment to the option trade was only $105 ($1.05 x 100 shares) per contract, far less than that needed to short one hundred AMZN shares. This also shows how the power of leverage allows one to put less capital at risk during turbulent markets.

If an individual's market view is bullish, he can buy stocks and mutual funds, or he can buy call options, which in essence lease the movement of the underlying stock for a limited time period. The advantages of these options—leverage and a lower capital commitment—are discussed above.

But what about a bearish view? For the mutual fund investor, there are funds directed toward profiting in downward markets, but they are relatively small in number and usually large in minimum account sizes. For stock traders, there is short selling—borrowing shares to sell now in hopes of replacing them with others bought in the market later at a lower price. But, short selling has what we refer to as negative convexity—higher potential losses than gains. A stock shorted at $50, for example, conceivably could rally to $100 or $150, costing the short seller $50 to $100 per share. However, because the shares cannot trade below zero, the gain in this case is limited to $50.

A Simple Strategy: Put Buying

For positive convexity, consider put buying. While the option position appreciates just as much as the short sale on a decline in the share price (once the premium paid for the put is exceeded), its losses are limited to the premium no matter how much the stock rallies. Its profit potential, however, is far greater (though not unlimited since a stock can't decline below zero), resulting in positive convexity.

To illustrate this concept, let's take stock XYZ that is trading at $100. We have a bearish outlook on the shares and can either short 100 shares of the stock or buy a 100-strike put option expiring in three months for $10 per share or $1,000 per contract. In other words, we are able to lease the price movement (hopefully to the downside) in the stock for three months for $1,000. If XYZ is trading at or above $100 at option expiration, the put expires worthless, and we lose our entire $1,000 premium. This also is the maximum loss for the option position. *Table 2* shows the profit outcomes of these two positions at various stock prices.

The short sale will lose one point for every point the stock gains. Therefore, the loss for the short seller will be less than that for the put buyer as long as XYZ gains less than $10. Note also that the break-even point for the put position is ten points below the short sale due to the premium paid. The short sale, however, begins to profit with any decline below $100.

Once their respective breakeven points are reached, each position profits point for point with each drop in the stock price. The major advantage for the put trade is comparing its maximum loss and profit. The most that can be lost on the option trade is the premium paid, in this case $1,000, while the maximum profit is $9,000 (in the unlikely event that the stock drops to zero). The maximum profit for the short sale is $10,000, but the maximum loss is theoretically unlimited because the stock has no maximum price. The put position also has a much lower capital commitment and will enjoy the benefits of leveraged gains. Plus, short sales cannot occur on downticks by the stock, while put positions can be initiated at any time.

The bottom line is that put buying is a bearish strategy that effectively deals with the real concerns about risk and negative convexity that have been associated with short sales.

Many Strategies in Options Trading

We also should mention that there are a number of option strategies that involve selling options in various combinations that can be profitable in flat or trading-range markets. The goal of these strategies generally is for the sold options to expire worthless so that the seller retains the premium. Taking advantage of a listless market with options is a great way to add income to a portfolio that otherwise would be in a holding pattern.

One more advantage of puts in a down market is their value as insurance for held stocks. Those who prefer to keep stocks in their portfolio despite a negative outlook for a short time can weather the expected downturn by buying a put. An at-the-money put will gain value on a point-for-point basis with the decline in the un-

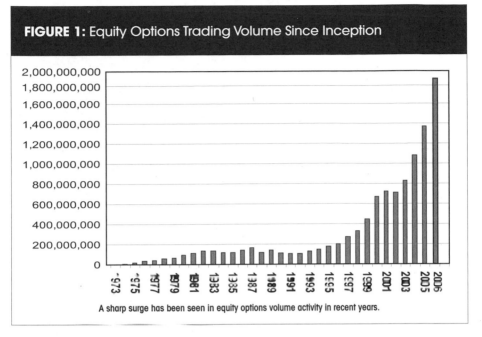

FIGURE 1: Equity Options Trading Volume Since Inception

A sharp surge has been seen in equity options volume activity in recent years.

derlying stock. Thus, the net value of the position remains stable, with the only cost being the premium paid for the put. In some situations, this premium may be less than the costs associated with selling the stock, especially if taxes are a consideration.

Still Not Convinced? Options Trading on the Rise

For those who still feel that options remain far removed from the mainstream, we offer the following facts. Since 1991, equity options volume has set a record every year except for 2002, which suffered a slight dip (see *Figure 1*). Volume in 2006 blew out the previous year's volume by nearly 35 percent and was more than double that recorded in 2003.

Adding to the legitimacy of options was the awarding of the 1997 Nobel Prize for Economics to Robert C. Merton and Myron S. Scholes for their outstanding achievement (along with Fischer Black) in developing the Black-Scholes model for valuing derivatives and stock options. This recognition inserted options and other derivatives squarely into the realm of authentic and usable financial instruments.

Answering the whys is only the first step. We urge those readers whose interest we've piqued to educate themselves about the hows and whats. Such education and understanding no doubt will increase the ability and potential to add profits to any portfolio.

Bernie Schaeffer is chairman of Schaeffer's Investment Research. His website, www.schaeffersresearch.com, has been cited by Forbes and Barron's as a top options website. Schaeffer's contrarian approach focuses on stocks with technical and fundamental trends that run counter to investor expectations. This article originally appeared in *SFO* in September 2004.

REDUCE RISK WITH BULL AND BEAR OPTIONS SPREADS

BY LAWRENCE MCMILLAN

Option traders have a whole range of strategies at their disposal. Each has its best use, and one size does not fit all, nor should it. There is no doubt that spreads bring some practical benefits to the table and, yet, they have some limitations like any strategy. Option traders sometimes establish a spread position rather than just buying an option outright and, while it generally reduces risk in dollar terms and may improve the probability of profit, novice traders would be well advised to grasp the potential drawbacks as well.

Simple Spreads

Let's get basic. A spread is the simultaneous purchase of one option, hedged by the sale of another option, rather than just the outright purchase or sale of an option.

Simple spreads fall into three basic categories: vertical, horizontal and diagonal. Originally, option prices were available mainly from newspaper listings, and these directional names came from the way in which option prices were, and still are, listed in the newspaper. The striking prices are listed vertically while the expiration months are listed horizontally (*Figure 1*). Logically, the vertical spread involves two options having the same expiration month but different striking prices. A horizontal spread involves two options with the same striking price but with different expiration months. A diagonal spread involves both different striking

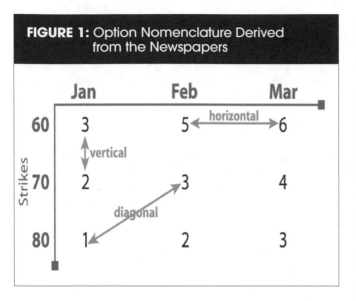

FIGURE 1: Option Nomenclature Derived from the Newspapers

prices and different expiration months.

To traders, vertical spreads are probably even more commonly known as bull or bear spreads, depending on whether the position profits from a bullish or a bearish move. And, horizontal spreads are more commonly called calendar spreads.

There is another classification that is sometimes placed on a spread, whether it is a credit spread or a debit spread. Bull and bear spreads are also credit or debit spreads and, in fact, can be either. The term "credit" or "debit" merely refers to whether money comes into an account when the spread is established (credit spread) or is expended (debit spread).

(For the bull and bear spreads discussed here, assume that the quantity bought and the quantity sold will match. There also are more advanced spreading strategies that involve buying and selling different quantities when the spread is established, like backspreads or ratio spreads.)

Spread Orders and Executions
In its purest sense, a spread is established as a single order, with the simultaneous purchase and sale of the two sides of the spreads. If a spread is not established in that manner, but is instead executed one side at a time (usually because a trader has an opinion about which way the underlying will move—thereby theoretically getting a better price for his spread), it is called "legging into the spread." Legging is not recommended for one reason: if a trader is wrong about the underlying direction after the first leg is established, an inferior spread will result.

OK, let's spread. Assume the following prices exist:

OPTION	BID	OFFER
Jan 50 call	4	4.5
Jan 60 call	2	2.50

If a market order to buy this spread is executed, the offering price for the Jan 50 call (4.50) would be paid, and the bid price for the Jan 60 call (2)—a debit of 2.50—would be received. On the other hand, suppose this spread is sold. The bid price for the Jan 50 call (4) would be received and the offering price for the Jan 60 call (2.50)—a credit of 1.50—would be paid. So, we could say the spread market is 1.50 bid, 2.50 offered. If market orders are placed on an electronic order-entry system, these prices are expected to be paid or received if trading the spread.

In reality, market makers often will make a better market. If a spread market is requested from the trading crowd in the pit, the broker might say that the spread market actually is 1.75 bid, offered at 2.25. In other words, a trader who is willing to trade a two-sided position (i.e., a spread) may find that his order is more attractive to some of the traders in the crowd, and they may make a better market than otherwise would appear possible.

With the computerization of option markets, the inability to provide a crowd to make an inside market for spread transactions is a big problem. It is virtually impossible for market makers to make markets in all possible spreads continuously—there simply are too many. For example, if stock XYZ has 20 various call options trading, at different striking prices and in different expiration months, there would be (20/2) possible two-sided spread combinations, or 190 in total.

In the traditional market setting, if a trader wants to trade a particular spread, all he needs to do is send a floor broker into the crowd, and the crowd will quote him a market. This is much harder to do in an electronic marketplace because there is no such central place for the various electronic market makers to make a spread market. This fact has not been lost on the International Securities Exchange (ISE), the electronic option exchange. They are attempting to address this, perhaps by having a chat room where spread markets could be requested.

Spread trading has been a key part of option trading since its existence. Almost any strategy involves rolling options at expiration from the current month to a later expiration date. Covered writers and outright option buyers do this quite often even though they are not spreaders, per se, in their basic strategy.

When a spread order is placed with a broker, whether human or electronic, certain basic facts must be stated, preferably in the order shown in the following example:

To place a spread order:
1) Specify the option to be bought and the quantity;
2) Specify the option to be sold and the quantity;
3) Specify the price you are willing to pay, including whether it is a debit or credit.

To buy the spread in the previous example ten times at a price of 2.25, enter the spread order as "Buy 10 XYZ Jan 50 calls, and Sell 10 Jan 60 calls, for a debit of 2.25." With an electronic broker, the information is entered on a spread order form. If the broker takes electronic spread orders, the form generally asks for this information in the order shown above.

Bull Spread Basics

One of the more popular types of spreads is the bull spread, although in my opinion, it is overused. It is a vertical spread that makes money if the underlying rises in price, i.e., it is bullish. A bull spread can be implemented with either calls (as a debit spread) or with puts (as a credit spread). The bull spread always follows the following construction:

Bull Spread: buying an option at one striking price and simultaneously selling an option with a higher striking price, where both options expire in the same month. This definition is true whether using calls or puts to establish the bull spread.

Example:Assume a bull spread using calls is established. The following prices exist:
XYZ stock price: 32
Buy one Oct 30 call: 4
Sell one Oct 35 call: 2

The following columns illustrate how each option would perform at expiration. The spread result is the sum of the two.

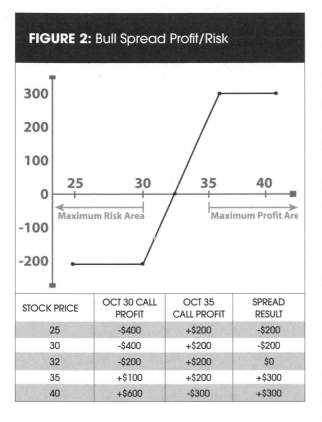

FIGURE 2: Bull Spread Profit/Risk

STOCK PRICE	OCT 30 CALL PROFIT	OCT 35 CALL PROFIT	SPREAD RESULT
25	-$400	+$200	-$200
30	-$400	+$200	-$200
32	-$200	+$200	$0
35	+$100	+$200	+$300
40	+$600	-$300	+$300

Figure 2 shows these tabular results in graph form. A bull spread always has the shape shown in the graph. There is a maximum, but limited, risk area below the lower striking price of the spread, and there is a maximum profit area, also limited, above the higher striking price of the spread. In between, there is a breakeven price—32 in this case (excluding commission)—where the spread neither makes nor loses money.

In most cases, spreads have to be executed in a margin account, and the margin required to establish the spread is the maximum risk involved. In the previous example, the maximum risk was $200, and that also is the margin requirement. Hence, 100 percent of the investment in a spread is risked, and profits, while limited, can be large in percentage terms (150-percent maximum return in this example).

These simple formulas can be used to quickly compute the pertinent profit and risk figures for a bull spread, established with call options as a debit spread:

- Maximum risk = debit paid for the spread
- Maximum profit potential = difference in strikes - debit paid
- Breakeven point = lower striking price + debit paid

In the example above, these formulas would yield the following answers:

Debit paid: 2 points

Maximum profit potential =

difference in strikes - debit = (35 - 30) - 2 = 3 points

Breakeven point = lower striking price + debit paid = 30 + 2 = 32

Bull Spread Philosophy

A spread is usually established to reduce the risk of outright owner-ship of an option. In the above example, the XYZ Oct 30 call, which sells for a price of 4, is too expensive. However, if the Oct 35 call is also sold, the risk is reduced. This particular concept of risk-reduc-tion often is overrated and, in fact, may be harmful to profit po-tential. In the spread example above, the most that can be made is $300. However, if a trader merely owns the Oct 30 call outright, the profit potential would be unlimited.

Novices often make the mistake of establishing a bull spread, not fully realizing that it will not expand to anywhere near its maximum-profit potential if there is a substantial amount of time left until expiration. For example, if one buys a 90-day spread to begin with, and the stock makes a move to or above the higher striking price of the spread, that spread won't widen to its maxi-mum profit potential unless 1) the stock trades well above the higher striking price of the spread, or 2) expiration nears.

The graph in *Figure 3* depicts the profit potential of a 10-point bull spread (buying a call with a 90 strike and selling a call with a 110 strike). Assuming the cost of the spread is 10 points, the risk and the maximum profit potential are both 10 points at expira-tion. Notice that, initially, the spread had 90 days of life remaining. However, the profit picture is substantially different when viewed after either 30 or 60 days. When 30 days have passed, the spread profit is only $500, even if the stock has risen all the way to 140—well past the higher striking price of the spread. In any specific situation, this profit potential prior to expiration is dependent on the volatility of the options, but *Figure 3* shows the general concept. After 60 days have passed, the profit potential curve in *Figure 3* is beginning to take on more of the shape one would expect to see at expiration (as in *Figure 2*).

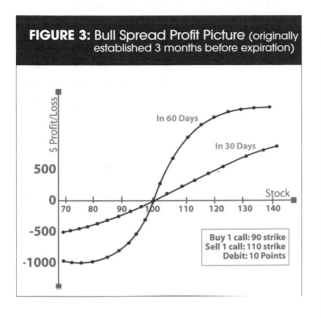

FIGURE 3: Bull Spread Profit Picture (originally established 3 months before expiration)

In 60 Days

In 30 Days

$ Profit/Loss

Stock

Buy 1 call: 90 strike
Sell 1 call: 110 strike
Debit: 10 Points

Many novice traders establish a bull spread and are pleased when the underlying stock quickly rises in price. However, their pleasure turns to disappointment when they realize that the bull spread has not made much money and is nowhere near its maximum profit potential. In fact, it will not get to its maximum profit potential until some time passes—when expiration is much closer.

The bull spread is most feasible when the options are expensive, because that is a situation in which call option buying does need some risk reduction. The problem of the spread not widening quickly, as shown in *Figure 3*, cannot be entirely overcome, but it can be mitigated by widening the distance between the strikes of the spread. This means that the maximum profit potential is larger, and if the spread widens out to, say, only 50 of the 60 percent of its maximum- profit potential, at least that will be a larger number if the strikes are widely spaced.

By widening the strikes in that manner, more risk is assumed. The call that is sold is lower priced than a call would be at a lower striking price. Some spreaders do not like assuming this additional risk (although if one is bullish on the underlying stock, he should expect it to rise in any case). This problem can be offset somewhat by using out-of-the-money calls in the spread. By doing this while still keeping the striking prices wide apart, the trader will have a relatively low-cost spread with decent profit potential, which really is the ultimate objective of the bull spreader.

Put Credit Spreads

Each of the examples above shows the bull spread implemented as a call debit spread. However, a put credit spread is another type a bull spread. The put spread is very similar to the call spread—the put with the lower striking price is purchased, and the put with the higher striking price is sold. The profit graph has the same shape—limited loss below the lower striking price and limited profit above the higher striking price. For the put credit spread, the following formulas apply:

- Maximum profit potential = initial credit received
- Breakeven price = higher striking price – credit received
- Risk = distance between strikes - credit received = margin required

Put credit spreads usually are implemented with out-of-the-money puts so that both puts in the spread expire worthless, and the credit received is kept as a realized profit. Thus, a small amount of money is usually taken in, but there is a low probability that the stock will fall far enough to cause problems.

Example: XYZ is at 80. A put credit spread is established as follows:
Buy 1 Jan 65 put at a price of 1.00
Sell 1 Jan 55 put at a price of 0.50

Credit received = 0.5 points = maximum profit potential
Breakeven price = 65 - 0.5 = 64.5
Risk = 65 - 55 - 0.5 = 9.50

The spreader is risking 9.50 points to make 0.50 points but, because the stock is at 80, and the entire credit will be kept as profit as long as the stock is above 65 (the higher striking price) at expiration, there is a fairly large probability of keeping the credit.

The strategy of selling put credit spreads is one that does not appeal to everyone. Understandably, most people are not comfortable with risking 9.50 points to make 0.50 points. At those odds, it would take only one maximum loss to wipe out 19 winners. In reality, the overall return from this strategy is small after slippage and commissions are taken into account. There is a high probability of making a little money and a small probability of losing much more.

Some proponents of the put credit spread strategy attempt to place the spreads only when the puts are expensive. Even so, what does a trader really gain by selling an expensive option and then hedging it by buying an-

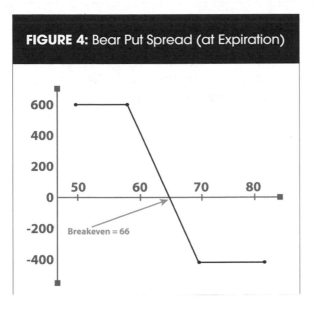

FIGURE 4: Bear Put Spread (at Expiration)

other expensive option? A little, perhaps, but not enough to change the overall assessment of this strategy—akin to betting on a heavily favored horse to win at the race track, race after race. It's lots of small profits with occasional large losses.

Bear Spreads

In a bear market, the bear spread may be preferable to bull spreads. Essentially, the bear spread is just the bull spread turned around:

Bear Spread: buying an option with a higher striking price and simultaneously selling an option with a lower striking price, where both options expire in the same month.

A bear spread profits if the underlying declines in price. Like before, this spread can be established either with puts or calls—that's why the definition above does not specify the type of option. With this definition the call bear spread is a credit spread, while the put bear spread is a debit spread.

Example: XYZ is at 65. A bear spread is established with the following trades:
Buy 1 April 70 put for 7
Sell 1 April 60 put for 3
Risk = initial debit = 4 points
Profit potential = difference in strikes - debit = 10 - 4 = 6 points
Breakeven price = higher strike - debit = 70 - 4 = 66

These points also can be observed from the profit graph above (*Figure 4*).

The other points made earlier regarding bull spreads normally are applicable to bear spreads as well. For example, they won't widen out as quickly as one might hope. The best way to counter this situation is to spread the strikes farther apart, a move that allows for greater widening of the spread if the underlying drops in price.

Bull and bear spreads both feature viable ways to reduce risk with options. However, novice traders tend to overuse the strategy, only to find that the performance of the spread is not as good as they originally had expected. Speculators probably are best served by taking outright option positions most of the time, reserving the spread strategy for cases in which the options are overpriced. In those cases, they would use the bull spread or bear spread to ensure that there is a fairly wide distance between the striking prices of the spread; thus, it increases the chance to widen and produce a profit on a quick move by the underlying. When approached in this manner, the bull and bear spread can be a valuable addition to the strategy arsenal of the option trader.

Lawrence G. McMillan, author of several books, including the best-selling *Options as a Strategic Investment* (Prentice Hall Press, 4th edition 2001), is president of McMillan Analysis Corp. www.option-strategist.com. McMillan Analysis publishes several option trading newsletters, has a wide array of option research material, educational material and seminars available, and manages individual accounts in the option markets as well as a hedge fund. The company also sells software, such as a stand-alone version of the Black-Scholes model. McMillan formerly was a proprietary trader for the brokerage firms of Thomson McKinnon Securities and Prudential-Bache Securities, prior to founding McMillan Analysis Corp in 1991. He has an undergraduate degree in math from Purdue University and a Masters in applied math and computer science from the University of Colorado. This article originally appeared in *SFO* in August 2002.

EXPLOIT MARKET VOLATILITY WITH OPTIONS

BY GEORGE FONTANILLS & FREDERIC RUFFY

Confusion, chaos, mayhem, plunging stock prices, cries of pain from the bulls, screams of joy from the bears...market volatility reigns. If you have spent many years in the stock market, you have probably experienced, if not endured, some of these moments of extreme market turbulence. There was the great crash of 1987, the global financial crises in 1998, and the grueling bear market that lasted from 2000 to 2003. These periods of market panic, of course, occur from time to time and are an inevitable part of investing.

Yet, while periods of high market volatility occur on occasion, often times the market trades quietly as well. In fact, stock prices can go through prolonged periods of time without moving dramatically higher or lower. In addition, because investors generally are attracted to fast-moving markets, sideways trading or horizontal movements can make it more difficult for traders to make investment decisions. Should I buy stocks and go long, or sell stocks and go short?

There are some very appropriate options strategies for both quiet periods, anticipating that market volatility will increase going forward, and periods of high volatility, which are often short-lived, and generally followed by more stable trading. This discussion explores those strategies and outlines specific ways to exploit both high and low volatility.

Volatility Defined

In order to understand volatility trading, let's first define what we mean by volatility. Volatility is a measure of a stock, commodity or option's tendency to move up and down in price based on its daily price history over a period of time. Generally, when people talk about volatility, it is in reference to falling stock prices. For example, if Brian Williams or one of his cohorts reports on the evening news that the S&P 500 endured volatile price moves, he probably means that stocks fell. But for options traders, the definition of volatility is not so one-sided. Options traders generally agree that volatility does not only occur when stocks move lower. In fact, the market will, and often does, make volatile moves to the upside. Traders also use different measures of volatility to gauge the price movements of stocks, such as historical volatility, which measures past price movements, or implied volatility (IV), the focus of this discussion.

Unique to the options market, implied volatility can only be computed using options prices and a model. To compute implied volatility, one first must have access to an options-pricing model, such as the Black-Scholes model, and a set of variables, including the option price, the underlying asset price, the strike price and the time left until expiration. These variables, along with the model, are used to compute implied volatility.

Because computing implied volatility on a large number of different stocks is somewhat cumbersome, traders generally do not bother with the model or the computation. Instead, they can access implied volatility information from a wide variety of sources. For example, Optionetics.com's Platinum Site offers IV for stocks and indexes as do online brokerage firms that specialize in options trading. In addition, traders also can view implied volatility using the CBOE Volatility Index ($VIX), which is the current implied volatility of the S&P 500 Index ($SPX) options.

Reversion to the Mean

The next step in identifying trades using a volatility approach is to understand the concept of reversion to the mean. That is, even though volatility is always in a state of flux, the volatility of stocks or indexes can usually be assigned a normal or average value, the volatility around which a stock or index tends to center around over time. In

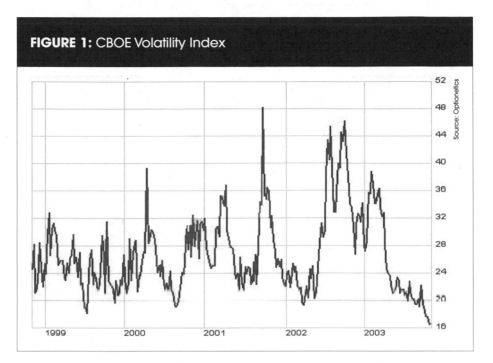

FIGURE 1: CBOE Volatility Index

statistics, the average is also known as the mean. When volatility diverges greatly from that mean, there is a tendency for it to revert back to that average or normal level. Therefore, if the volatility of a stock is low relative to its average over a long period of time, we can expect it to revert back to its mean. Conversely, when it is high relative to its mean, there is a greater probability that implied volatility will fall back toward more normal levels.

So, when creating trades based on volatility studies, we often expect periods of high volatility to follow periods of quiet trading. Alternatively, periods of low volatility often occur after a period of extreme market volatility. The goal is to find out what is normal or typical for a given security and look for deviations from the normal pattern.

Another important factor to consider is the impact of implied volatility on option premiums. *Figure 1* shows VIX over the past five years. As we can see, the index rises and falls through time. In 2001 and 2002, VIX moved above 40 percent on more than one occasion. During those times, implied volatility or expected volatility of S&P 500 Index options was high. Furthermore, because implied volatility is one of the factors used to determine an option price, as it rises, so does the option price. High levels of IV indicate that options traders

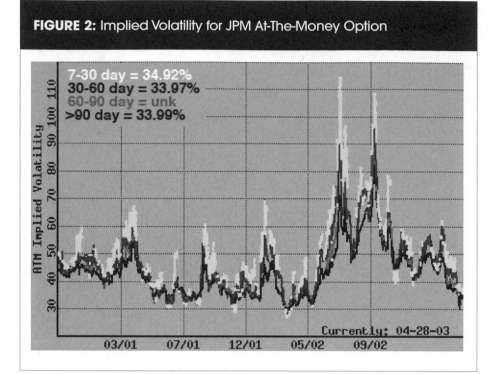

FIGURE 2: Implied Volatility for JPM At-The-Money Option

7-30 day = 34.92%
30-60 day = 33.97%
60-90 day = unk
>90 day = 33.99%

expect the underlying asset to exhibit higher volatility in the future, and those expectations are being priced or implied into the option premiums. Simply put, when implied volatility rises, the option premiums are becoming more expensive.

On the other hand, when the volatility index falls to the lower end of its range, or below 12 percent, it suggests that implied volatility in the S&P 500 Index market is low. In this case, the decline is a sign that option premiums are also declining. During the period from 2004 to 2006 VIX experienced a long-term decline and fell to multi-year lows of less than 11 percent. Options on the S&P 500 became very cheap on a historical basis due to a protracted decline in expected or implied volatility.

While VIX measures the implied volatility of S&P 500 Index options, similar graphs can be computed for any optionable stock or index. Let's consider an example of implied volatility to see how it tends to change over time. *Figure 2* shows the implied volatility of JP Morgan (JPM) options from 2001 until 2003. Each line on the graph represents options with different periods left until expiration. For instance, the lightest line that tends to show the greatest swings represents the implied volatility of options with less than thirty days left until expiration. Options with less time left until expiration are more likely to see more dramatic changes in implied volatility. Further, notice that an average or normal range for the IV of this stock is between 30 and 50 percent.

During the fall of 2002, the implied volatility of JP Morgan options spiked higher. Indeed, this trend was prevalent throughout the stock market as investor anxiety rose to high levels. Bank stocks like JP Morgan were hit especially hard as investors worried about myriad challenges, including the economy and loan defaults, as well as bank exposure to troubled markets in Brazil and other parts of the world. There also was talk that JP Morgan might cut its dividend. Due to a variety of factors, investors grew worried, and market anxiety levels became quite high. Bank stocks sold off, and the implied volatility on JPM options rose into the triple digits—well above the normal range for the stock. The options became quite expensive.

Back to the Basics

It is better to be an option seller when implied volatility is high and options become expensive. Let's consider one of the most basic stock option strategies—the covered call—to see why. Also known as the "buy write," this strategy combines the purchase of stock against the sale of call options.

There are two ways to establish a covered call position: 1) simultaneously purchase the stock and sell a call or 2) sell call options against a stock that is already held in a portfolio. Either way, one call is sold for every one hundred shares of stock that are held. The call writer receives cash for selling the calls. The money received is equal to the premiums of the call option, or the call option's price in the market. As a result, the call writer will receive more premium when implied volatility is high.

In exchange for the premium, the call writer agrees to sell the stock (100 shares per every one call sold) at the option's strike price until the expiration of the call option—the Saturday following the third Friday of the option's expiration month. When a covered call writer is forced to sell his or her stock, it is known as assignment. So, the covered call writer holds shares of stock and receives premium for

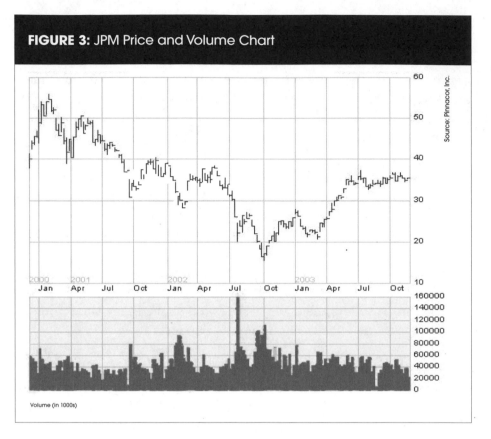

FIGURE 3: JPM Price and Volume Chart

Source: Pinnacor, Inc.

Volume (in 1000s)

selling the call. However, the sale of the call is also a contract, one that will require the trader to sell the stock at the option's strike price if assigned.

Let's work this through using the JP Morgan example. Generally, the buy write strategy is established using out-of-the-money calls. In other words, the call options that are being sold have strike prices above the current market price for the stock. For example, in mid-October 2002 when IV spiked up to the triple digits, JP Morgan was trading near $20 a share. With IV near 75 percent, the strategist could buy 500 shares of JP Morgan for $10,000 and offset some of that cost by selling the five March 25 calls for $2 a contract. The premium earned on the sale totals $1,000 [or 5 x $2 x 100 (the multiplier)]. Therefore, the total cost of the trade is $9,000, and the breakeven is lowered to $18 a share ($9,000/500).

Always Calculate the Risk

What is the risk to this trade? First, the stock could fall below $18 a share. Anything less than $18 a share when the options expire will result in a loss. Second, JPM might stay between $25 and $18 through expiration. If so, the options expire worthless. In that case, the trader keeps the premium ($1,000) and can sell more calls, hold the stock, or exit the position entirely. Third, the stock could rise to greater than $25 a share. In this case, the stock could be called away from the investor. If so, the 500 shares are sold at $25 a share, and the strategist keeps the premium from the sale of the calls, plus the money accrued from the rise in JPM from $20 (initial price at purchase) and $25 (price at sale).

In all likelihood, the second scenario would have occurred in our JP Morgan example. That is, the options would expire worthless and the stock could be sold at a profit. *Figure 3* shows the three-year price action of the stock. By March expiration, the stock was near $22.50 a share. As a result, the options have no value and, therefore, will expire without assignment. At that point, the position can be closed at a profit of $2,250, or 25 percent [($22.50 x 500) - $9,000.00].

Now, consider what would happen if the covered call is established when implied volatility is low. Recall that in the first example, implied volatility of the JPM options is 75 percent, and the March 25 calls are trading for $2 a contract. Let's assume now that implied volatility is at the lower end of the range, or 25 percent. The same JPM March 25 calls carry a premium of only 25 cents. If we establish the same position, the cost or risk of the trade is $9,875 {[500 shares x $20.00 a share] – [5 x $0.25 x 100 (the multiplier)]}. In this case, the breakeven is $19.75 and the profit from the success of the trade when JPM hits $22.50 at expiration is only $1,375, or 13.9 percent [($22.50 x 500) - $9,875]. Thus, in this case, the difference in the implied volatility assumptions makes an enormous difference to the profit or loss associated with the trade.

Exploiting High Volatility

The covered call strategy yields the best results when a stock makes a gradual, steady climb higher, underscoring the benefit of selling options when implied volatility is high. First, when implied volatility rises well above normal or average levels, it often will revert back towards the mean. Therefore, expensive options become cheaper. It is time to sell high. Second, periods of extremely high implied volatility often reflect extreme angst, or even panic, among investors. During these times, stocks often get washed out, and the next logical move in the stock is to the upside. That certainly was the case in our JPM example in October 2002.

While the risk/reward of the covered call improves when implied volatility shoots higher, it is not always the best strategy because it is not a low-risk trade. Basically, by using the strategy, the investor is offsetting some of the cost of purchasing a stock with the sale of calls. As a result, the covered call is only moderately less risky than simply owning the stock, and it offers less reward potential. It also requires a relatively large commitment of one's trading capital. Consequently, despite its popularity among some investors today, it is less than ideal during many situations.

Bull Put Spreads

Instead of the covered call, there are a number of ways to create interesting risk-reward scenarios in a high volitility environment. For example, if a trader expects the stock to make a significant move higher, he might sell an at-the-money put and hedge that bet by purchasing a put with a higher strike price. This trade is known as a bull put spread and can be used to take advantage of high levels of implied volatility.

A bull put spread is created by purchasing a lower strike put and selling a higher strike put with the same expiration dates. This strategy is a credit spread and can be used to take advantage of a bullish market—thus, the name. The net credit received from placing the combined position is the maximum profit that can be made on the position. In the best scenario, the underlying stock moves above the higher strike price by expiration, and the options expire worthless. If the underlying stock falls below the lower strike, the maximum risk is limited to the difference between strikes minus the credit received. In order to choose the options with the best probability of profitability for a credit spread, it is important to balance out the following factors:

• Because the profit on these strategies depends on the options expiring worthless by expiration, it's best to use options with forty-five days or less until expiration. This gives the underlying stock less time to move into a position where the short put will be assigned and the maximum loss occurs.

- Because the maximum profit is limited to the net credit initially received, keep the net credit as high as possible to make the trade worthwhile.
- Keep the short strike at-the-money and try to avoid selling an in-the-money put.
- The difference between strikes must be small enough so that the maximum risk is low enough to make the trade worthwhile.
- Make sure the breakeven is within the underlying stock's trading range.

Let's create an example of a bull put spread by going long one April XYZ 65 put at $2.00 and short one April XYZ 75 put at $8.00. The profit on this trade relies on the short put expiring worthless by expiration. To exit this trade profitably, you need XYZ to move above the strike price of the short option and stay there until expiration so that the short options will expire worthless. The maximum profit is limited to the net credit received on the trade, or $600 [(8 - 2) x 100 = 600]. The maximum risk is calculated by subtracting the net credit from the difference in strike price. The maximum risk of this trade is $400 {[(75 - 65) – 6] x 100 = $400}. The breakeven of a bull put spread is calculated by subtracting the net credit from the higher strike put. In this example, the breakeven is 69 (75 – 6 = 69). This trade theoretically makes a profit when XYZ stays above 69.

To exit a bull put spread, you have to monitor the daily price movement of the underlying stock as well as the implied volatility of the options. Although each trade is unique, let's explore what happens to the trade in the example in the following four scenarios:

- XYZ rises above the short strike (75). Let the options expire worthless, and keep the maximum credit received when the trade was initiated.
- XYZ stays above the breakeven (69), but does not rise above the short strike (75). The short put may be assigned and exercised by the option holder, and you are obligated to purchase 100 shares of XYZ from the option holder at $75 a share. You can sell the shares at the current price, which is above the strike price of the long put and incur a small loss that can be offset by the initial credit received. You can also sell the long put for additional profit.

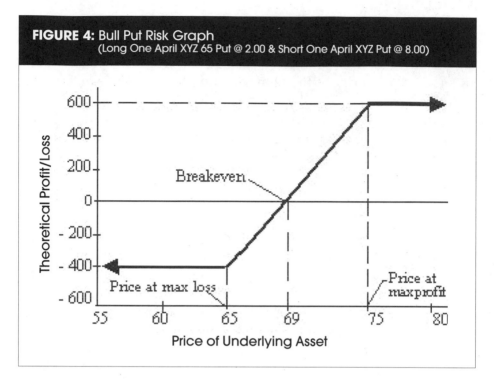

FIGURE 4: Bull Put Risk Graph
(Long One April XYZ 65 Put @ 2.00 & Short One April XYZ Put @ 8.00)

- XYZ falls below the breakeven (69), but stays above the long strike (65). Once again, the short put may be assigned and exercised by the option holder, and you are obligated to purchase 100 shares of XYZ from the option holder at $75 a share. You can sell the shares at the current price, which is slightly above the strike price of the long put. In this case, the loss on the shares will not be balanced out by the credit received. Selling the long put may bring in additional money to mitigate the loss.
- XYZ falls below the long strike (65). If the short put is assigned and exercised by the option holder, you are obligated to purchase 100 shares of XYZ from the option holder at $75 a share. You can now exercise the long put to sell the shares at $65 each, incurring the maximum loss of $1,000, which is balanced by the $600 credit received at initiation, for a total loss of $400.

A risk profile of a bull put spread (as shown in *Figure 4*) shows the profit/loss line slanting upward from left to right displaying its bullish bias. If the underlying stock rises to the price of the short put, the trade reaches its maximum profit potential. Conversely, if the price of

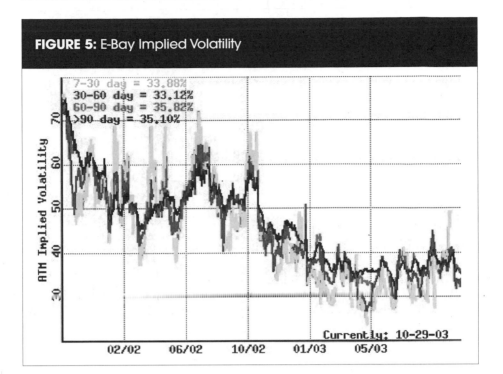

FIGURE 5: E-Bay Implied Volatility

7-30 day = 33.88%
30-60 day = 33.12%
60-90 day = 35.82%
>90 day = 35.10%

ATM Implied Volatility

Currently: 10-29-03

02/02   06/02   10/02   01/03   05/03

the underlying stock falls to the strike price of the long put, the maximum limited loss occurs. Always monitor the underlying stock for a reversal or a breakout to avoid the maximum loss.

Various types of calendar and diagonal spreads also can work well when the strategist expects the period of high volatility to pave the way for quieter and more normal trading in the underlying stock.

Straight Puts and Calls

The simplest strategy for a low volatility environment is the purchase of a put or call. This is not a trade that I normally recommend, but for purposes of our discussion on volatility, let's consider the straight call purchase on eBay (EBAY). In November 2006, eBay is trading for $32.75 a share. We decide to buy the EBAY April 35 calls for $2.50 a contract. Each call gives us the right to buy 100 shares of eBay until the options expire in April 2007, which is 165 days away.

Using a model, we compute the implied volatility of these April 2007 calls, and it currently equals roughly 35 percent. As we can see from *Figure 5*, 35 percent is a historically low level for eBay implied volatility. In fact, within the last year, the IV of these options has spiked to almost twice that level on more than one occasion. So, these options are relatively cheap. In fact, if all other factors stayed the same, and implied volatility rose from 35 percent to 70 percent, the option price would increase from $2.50 to $5.50—a 120-percent gain from the rise in implied volatility alone!

Put buyers are more likely to benefit from increasing implied volatility than call buyers because IV tends to rise when a stock or index moves lower. Stated differently, rising stock prices often lead to falling levels of implied volatility. Why? Falling stock prices generally lead to higher levels of IV because of market psychology and the way traders react to market declines. Specifically, when a stock or market takes a nosedive and the move triggers mounting levels of investor anxiety, traders will begin pricing in (or implying) greater levels of volatility into options prices. For that reason, put buyers are more likely to benefit from rising implied volatility than call buyers.

It is important to note at this point, however, that the success of both straight call buying and straight put buying depends largely on the underlying asset moving in the anticipated direction before expiration. In addition, as seasoned option traders know well, time decay also can have a negative impact on the long call or long put. Specifically, because options have a fixed expiration date, they lose value as time passes. For that reason, options are sometimes called wasting assets.

In sum, the price of the underlying asset is the most important factor to consider when implementing trades like straight calls or straight puts. Implied volatility and time decay are generally secondary considerations, but extremely important nonetheless. So, one would not buy a call simply because implied volatility is low. If the stock tanks, the call will lose value even if IV shoots higher. Yet, the odds of success associated with call and put purchases are better when options are cheap and IV is low, but the strategist expects a significant move higher or lower.

Straddles Ahead of Breakouts

A straddle is the purchase of both a put and a call. Generally, the strategist will buy puts and calls with the same strike prices (which are very close to the actual market price) and the same expiration dates. Using the eBay example, instead of buying EBAY 35 calls, the trader buys an EBAY April 32.5 straddle. In that case, she would buy the EBAY April 32.5 calls for $3.70 and the EBAY April 32.5 puts for $2.80. The implied volatility of both these options equals 35 percent at the time of the trade, and the total cost is $6.50 per straddle ($3.70 + $2.80).

Ideally, the straddle buyer wants the underlying stock to make a dramatic move higher or lower before these options expire. For example, if eBay rises above $39.00 (the strike price plus the cost of the straddle) at expiration, the calls will yield profits. On the other hand, should the stock fall below $26.00 (or the strike price minus cost of the trade), the appreciation in the put option will make the straddle profitable. Either way, the options strategist wants to see the stock make a dramatic move higher or lower after buying a straddle.

Implied volatility can also have an important influence on the value of a straddle prior to expiration. As we saw earlier, if all other factors remain the same and the implied volatility of the April 32.50 calls increases from 35 percent to 70 percent, the price of the call will rise from approximately $2.50 to $5.50. Similarly, if the implied volatility of the put increases from 35 percent to 70 percent, the value of the 32.5 straddle will also increase. For example, all else being equal, if implied volatility rises from 35 percent to 70 percent, the value of the straddle will increase from $6.50 to approximately $12.00 per straddle.

Of course, all things are rarely equal, and it is highly unlikely that the implied volatility of both options will increase and everything else will stay the same. Implied volatility tends to rise over time, during a period of weeks or months. It rarely spikes higher from one day to the next. Therefore, the straddle buyer can benefit from increasing implied volatility, but other factors also will affect the trade. The most important element to success will be a significant movement in the underlying asset. In this case, the strategist expects a big move in Ebay. In addition, the straddle buyer also will be fighting the forces of time decay. Both the put and the call will lose value due to time decay. In this example, there were 165 days left until the April expiration. The strategist wants the price of the underlying asset to move fast enough to offset the negative impact of time decay, which rots away at the premium with each passing day. So, the sooner the stock makes its move, the better. Implied volatility will also affect the trade. It is an extremely important secondary consideration.

Keep an Eye on the Price of the Underlying Asset

Option strategies can offer unlimited profit opportunities once traders understand how to maximize the odds of success. In many cases, the success of the strategy will depend on the underlying asset moving in the anticipated direction. Straight calls and puts, different types of spreads and covered calls, for example, are all strategies that hinge on the underlying stock moving higher or lower. Therefore, in addition to focusing on implied volatility, many traders focus on predicting price movement when establishing options positions. Implied volatility is an essential ingredient in option pricing.

The key is to specialize in a handful of options strategies that can work in a high-or low-volatility environment. Optionetics.com offers information and free educational articles on these and a host of other strategies, as do other firms involved in educating options consumers. It's worth the time to study them, as understanding the inner workings of volatility during wild and not-so-wild periods may spell the difference between success and failure.

George Fontanills is the president of Pinnacle Investments of America and president emeritus of Optionetics www.optionetics.com. He actively trades equity options and stocks and is a registered investment advisor and hedge fund manager with a number of offshore trading organizations, professional trading firms and large financial institutions. He has written best-selling books including, *The Options Course: High Profit & Low Stress Trading Methods* (Wiley Trading, 2nd Edition 2005), *Trade Options Online* (Wiley, 2000), and *The Volatility Course* (co-written with Tom Gentile, Wiley, 2002).

Frederic Ruffy is senior writer and index strategist for Optionetics. He specializes in trading options on exchange-traded funds and index products. Prior to working with Optionetics, Ruffy worked in New York for the trading firm Miller Tabak + Co. A version of this article first appeared in *SFO* in February and March of 2004.

COMMON MISTAKES OF THE OPTIONS TRADER

BY LAWRENCE McMILLAN

Many traders feel they are fairly adept at picking stocks and trading them; but when they try to translate that activity into the options market, they lose money. Frustrated, they sometimes blame the options market itself, the market makers, and specialists for the failure of options to produce a profit. Realistically, if one successfully trades stocks or has a successful trading system, there is every reason to believe that it can be translated to options successfully. In fact, using options may even increase the trader's profitability. Traders make several common mistakes that are easily identified and remedied.

In general, option buyers' mistakes fall into three categories: choosing the wrong striking price, buying an incorrect quantity of options, and failing to perform a reasonable what-if analysis. The remedies generally have to do with some common sense techniques that are founded on sound statistical analysis, as found by using an option-pricing model. It is not necessary to be a mathematician or statistician in order to understand trade options. However, it is necessary to understand how to use some of the basic outputs of an option-pricing model.

Therefore, it is critical for all option traders to use an option-pricing model when they trade. If you do not use a model, you will surely suffer at the hands of those option traders who do, which is just about everyone else.

The most common option-pricing model is the Black-Scholes model. A free version of it is available at the CBOE's Web site (cboe.com). Fancier versions can be purchased from a variety of software and option trading companies, the cost of which ranges from approximately $100 for the stand-alone models (in which the user enters the prices himself) to $1500 or more for sophisticated models that are connected to real-time streaming prices. In general, it is not necessary to spend a lot for modeling software. If the cheaper version gives you the analyses you need, then don't spend a thousand dollars more to buy functionality that you will not even use.

Choosing The Best Option To Buy

Many successful stock traders have trouble choosing the proper option to buy when trying to translate their trading system to options. There is actually a rather simple method of deciding which option to buy to fit in with the trading system that you are presently using for stocks. It involves knowing and using the delta of the option. The delta of an option is a number that defines how far the option will move when the stock moves, or more specifically, what percentage of a stock price move will be captured by the option. Delta ranges between 0 and 1 for call options. If the delta of a particular call option is 0.50 (50 percent), then the call will move half as fast as the stock. (For example, if the stock is up 80 cents, one would expect this call to increase in value by 40 cents.) The delta of an option is obtained as an output from an option-pricing model. The general rule of thumb is this: the shorter the term of your trading system, the higher the delta should be of the option you purchase.

Some examples will explain this. The shortest-term trading system is day trading. Thus, according to the rule, day traders would want the instrument with the highest delta. The instrument with the highest delta is the underlying stock itself; it has a delta of 1.00 at all times. Thus, what we are saying here is that day traders should probably stick with trading the underlying stock and not use options at all. Stock is more liquid than options and has tighter markets, so it is much better for day trading than options.

However, just about any trading system, other than day trading, can benefit from options. Suppose you have a short-term stock trading system, in which your holding period can be as short as two or three days, and perhaps as long as a week or two. That system can utilize options, even though it is a very short-term system. Again, according to the rule, you would want to buy an option with a high delta. In fact, a short-term, in-the-money option is warranted here. For example, if the stock is at 50 and you get a buy signal on the first day of August, then you would want to buy the August 45 call. Such an option has very little time value pre-

mium, and thus has a very high delta, perhaps as high as 0.85 or so. It be-
haves very much like stock, sort of a stock substitute. I would not buy an
option with less than a week to go, but since this trading system appears
to be in and out of a position in less than two weeks most of the time, it is
certainly appropriate to buy August options on the first of August.

Longer-term stock trading systems can utilize different options.
Suppose you are following an intermediate-term system (three to six
months). If you want to buy an option after getting a buy signal from your
intermediate-term stock trading, you could buy an at-the-money, three-
month call. Such an option has a delta of 0.55 or so, but for an intermediate-term system, you don't need a really high delta. For example, suppose
the stock is trading at 50 on August 1 and you get a buy signal for your
intermediate-term trading system. The proper option to buy would be the
November 50 call.

Finally, if your stock trading system is truly long-term oriented (more
than a year's holding period), then you could buy Long-term Equity Anticipation Security (LEAPS) options, which is just a fancy name given to
options that expire more than nine months from the current date. Since
these are such long-term options, even out-of-the-money calls have fairly
high deltas. Hence, this is one of the few times where the purchase of an
out-of-the-money option could be considered. Again, with the stock at 50
and a buy signal from a long-term trading system, one might consider the
purchase of the LEAPS August 55 calls, expiring in January two years
later, about 17 months away. Such an option would have a delta of 0.60 or
so, depending on the volatility of the underlying stock.

This simple rule can generally cure many of the ills that befall option
traders, buying options that are too far out-money, for example. By using
this rule, coupled with a successful stock-trading system, your option
purchases should be profitable as well.

Deciding How Many Options to Buy

Many option traders hurt their profits by buying the wrong quantity of
options. That does not necessarily mean they buy too many, buying too
few is just as bad. So how does one decide what is the correct number of
options to buy? There is, once again, a fairly simple standard that can
be applied: risk the same percentage of your account on each trade you
make. Further, that percentage should be in the 3 or 4 percent area, not
something much higher or much lower. If you risk 3 percent of your trad-

ing account on each trade, you will have plenty of action. In addition, if you are hot and are trading successfully, you will automatically be buying more options, since 3 percent of your trading is a larger dollar figure as your account grows. Conversely, if you hit a losing streak, as we all do, then 3 percent of your trading account will be a shrinking number, and using this rule will force you to cut back on the size of your trades.

This is the proper approach. Increase your trading size when you are hot, and reduce it when you are cold. If you have heard the opposite, you are trading something akin to what mathematicians call a Martingale system, which is the road to ruin. A mathematician named Martingale showed that you can always make $1 from a 50-50 betting proposition. Bet $1 on the first bet. If you lose, bet $2. If you lose that, bet $4, and so on. Eventually, you will win and make the dollar (as an example, suppose you lose the first 5 bets and then win the sixth, you would have these results: -$1 -$2 -$4 -$8 -$16 + $32 = +$1). This strategy works only in theory, because in real life there are limits to what we can invest. If you doubled up your trading size every time you lost, you would eventually run out of money if a long losing streak developed, and long losing streaks do develop, especially if you tempt fate when you cannot afford it.

Say we decide to risk 3 percent of our account on each position we take. (Note the rule does not say to invest 3 percent of your account, but to risk 3 percent.)

Suppose you are watching a stock and see it break out to a new high at a price of 100. In looking at the chart, you decide that if you bought it, you would stop yourself out if it fell back to 95, that such a retracement would indicate it was a false breakout. So your risk is five points on this trade. Furthermore, assume you have a $100,000 trading account and want to risk 3 percent on each trade. You would want to risk $3,000. Since your analysis of the stock shows that you would risk five points on this stock trade, you would therefore buy 600 shares of stock to trade this position ($3,000 total risk divided by the 5 points risk per share = 600 shares of stock to buy). Note that you would be investing $60,000 to buy 600 shares at $100 per share, but your risk is $3,000 if you stop yourself out at 95.

A similar strategy can be applied to the option market. Suppose that you decide to buy an option that costs ten points, or $1,000, instead of buying the stock. Presumably, that option would be selected in accordance with the previous rule, deciding which option to buy based on the time horizon of your trading system. It seems at first glance that you would buy three options, the $3,000 you want to risk from your $100,000 trading account divided by the $1,000 cost of each option. However, that is not the right answer! Are you really risking $1,000 on this option trade if you plan to stop yourself out if the stock trades down to 95? Probably not. There would almost assuredly be some value left in the option if that happened.

The correct analysis is to use an option-pricing model to determine what the value of the option would be if and when the stock declined to 95. As an example, suppose that you determine that the option would be worth seven points if the stock declined to 95 in two weeks, the supposed time horizon of your trading system. In that case, your risk for each option contract is $300, the original cost was ten and the estimated worth is seven. So, if you plan to risk $3,000 on this trade (3 percent of your trading account), then you would buy ten options: $3,000 divided by the $300 risk on each option contract.

This is quite a difference, buying ten options instead of three, but it is the correct quantity to buy if your analyses are correct. It is just as egregious an error to buy too few options, as it is to buy too many. I sometimes liken it to poker, where a good player will not waste money chasing every hand to its conclusion but realize that he must bet his good hands to their fullest. In option trading, it is foolhardy to risk too large of a portion of one's assets on any one trade. However, each potentially successful trade must be invested to the fullest extent within the risk parameters. Hence, it is correct to buy ten options in this case, not three.

Performing a What-If Analysis

The final step that an option buyer should take is to ensure that he has properly accounted for reasonable market outcomes when buying his options. This can only be done with an option model, but it is very important. If he buys options by convenience or by gut feeling, he will assuredly run afoul of events that he could easily have anticipated had he just done some advance planning.

In order to demonstrate this, let's use an example. Suppose that he sees a stock breaking out to new highs at 115 and decides he wants to buy options on it. The date is July 1, but he wants to buy September options to give himself some time. In looking at the option prices, he sees the following:

STOCK PRICE: 115
Sept 110 call: 17.5
Sept 115 call: 15
Sept 120 call: 13
Sept 125 call: 11
Sept 130 call: 9

Looking over this list of options, the trader (incorrectly) assumes that he would rather buy the Sept 130 call because it is a single digit cost (nine points). He has no interest in buying the at- or in-the-money options because they appear to be too costly. The Sept 130 call is the one he concentrates on. It is bid at eight and offered at nine. It is often the case that fairly illiquid options on volatile stocks have a wide market, such as the one point market exemplified here. Furthermore, suppose that the trader uses his option modeling software and determines that the delta of the Sept 130 call is 0.46.

Overcoming the Bid-Asked Spread

One of the first things a trader should do is determine how far the stock needs to advance in order to merely overcome the bid-asked spread in the option he has selected to trade. In this case, the bid-asked spread is one point (eight bid, nine asked) and the delta is 0.46. So, dividing the spread by the delta: $1/0.46 = 2.25$ means the stock needs to move up by 2.25 points just to recover the bid-asked spread! That is, if you pay nine for the option now (likely, since market makers won't let you trade between the bid and offer in an illiquid option), then the stock will need to rise by 2.25 points just to make the option have a bid of nine. That's a heavy toll to begin with.

Other Considerations

Furthermore, another thing that an option model can convey is how the option will react to changes in implied volatility. Suppose the option is currently trading at an implied volatility of 95 percent, as opposed to its usual implied volatility of 85 percent, due to the fact that it is breaking out to new highs. The option model can tell you that the vega of this option is 16 cents (0.16). That is, the option will gain or lose 16 cents of value for each percentage point that implied volatility increases or decreases.

The option trader decides to buy this Sept 130 call at a price of nine. He has not necessarily ignored the warnings from the option modeling software, but he has not taken them fully into consideration either.

Three days later, the stock is four points higher, so the trader calls his broker or checks his online quotes and finds to his dismay that the option he paid nine for now has a bid of 8.25, even though the stock has traded four points higher. At this point, the trader might issue epithets about option markets, market makers, and the like. In reality, if he had been more careful about his what-if analysis, he would have realized this could happen.

Let's look at the evidence: first, the stock gained four points and the delta was 0.46, so the option should have gained 1.84 points of value (4 x 0.46). In fact, it did. It's just that other factors cost more than that. Furthermore, assume that a couple days after the breakout, the options returned to their usual, implied volatility of 85 percent. That's a drop of ten percentage points from the 95 percent implied volatility at which the option was bought. Since the model had warned that each percentage point drop would cost 16 cents in option value, this is a loss of 1.60 points (10 x 0.16). Finally, there is the bid-asked spread of one point. A buyer who buys on the asked and sells on the bid will lose one point due to the width of the spread.

In summary, then, the option trade produced these results:
Delta: Gain of 4 points x 0.46 = +1.84
Volatility decline: loss of 10 percentage points x 0.16 = -1.60
Bid-asked spread: -1.00
Net Option Loss -0.76

In other words, if this trader had done a "what-if" analysis with the option model, asking what would happen if the stock rose four points, while implied volatility returned to its usual levels, and the bid-asked spread remained the same, the model would say that the option would lose roughly three-quarters of a point—which is exactly what happened!

How could this have been avoided? First of all, if this trader had remembered that one should buy a short-term, in-the-money option for a short-term stock trading system, then he would have bought a July 110 call. That call would have had a much higher delta than 0.46 with much less exposure to a volatility decrease. So the top line (delta gain) would have been a bigger gain and the second line (volatility loss) would have been a much smaller loss. Moreover, the bid-asked spread would assuredly be narrower for a short-term option. Thus the whole transaction would have resulted in a profit.

While it appeared that buying the out-of-the-money option for a single-digit price was a way to limit risk, it turned out it was merely a way to eliminate profits. A proper usage of the option modeling software would have told the trader these facts in advance. However, even lacking the power of the option model, if he had merely adhered to the first rule presented in this article—the shorter the time horizon of the trade, the higher the delta should be—he would have bought a short-term, in-the-money call option and come out okay. This is a classic example of how trusting your gut when you are not an experienced option trader can get you into trouble, even though you have selected a winning trade in the underlying stock.

Many option traders can improve their profitability by just adhering to the simple rules presented in this article. First, remember that the shorter the term of your stock-trading system, the higher the delta should be of the option you purchase. Second, remember to accurately assess your option risk with a model so you buy enough options when making a trade. Finally, utilize the delta risk and volatility risk, again, with a model, so that you can perform a realistic what-if analysis on the option you are considering purchasing. With these simple procedures, anyone with a successful stock-trading system should be able to convert it to a successful option-trading system and probably increase his rate of return while actually decreasing risk.

Lawrence G. McMillan, author of several books, including the best-selling *Options as a Strategic Investment* (Prentice Hall Press, 4th edition 2001), is president of McMillan Analysis Corp. www.option-strategist.com. McMillan Analysis publishes several option trading newsletters, has a wide array of option research material, educational material and seminars available, and manages individual accounts in the option markets as well as a hedge fund. The company also sells software, such as a stand-alone version of the Black-Scholes model. McMillan formerly was a proprietary trader for the brokerage firms of Thomson McKinnon Securities and Prudential-Bache Securities, prior to founding McMillan Analysis Corp in 1991. He has an undergraduate degree in math from Purdue University and a Masters in applied math and computer science from the University of Colorado. This article originally appeared in *SFO* in July 2002.

CONCLUSION

Lastly, some advice on how to avoid some of the most common (and costly!) mistakes of online traders. Boris Schlossberg, noted currency trading expert, shares his first-hand experience with seven of the worst trading mistakes and time-tested strategies for avoiding them. Whether you're just beginning to trade or already an active trader, you'll likely recognize at least a couple of these scenarios and learn something from the discussion.

28

THE SEVEN DEADLY SINS OF TRADING

BY BORIS SCHLOSSBERG

Pride, envy, gluttony ... these, among others, are the seven deadly sins. We are familiar with each of them and the damage they cause to body and soul. In trading, do we make similar transgressions that hurt our confidence and destroy our capital? Yes. These are seven of the worst trading mistakes and some possible ways to avoid them. How do I know? I've made them all.

1. No Good Reason to Trade

Ask a novice trader why he is in a trade, and he most likely will look at you dully and mumble, "I dunno, it sold off so I bought it."

Ask a semi-pro trader, and he may say something like this: "Well, the MACD diverged with price on the five-minute chart on the long side so I shorted it." Then ask the semi-pro, "So then, why did you go back into the trade after getting stopped out?" And he'll say something like this: "Well, it's got to go down sometime."

Finally ask a truly professional trader what he is trading, and more often then not he'll simply state, "I'm not trading anything right now because I see no set-ups."

Clueless, impulsive trading is the principal reason why most traders lose money quickly. Lost in a sea of seemingly random price movement, conflicting fundamental advice and a bewildering array of economic, political and technical price information, many traders lurch from one trade to the next like desperate shipwreck survivors trying to find shore. They try to trend on choppy days and fade on

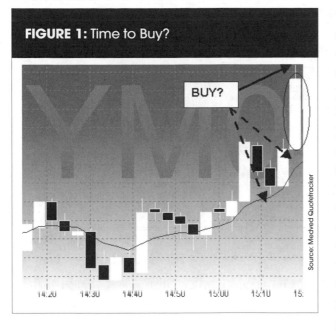

FIGURE 1: Time to Buy?

BUY?

Source: Medved Quotetracker

14:20   14:30   14:40   14:50   15:00   15:10   15:

trend days. After one good trade, drunk with power of winning, they plunge right back into the market and proceed to give it all back...and then some. Finally, frustrated and bewildered, many traders turn to gurus or trading systems that often charge thousands for nothing more than a glorified moving average crossover strategy.

Guess what? Trading a black box system that made two trillion dollars of pretend money in the last twelve months is not a good reason to trade. Buying the E-mini S&P in the midst of a freefall because it "looks like it's gone down enough" is not a good reason to trade. Selling bond futures because some staid economist on CNBC said rates are going up soon is not a good reason to trade.

How do you find good reasons for a trade? There is, after all, no magic pill. Simply, you must put in the work. If you trade stocks and stock indexes, which lend themselves to technical trading, you have to look at potentially thousands of hours of charts until you are able to isolate price patterns that appear with regularity and that you personally will be comfortable trading. Then you have to spend hundreds of hours practicing trading only these specific patterns on the simulator and then doing it in real life.

If you trade bonds or currencies—two markets that lend themselves well to fundamental trading—you have to really know the triggers that move those markets. Quick—name the seven major central bank governors and their respective monetary policies. What's the last six-month trend for German factory orders? Who amongst the G-7 is most vulnerable to spikes in oil prices, and whose currency is most oil-positive? If you

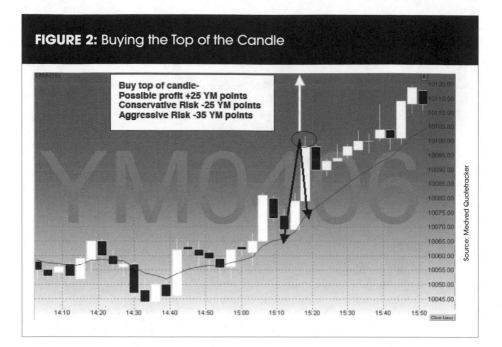

FIGURE 2: Buying the Top of the Candle

> Buy top of candle-
> Possible profit +25 YM points
> Conservative Risk -25 YM points
> Aggressive Risk -35 YM points

Source: Medved Quotetracker

are trading those markets and don't know the answers to these questions, then you are not trading with a good reason.

2. Chasing Price

Let's make this point simple and visual. Take a look at *Figure 1*. Looks good to buy, doesn't it? Actually, no. Even if price skyrocketed 50 YM points, buying this candle is a sucker bet. Why? Because it presents a terrible risk-to-reward ratio. Let's deconstruct the trade in more detail. What would be a reasonable profit target on this trade? Let's say it would equal the amplitude of the breakout candle. And what would be the logical point of failure where a trader would place a stop? A risk-averse trader would place a stop just below 10 EMA support, while a more aggressive trader would place a stop one tick below the low of two candles back.

But let's see how the possibilities evolve on the following few charts.

Notice that when comparing *Figure 2* and *Figure 3* how the dark arrows suddenly get much smaller and the light arrows much larger. What's so different about the second set-up in *Figure 3*? Nothing much. We still followed the same reason to trade, but we simply waited for the price to come to our target. Yet, note what a drastic difference in risk and reward we've achieved. In the first case (*Figure 2*), the

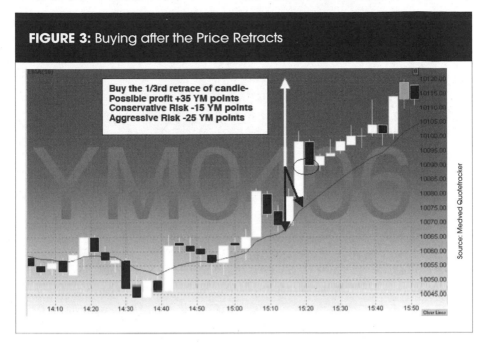

FIGURE 3: Buying after the Price Retracts

Buy the 1/3rd retrace of candle-
Possible profit +35 YM points
Conservative Risk -15 YM points
Aggressive Risk -25 YM points

Source: Medved Quotetracker

trade presented 1:1 and 1:1.4 reward-to-risk ratios. In the second case (*Figure 3*), the trade presented 2.3:1 and 1.4:1 reward-to-risk ratios.

Buying tops and selling bottoms is a very expensive mistake. Even if the direction is right ultimately, the trader puts himself into a vulnerable position by either being shaken out of the trade on too tight a stop or having to take a stop far in excess of possible profit.

Many traders ask me what happens if they don't get their retrace price—if price continues to trend in one direction. The answer is simple. Don't chase price.

3. Not Letting Profits Run

By this point, even the most stubborn traders have been taught to cut losses short. With the proliferation of auto-execution software, which automatically embeds stop-loss orders the moment your trade is executed, most traders don't even have to consciously think about cutting losses short.

Letting profits run, however, is another matter. Why is it so hard to let profits run? Well, for one thing, losses always are absolute, and profits are potentially infinite. We all have a limited amount of capital, and this is the absolute loss that brackets us to the downside. Profits however, can be practically boundless.

Imagine owning $1,000 of MSFT (Microsoft) IPO stock. Present value? – about $1MM. The MSFT example, of course, is absurdly extreme, but it demonstrates an important point. The reason to trade the market is to let profits run, not to cut losses short.

We tend to punish ourselves for taking losses and reward ourselves for taking small profits. In fact, we should be doing the opposite. We should compliment ourselves for taking proper losses to preserve capital and control risk. And we should admonish ourselves for taking small profits, when much larger gains are possible. How can we expect to pay for those losses if we don't generate enough profit? In most businesses, 20 percent of transactions account for 80 percent of the profit. Why should trading be any different?

Trading, however, is very different in one respect. In a regular business, frequently we know or have a very good idea ahead of time which are the 20 percent of most profitable transactions. We can anticipate needs and devote enough resources to make sure that we attract and preserve that business. No such luck in trading. In a series of one hundred trades, no one can predict with any certainty which twenty will generate 80 percent of the profit. This is one of the maddening aspects that makes trading so difficult.

How do you let profits run in a business that can take them away in an instant? The only way that I've observed successful traders do it is by the scale-out method. Our human need to ring the register is so great that if we do not relieve some pressure right away we will sabotage the trade. Therefore, many successful traders will take one-third of the position off when it reaches a very quick profit (say, one ES or 10 YM points), sell the second lot at their intermediate target (e.g., +3ES +30YM), and hold the third and final lot for that potential homerun day trade (+10ES +100 YM).

Those who choose to do the math will discover that the scale out method is actually less profitable than a single exit method (because of the rarity of achieving the third-lot target). However, in markets, what is mathematically optimal often is not what is psychologically optimal. That is why streetwise guys in the pits of Chicago and New York take money away from quantitative PhD desk traders every day.

What if you are only a one-lot trader? The honest answer is that you are trading too large for your size. One possible solution is to trade single stock futures (SSF) instead of E-mini indexes. For example, you could trade DIA SSF in lieu of YM and QQQ SSF in lieu of NQ in order to enable the scale-out method.

4. Seeking High-Probability Trades

What if I told you that the single best hedge fund trader in the world—a guy so good he takes 50-percent profit fees while all others charge 20 percent—makes most of his money on only 5 percent of his trades? That's right, Steve Cohen, who runs SAC Capital Associates, the highly secretive and successful $4-billion Greenwich, Connecticut, hedge fund, is not afraid of being wrong. Cohen, who is an old school news-flow trader, will put on many trades that will fail his expectations. He trades for the "big thing," not the "sure thing." In an interview with Jack Schwager, Cohen said, "Most of my traders make money only 50 percent of the time. That means you are going to be wrong a lot. If that is the case, you better make sure your losses are small as they can be, and that your winners are bigger."

The lesson from Cohen's success is clear. The stock market is hardly a highly predictable environment. Instead of always looking for high-probability trades with low payouts (and trust me, there are no high-probability trades with high payouts), traders should seek trades with greater payout potential but less accuracy. The tried and true method of making 2:1 reward-to-risk trades with 50 percent accuracy still rings true. Any trader who can even approach those numbers will be extremely profitable in the long run.

5. Assuming the Trend Is Linear

One of the worst myths perpetrated on novice traders is that all you have to do to make money in trading is trade with the trend. Novices then instantly imagine smooth linear slopes as prices rise from point A to B, and their account equity grows exponentially. Often prices do rise from point A to B but very few traders have positive equity at the end of the run. If trends happen so frequently, why do so few people profit from them?

Take a look at *Figures 4, 5 and 6*. Certainly in hindsight, the trend looks obvious. But look at the individual time frames again. These charts hardly inspire confidence in the long side. Markets try to shake traders out all the time. That's why those who think that trading the trend is easy are operating under a deadly illusion. And those who trade trend effectively have an enormous reservoir of conviction.

6. No Averaging Down

Let's run a very simple scenario. I own 100 shares of $100 stock. The stock moves down to $90. I buy 200 shares at $90. The stock moves to $80, and I buy 400 shares at $80 and put in a stop loss at $75. I now have given

FIGURE 4

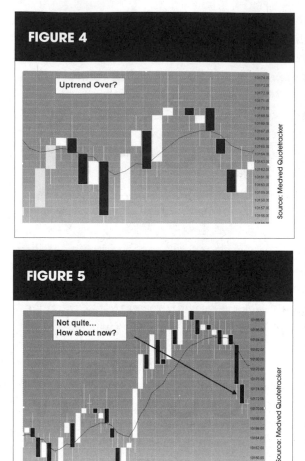

Uptrend Over?

Source: Medved Quotetracker

FIGURE 5

Not quite...
How about now?

Source: Medved Quotetracker

FIGURE 6

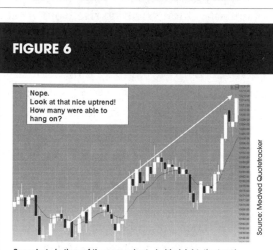

Nope.
Look at that nice uptrend!
How many were able to
hang on?

Source: Medved Quotetracker

Snapshots in time of the same chart. In hindsight, the trend seems obvious, but it's not so clear in real-time.

myself a very wide band of price movement, and I've used a much more aggressive double-down strategy (1 x 2 x 4) versus the standard (1 x 1 x 1) to bring myself as close as possible to current market price. Furthermore, let's assume I will only target $90 as my exit price to give me the highest probability of profit. How much of a probability? Let's assign a 75-percent win rate—almost unheard of in real trading conditions.

We have now rigged the strategy to make it as attractive as possible to average down. What happens? At the 75-percent accuracy rate, we make $37.50 on the trade. "Not bad," you say. But wait. What if our odds slip to 70 percent? We lose $15. And what if the odds go down just a tad more to 65 percent? Then we are losing $67.50. Here we have a strategy that is winning two out of three times, and we still lose $67.50.

One final question. What if we enter a prolonged down phase in the market, and our rate of success drops to 55 percent. We still have a net positive strategy. What happens? Our loss after every ten trades is a whopping $172.00! With a relatively small 20 percent decrease in odds, we incur a loss 450 percent greater than our best profit.

Averaging down is the Russian roulette of trading strategies. You can escape the odds for some time, but one day it will get you and wipe you out.

There is one exception to the average down rule, and it is the reverse of a scale-out strategy mentioned in mistake #3. If your original position size is going to be 300 shares, you may average into your position 100 shares at a time as long as you are honest with your stops. For example, if you were going to buy 300 shares at $100 with a stop at $90, risking 30 points in total, you may scale in by buying 100 at $100, 100 at $95, and 100 at $90 with a stop at $85. Many traders prefer this approach because it offers them a better blended price and a little further absolute stop. If you do follow this approach, do it from the outset. Don't double up your original position size and call it scaling in—the only person you will be fooling is yourself.

7. Overtrading

You have $10,000 of risk capital. You open an account with a direct access futures broker that charges you rock bottom rates of $5 per round turn. You download the latest free auto-execution software and start trading. Because you don't want to risk wide stops, you decide to be scalper and make ten round-turn trades per day. How well are you doing? Much better than most. You are consistently breaking even. You didn't expect to be profitable right away, but you are learning and not giving an inch to the market.

Assume that 200 days forward your losses and wins even out completely, and you haven't given up even one point of capital to the market. How much money is left in your account? Zero.

That's right! Your broker turns out to be some partner. And you can't blame him—he offers the lowest rates in town! The fault lies in overtrading, an extremely insidious trading sin, the true cost of which is never obvious right away.

If active traders were to compare their yearly commission bill to their year-end profit-to-loss ratio, they might be shocked to see the numbers. Most traders pay more in commissions than they ever take out of the market.

So, what is a reasonable amount of round trips a day trader should make? There is no hard and fast rule, but, generally, it should not average more then three to five trips per day. If you are doing more than ten round trips per day, and you are not a hyperactive scalper with an incredible, short-term feel for the market, you are overtrading. In the end it will cost you.

Avoiding the seven sins of trading will in no way guarantee you a profit; only your skill and determination will determine that. But successful trading is as much an act of avoidance as it is an art of action. Avoiding the seven deadly sins of trading may not make you a good trader, but it will prevent you from being a bad one.

Boris Schlossberg serves as senior currency strategist at FXCM, one of the largest retail forex dealers in the world. He is the author of *Technical Analysis of the Currency Market: Classic Techniques for Profiting from Market Swings and Trader Sentiment* (Wiley Trading, 2006). This article originally appeared in *SFO* in August 2004.

GLOSSARY OF TERMS

A

Algorithm: An advanced mathematical model that can be used in a trading system to make transaction decisions in the financial markets.

American Stock Exchange (AMEX): A stock exchange; a private, not-for-profit corporation, located in New York City and founded in 1842. Also called AMEX and the curb exchange.

Application Program Interface (API): a function in a computer software program that sends a trading order to the "back end," which includes the hardware involved in processing the order.

Arbitrage: The simultaneous purchase of one asset against the sale of the same asset (usually in different exchanges or marketplaces) in an attempt to profit from different prices for the same security, commodity, or financial instrument in different markets.

Arcade: A trading room set up for a group of individual traders.

Ask: The price a seller is willing to accept for a security, futures contract or other financial instrument. Also called the offer.

At or better: (1) In a buy order for securities, futures, or other financial instruments, a purchase at the specified price or under it (2) For a sell order, a sale at the specified price or above it.

At-the-money: An option with a strike price equal to the current price of the instrument, such as a stock, upon which the option was granted.

At-the-opening order: An order that specifies it is to be executed at the opening of the market or of trading or else it is to be canceled. The order does not have to be executed at the opening price, but within the opening range of prices.

B

Backspread: A type of options spread in which a trader holds more long positions than short positions. The premium collected from the sale of the short option is used to help finance the purchase of the long options. This spread can be created using either all call options or all put options.

Bear market (bear, bearish): A market in which prices are declining. A period of generally falling prices and pessimistic attitudes.

Bear spread: A simultaneous purchase of one option, hedged by the sale or another option, where the options have the same expiration month but different striking prices and will profit from a decrease in prices.

Beta: A measure of an investment's volatility. The lower the beta, the less risky the investment.

Bid: The price a buyer is willing to pay for a security, futures contract or other financial instrument.

Beta coefficient: A means of measuring the volatility of an individual market (security, future, financial instrument) in comparison with the market as a whole.

Black Box System: A software trading program where the inner workings, or algorithms, are unknown, and the variables cannot be modified. A "gray-box system" is similar in that the algorithms are unknown, but the variables can be modified.

Black-Scholes Model: A widely used option pricing equation developed in 1973 by Fischer Black and Myron Scholes. Used to evaluate OTC options, option portfolios, or option trading on exchanges.

Board of Trade: Any exchange or association of persons engaged in the business of buying or selling a commodity. Usually an exchange where commodity futures and/or options are traded. Sometimes referred to as Contract Market or Exchange.

Bollinger bands: A method used by technical analysts that indicates if a market is overbought or oversold. Fixed lines above and below a simple moving average. As volatility increases, the bands widen.

Bond: A debt instrument that pays a set amount of interest on a regular basis. The issuer promises to repay the debt on time and in full.

Book value: The value of a financial instrument as shown by accounting records, often not the same as the instrument is valued by the market.

Booked: The point at which a transaction is processed. Though funds may not yet be available, the system has posted it and marked it as having a value date in the future.

Booking date: The date the payment is to be booked and executed. The date the payment will be passed to the automated system to book.

Bookings: A collection of records of financial transactions processed by automated systems. Booking are also called postings.

Bracket order: A three-part order, including the entry order, stop exit order and target exit order. When one exit order is fulfilled, the other is cancelled.

Break: A rapid and sharp price decline.

Break-even point: (1) The point at which gains equal losses. (2) The price a market must reach for an option buyer to avoid a loss if he or she exercises.

Broker: (1) An individual or firm that charges a fee or commission for executing buy and sell orders placed by another individual or firm. (2) A floor broker in commodities futures trading, a person who actually executes orders on the trading floor of an exchange.

Brokerage: A fee charged by a broker for execution of a transaction.

Broker-dealer (BD): A person or firm in the business of buying and selling securities. A firm may act as both broker (agent) or dealer (principal), but not in the same transaction. In the United States, broker-dealers must register with the SEC and any state in which they do business.

Bucket (bucketing): (1) The illegal practice of accepting orders to buy or sell without executing such orders on an official Board of Trade. (2) The illegal use of a customer's funds without disclosing such use.

Bull market (bull, bullish): A market in which prices are rising. A trader who believes prices will move higher is called a bull.

Bull spread: A simultaneous purchase of one option, hedged by the sale or another option, where the options have the same expiration month but different striking prices and will profit from an increase in prices.

Buy in: A purchase to offset, cover, or close a short position.

Buy stop order: An order to buy a market that is entered at a price above the current offering price and that is triggered when the market price touches or goes through the buy stop price.

C

Calendar spread: See horizontal spread.

Call option: Publicly traded contract granting the owner the right, but not the obligation, to buy a commodity or other financial instrument at a specified price at a stated future date.

Candlestick Chart: A price chart that includes information on the opening price, closing price and direction of movement during a trading session. Also called a Japanese candlestick chart.

Cap: An investment product that compensates the holder when interest rates rise above a certain level.

Carrying broker: A member of a commodity exchange, usually a clearinghouse member, through whom other brokers or customers clear all or some trades.

Carrying charges: Costs incurred in warehousing the physical commodity, generally including interest, insurance, and storage.

Cash market: The underlying commodity, security, currency, or money market in which transactions for the purchase and sale of cash instruments which futures and derivative contracts relate to are carried out.

Charting: The use of graphs and charts in the technical analysis of markets to plot trends of price movements, average movements of price volume, and open interest.

Chicago Board Options Exchange (CBOE): An exchange at the Chicago Board of Trade to trade stock options. The CBOE has markets in equities, options, and over-the-counter securities.

Chicago Board of Trade (CBOT or CBT): The oldest futures exchange in the United States, established in 1848. Announced intention (in late 2006) to merge with the Chicago Mercantile Exchange (and operate under the name of the CME). The exchange lists agricultural commodity futures such as corn, oats, and soybeans, in addition to financial instruments—e.g., Treasury bonds and Treasury notes.

Chicago Mercantile Exchange (CME): Announced intention (in late 2006) to merge with the Chicago Board of Trade to become the largest futures exchange in the world. The Exchange operates the International Monetary Market (IMM), the Index and Options Market (IOM), and the Growth and Emerging Markets (GEM), and will eventually operate Chicago Board of Trade agricultural commodity futures such as corn, oats, and soybeans, as well as financial instruments such as Treasury bonds and Treasury notes.

Clear: The formal completion of a trade.

Clearing member: A member of a clearing house or an association. All trades of a non-clearing member must be registered and eventually settled through a clearing member.

Clearing house: An agency or separate corporation connected with an exchange responsible for settling trading accounts, clearing trades, collecting and maintaining margin monies, regulating delivery and reporting trading data. Clearing houses act as third parties to all futures and options contracts.

Clearing: The procedure through which trades are checked for legitimacy When trades are validated, the clearinghouse or association becomes the buyer to each seller and the seller to each buyer.

Close: The period at the end of a trading session during which all transactions are considered to be made at the close.

Closing balance: The balance of entries posted to the account at the close of the statement period.

Closing price: The price at which transactions are made just before the close on a given day.

Closing range: A range of closely related prices at which transactions took place at the closing of the market; buy and sell orders at the closing might have been filled at any point within such a range.

Commission broker: A member of an exchange who executes orders for the sale or purchase of financial futures contracts.

Commission Merchant (also Futures Commission Merchant, FCM): One who makes a trade, either for another member of the exchange or for a nonmember client, in his or her own name and becomes liable as principal to the other party to the transaction.

Commission: (1) A fee charged by a broker to a customer for performance of a specific duty, such as the buying or selling of futures contracts. A commission must be fair and reasonable, considering all the relevant factors of the transaction. (2) Sometimes used to refer to the Commodity Futures Trading Commission (CFTC).

Commodity: An entity of trade or commerce, services, or rights in which contracts for future delivery may be traded. Some of the contracts currently traded are wheat, corn, cotton, livestock, copper, gold, silver, oil, propane, plywood, currencies, Treasury bills, Treasury bonds, and stock indexes.

Commodity Channel Index (CCI): An oscillator used in technical analysis to help determine when an investment vehicle has been overbought and oversold. The index quantifies the relationship between the asset's price, a moving average (MA) of the asset's price, and normal deviations (D) from that average.

Commodity Exchange of New York (CMX): A division of the New York Mercantile Exchange.

Commodity Futures Trading Commission (CFTC): The federal agency established by the Commodity Futures Trading Commission Act of 1974 to ensure the open and efficient operation of the futures markets.

Conditional order: An order that is automatically submitted or cancelled only when specified criteria are met.

Confirmation statement: A statement sent by a commission house to a customer when a transaction is made. The statement confirms the number of contracts bought or sold and the prices at which the contracts were bought or sold.

Congestion: Sideways movement in the market.

Consolidation: A technical analysis term. A pause in trading activity in which price moves sideways, setting the stage for the next move. Traders are said to evaluate their positions during periods of consolidation.

Contract date: Date on which the contract is agreed between the parties.

Contract month: The month in which deliveries are to be made in accordance with a futures contract.

Contract: (1) An agreement between at least two parties to buy or sell, on certain conditions, a certain product, as a result of which a legal status concerning rights and duties of the parties exists. (2) A term of reference describing a unit of trading for a commodity.

Cookie: A small text file of information that certain Web sites attach to a user's hard drive while the user is browsing the Web site. A Cookie can contain information such as user ID, user preferences, or archived shopping cart information.

Corner: To secure control of a market so that its price can be manipulated.

Correction: A technical analysis term. A price reaction against the prevailing trend of the market. Sometimes referred to as a retracement.

Cover: The action of offsetting a futures securities or other financial instrument transaction with an equal and opposite transaction. Short covering is a purchase to offset an earlier sale of an equal number of the same delivery month. Liquidation is a sale to offset the obligation to take delivery.

Covered: An investment strategy in which the seller owns the underlying security.

Credit spread: The simultaneous purchase of one option, hedged by the sale of another option, when payment comes into the account when the spread is initially established.

Cross hedging: The hedging of a cash instrument on a different, but related, futures or other derivatives market.

Customer daily position: A statement produced daily showing the position of a customer's account or group of accounts.

D

Day order: An order that if not executed expires automatically at the end of the trading session of the day it was entered.

Day trader: Traders who take positions in the market and then liquidate them prior to the close of the trading day.

Dead Cat Bounce (DCB): A chart pattern that occurs when a price drops 30 percent to 70 percent in one session, then bounces upward before the decline resumes.

Dealer option: A put or call on a physical commodity, not originating at or subject to the rules of an exchange, written by a firm which deals in the underlying cash commodity.

Dealer: An individual or company that buys and sells financial instruments for its own account and customer accounts.

Debit spread: The simultaneous purchase of one option, hedged by the sale of another option, when payment comes into an account when the spread is expended.

Defrag: Short for Defragment. The process of collecting fragments of computer files and sorting them into contiguous sections on the hard drive, thus speeding up file management, and facilitating faster online trading.

Delta hedge: The partial offset of the exchange risk of a currency option by an opposite open currency spot position in the same foreign currency.

Delta: A measure of the relationship between an option price and its underlying futures contract or stock price. Measures how rapidly the value of an option moves in relation to the underlying value.

Demand: A consumer's desire and willingness to pay for a good or service.

Derivative: A complex investment whose value is derived from or linked to some underlying financial asset, such as a stock, bond, currency, or mortgage. Derivatives may be listed on exchanges or traded privately over-the-counter. For example, derivatives may be futures, options, or mortgage-backed securities.

Diagonal spread: A simultaneous purchase of one option, hedged by the sale of another option, where the two options have different striking prices and different expiration months.

Discount brokers: Brokers who charge lower commissions than full-service brokers.

Discount rate: The interest rate charged by the Federal Reserve on loans to member banks. This rate influences the rates these financial institutions then charge to their customers.

Divergence: A situation in which the price of an asset and an indicator, index or other related asset move in opposite directions. Can be positive or negative and is used in technical analysis to make investment decisions.

Drawdown: The peak-to-trough decline during a specific record period of a trade, usually quoted as the percentage between the peak and the trough.

E

Earnings per share (EPS): The portion of a company's profit allocated to each outstanding share of common stock. EPS serves as an indicator of a company's profitability and is often considered the single most important variable in determining the price of a share.

Equity curve: A chart that plots the ups and downs of the value of an account.

Elasticity: A characteristic which describes the interaction of supply, demand, and price. A commodity is said to be elastic in demand when a price change creates an increase or decrease in consumption. Inelasticity of supply or demand exists when either supply or demand is relatively unresponsive to changes in price.

Electronic Communications Network (ECN): The electronic system designed to allow traders to trade directly with each other when executing orders.

Electronic trading: The computerized matching of buyers and sellers of financial instruments. GLOBEX, Project A, and Access are examples.

Equity: The dollar value of a futures account if all open positions were offset at the current market price. In securities markets, it is the part of a company's net worth that belongs to shareholders.

Exchange: An association of persons or entities engaged in the business of buying and selling futures and/or options, usually involving an auction process. Also called a board of trade or contract market.

Execution date: The date on which a trader wishes to exercise an option.

Execution: (1) The completion of an order for a transaction. (2) The carrying out of an instruction.

Exercise date and striking price: The last day on which the option can be exercised, as well as the currency and price at which the market can be purchased or sold, on or before that date.

Exercise date: The date on which the buyer of an option chooses to exercise the buyer's right under the option contract with the seller of the option.

Exercise price: The price at which the buyer of a call (put) option may choose to exercise his right to purchase (sell) the underlying futures contract. Also called strike price or strike.

Exercise: By exercising an option, the buyer elects to accept the underlying market at the option's strike price.

Expiration date: Generally the last date on which an option may be exercised or a transaction made.

Exposure: A possible loss of value caused by changes in market value, interest rates, or exchange rates.

F

Fed: The short name for the U.S. Federal Reserve Banks.

Federal Open Market Committee (FOMC): A committee of the Federal Reserve Banks that makes decisions concerning the Fed's operations to control the money supply. Their primary purpose is the purchase and sale of government securities, which increases or decreases the money supply. It also sets key interest rates, such as the discount rate and Fed fund rate.

Federal Reserve: The central bank of the United States that sets monetary policy. The Federal Reserve and FOMC oversee money supply, interest rates, and credit with the goal of keeping the U.S. economy and currency stable. Also called the Fed.

Fibonacci Numbers (or Sequence): The sequence of numbers, used in technical analysis, discovered by the Italian mathematician Leonardo de Pise in the 13th century. The first two terms of the sequence are 0 and 1, and each successive number is the sum of the previous two numbers (0, 1, 2, 3, 5, 8, 13, 21, 34, 55, 89, 144, . .).

Fill: The act of completing an order (such as buy or sell) for a security or commodity.

Financial instruments: Also known as financial products or simply as instruments; includes bonds, stocks, derivatives, and other financial representations of assets.

Floor broker: An individual who executes orders on the trading floor of an exchange for any other person or entity.

Floor traders: Members of an exchange who are personally present, on the trading floors of the exchanges, to make trades for themselves.

Floor: (1) The lowest rate a financial market is allowed to fall. (2) The trading floor of an exchange.

Forward: A rate or the price of a financial instrument or event which is in the future.

Friction: The implicit and explicit costs associated with market transactions.

Front end: The software program that resides in your computer, from which you place a trading order.

Full-service brokers: Brokers who execute buy and sell orders, research investments, help investors develop and meet investment goals, and give advice to investors.

Fundamental analysis: An approach to the analysis of markets which examines the underlying factors which will affect the supply and demand of the market, overall economy, industry conditions, etc.

Futures Commission Merchant (FCM): An individual or organization which solicits or accepts orders to buy or sell futures contracts or commodity options and accepts money or other assets from customers in connection with such orders.

Futures contract: A standardized, binding agreement to buy or sell a specified quantity or grade of a commodity at a later date. Futures contracts are freely transferable and can be traded only by public auction on designated exchanges.

Futures option: An option on a futures contract.

G

Gap: In technical analysis, a trading day during which the daily price range is completely above or below the previous day's range

Globex: A global, after-hours electronic system for trading in derivatives, futures and commodity contracts. A Reuter's system for the Chicago Mercantile Exchange.

Good 'Til Cancelled (GTC) order: An order to buy or sell an asset at a set price that remains active until the customer cancels it, or it is filled.

H

Head and shoulders: A technical analysis chart pattern that has three peaks resembling a head and two shoulders. A head and shoulders top typically forms after a substantial rise and indicates a market reversal. A head and shoulders bottom (an inverted head and shoulders) indicates a market advance.

Hedge: An investment made in order to reduce the risk of an adverse price movement.

Hedging: A transaction strategy used by dealers and traders in foreign exchange, commodities, and securities, as well as farmers, manufactures, and other producers, to protect against severe fluctuations in exchange rates and market prices. A current sale or purchase is offset by contracting to purchase or sell at a specified future date.

Horizontal spread: A simultaneous purchase of one option, hedged by the sale of another option, where the two options have the same striking price but different expiration months. Also called a calendar spread.

I

Implied Volatility (IV): The estimated volatility of a security or commodity's price.

In-the-money: An option having intrinsic value. A call is in-the-money if its strike price is below the current price of the underlying futures contract. A put is in the money if its strike price is above the current price of the underlying futures contract.

Inelasticity: A characteristic that describes the interdependence of supply, demand, and price. A commodity is inelastic when a price change does not create an increase or decrease in consumption; inelasticity exists when supply and demand are relatively unresponsive to changes in price.

Initial margin: Customers' funds required at the time a futures or forex position is established, or an option is sold. Margin in futures or forex markets is not a down payment, as it is in securities.

Insider trading: (1) The legal trading of securities by corporate officers based on information available to the public. (2) The illegal trading of securities by any investor based on information not available to the public.

Instant Message: To send a text message in real time over the Internet.

Intercommodity spread: A trade involving the same (or close) delivery times and related commodities, generally on the same exchange.

Interdelivery spread: A trade involving the same commodity, usually at the same exchange, but different delivery times.

Intermarket spread: A trade involving the same commodity on different exchanges but with the same delivery time.

International Securities Exchange (ISE): The world's largest electronic equity options exchange.

Institutional investor: A person or organization that trades securities or other financial instruments in large enough quantities or dollar amounts that it qualifies for special treatment and/or lower commissions.

Interest: The charge or cost for using money; expressed as a percentage rate per period.

International Options Market (IOM): A division of the Chicago Mercantile Exchange.

Introducing Broker (IB): A firm or individual that solicits and accepts commodity futures orders from customers but does not accept money, securities, or property from the customer.

L

Level I: An online trading service consisting of real-time bid/ask quotes.

Level II: An online trading service consisting of quotes from individual market participants.

Leverage: The use of borrowed assets to enhance the return to the owner's equity, allowing an investor to establish a position in the marketplace by depositing funds that are less than the value of the contract.

Limit move: A price that has advanced or declined the limit permitted during one trading session as fixed by the rules of a contract market.

Limit order: An order to buy or sell as a specified price or better.

Liquid market: A market where selling and buying can be accomplished easily due to the presence of many interested buyers and sellers.

Liquidity: The ease of converting an asset to cash

Long hedge: Buying futures contracts to protect against possible increased prices of commodities. See also Hedging.

Long position: An excess of assets (and/or forward purchase contracts) over liabilities (and/or forward sale contracts) in the same currency. A dealer's position when net purchases and sales leave him or her in a net-purchased position.

Long: To own (buy) to a security, currency, futures contract, commodity, or derivative.

Long-term Equity Anticipation Security (LEAPS) options: Options that expire more than nine months from the current date.

M

Margin call: A call from a brokerage firm or clearing house to a customer or clearing member firm to bring margin deposits back up to minimum levels required by exchange regulations.

Margin: (1) In the futures industry, the amount of money deposited by both buyers and sellers of futures contracts to ensure performance against the contract. (2) In the stock market, the amount of cash that must be put up in a purchase of securities.

Market arbitrage: The simultaneous purchase and sale of the same security, futures, or other financial instrument in different markets to take advantage of a price disparity between the two markets.

Market impact cost: The price difference between the level at which an order is filled and the price level at it was optimally requested to be filled.

Market order: An order to buy or sell securities, futures contracts, or other financial instruments to be filled immediately at the best possible price. A limit order, in contrast, may specify requirements for price or time of execution.

Market: (1) Any area or condition where buyers and sellers are in contact for doing business together. (2) The generic term for a financial instrument.

Markup: The difference between the lowest current offering price among dealers and the higher price a dealer charges a customer.

Match trading: Financial transactions made outside of an auction or negotiation process. Buy and sell orders for the same financial instrument, at the same price, are paired and executed, often by computer.

Matching orders: Simultaneously entering identical (or nearly identical) buy and sell orders for a financial instrument to create the appearance of active trading in that market.

Measured Move Up (MMU): A chart pattern that signals a continuing upward price trend.

Mechanical system: A method of buying and selling stocks according to a screen based on results from predetermined indicators and other criteria.

Minis or E-Minis: Mini-sized versions of stock index futures traded electronically. Contracts are available on a wide range of indices such as the Nasdaq 100, S&P 500, S&P MidCap 400 and Russell 2000.

Momentum indicator: A line that represents the difference between today's price and the price of a fixed number of days ago. Momentum can be measured as the difference between today's price and the current value of a moving average. Often referred to as momentum oscillators.

Moving average: An average that changes over time, eliminating fluctuations in data. Moving averages emphasize the direction of a trend, confirm trend reversals, and smooth out price and volume fluctuations that can confuse interpretation of the market.

Mutual fund: An actively managed portfolio of securities in which all shareholders participate in the gains or losses of the fund. The shares are redeemable on any business day at the net asset value.

N

National Market System (NMS): A method of posting security prices simultaneously on regional exchanges. The system was widely adopted in 1975 to ensure trading activity met fair standards.

New York Stock Exchange (NYSE): The largest stock exchange in the United States. It is a corporation, operated by a board of directors, responsible for administering the Exchange and member activities, listing securities, overseeing the transfer of members' seats on the Exchange, and determining whether an applicant is qualified to be a specialist.

Normalizing: Adjusting data, such as a price series, to put it within normal or more standard range. A technique sometimes used to develop a trading system.

NYFE: New York Futures Exchange.

Nymex: New York Mercantile Exchange.

O

Offer: An indication of willingness to sell at a given price, also referred to as an ask, or asking price. The opposite of bid.

Offset: (1) The liquidation of a purchase of a futures contract, forward, or other financial instrument through the sale of an equal number of the same delivery months; (2) The covering of a short sale of futures forward or other financial instrument through the purchase of an equal number of the same delivery month. Either action transfers the obligation to make or take delivery of the actual financial instrument to someone else.

On-Balance Volume (OBV): A volume momentum indicator that correlates volume to price change. Originally developed by Joe Granville.

One-Cancels-All (OCA) order: An order to be cancelled when one of the other orders is executed.

Online broker: A retail securities, futures or options broker that provides services over the Internet.

Online trading: Using a computer and an Internet connection to place your buy and sell trading orders with an online brokerage firm, without the physical inclusion of a broker. Orders are entered and returned electronically via computer terminals.

Open outcry: Method of public auction for making bids and offers in the trading pits or rings of commodity exchanges.

Open: The period at the beginning of a trading session during which all transactions are considered made "at the open."

Opening range: The range of closely related prices at which transactions took place at the opening of the market; buying and selling orders at the opening might be filled at any point within such a range.

Option contract: The right, but not the obligation, to buy or sell a specific quantity of an underlying instrument on or before a specific date in the future. The seller of the option has the obligation to sell the underlying instrument (in a put option) or buy it from the option buyer (in a call option) at the exercise price if the option is exercised.

Option period: The period between the start date and the expiry date of an option contract.

Option premium: The money, securities, or property the buyer pays to the writer (grantor) for granting an option contract.

Option seller/writer: The party who is obligated to perform if an option is exercised by the option buyer.

Option: An agreement that represents the right to buy or sell a specified amount of an underlying security, such as a stock, bond, futures contract, at a specified price within a specified time. The purchaser acquires a right, and the seller assumes an obligation.

Order execution: The handling of an order by a broker, including receiving the order verbally or in writing from the customer, transmitting it to the trading floor of the exchange, and returning confirmation of the completed order to the customer.

Order to buy: An instruction to buy a given quantity of an identified financial instrument under specified conditions.

Order to sell: An instruction to sell a given quantity of an identified financial instrument under specified conditions.

Oscillator: A technical analysis tool that attempts to determine when an asset has become over- or under-priced. As the value of the oscillator approaches the upper extreme value the asset is deemed to be overbought, and as it approaches the lower extreme it is deemed to be oversold.

Out-of-the-money: A call option with a strike price higher, or a put option with a strike price lower, than the current market value of the underlying asset.

Over-the-counter-market (OTC): Trading in financial instruments transacted off organized exchanges, including transactions among market-makers and between market-makers and their customers.

Overbought: A technical analysis term market price that has risen too steeply and too fast in relation to underlying fundamental or other factors.

Oversold: A technical analysis term for a market price that has experienced stronger selling than the fundamentals justify.

Over-the-counter (OTC) derivative: A financial instrument whose value is designed to track the return on commodities, stocks, bonds, currencies or some other benchmark that is traded over-the-counter or off organized exchanges.

P

PC: Personal computer.

Parity: Equal standing.

Pip: Unit that expresses differences between exchange rates. The minimum incremental price change in the interbank markets.

Pit: A specially constructed arena on the trading floor of some exchanges where trading is conducted by open outcry. On other exchanges, the term "ring" designates the trading area.

Platform: A computer interface that provides the user with information and the means to place trades electronically.

Pledging: The act of putting up security for a loan or other financial transaction.

Point: The minimum fluctuation in prices or options premiums. Also called ticks.

Portfolio: A selection of financial instruments held by a person or institution, often designed to spread investment risk.

Position trader: A trader who buys or sells financial instruments and holds them for an extended period of time, as distinguished from the day trader, who will normally initiate and liquidate positions within a single trading session.

Position: A market commitment. For example, a buyer of futures contracts is said to have a long position, and, conversely, a seller of futures contracts is said to have a short position.

Premium: (1) The amount that an option buyer pays to an option seller. (2) The difference between the higher price paid for a financial instrument and the financial instrument's face amount at issue. (3) The additional payment allowed by exchange regulations for delivery of higher-than-required standards or grades of a commodity against a futures contract.

Price limit: Maximum price advance or decline from the previous day's settlement price, permitted for futures in one trading session by the rules of the exchange.

Price-to-earnings ratio (P/E): A measure of comparison of the value of different common stocks that is calculated by dividing the market price of the stock by the earnings per share.

Protective stop: An order to exit a trade if a price reaches a predetermined level, placed to defend against extreme loss.

Pullback: A fall in price from its peak.

Put (option): An option that gives the option buyer the right, but not the obligation, to sell the underlying financial instrument at a particular price on or before a particular date.

Put spread: The selling of a put at a lower strike price to pay for a put at a higher strike.

Q

Quote: The actual price, or the bid or ask price, of a security, commodity, futures, option, currency, or other financial instrument at a particular time.

R

Rally top: The point where a rally stalls.

Rally: An upward movement of prices.

Random walk theory: The theory that the past movement or direction of the price of a stock or other market cannot be used to predict its future movement or direction.

Range: The difference between the high and low price during a given period.

Ratio spread: An options strategy in which an investor simultaneously holds an unequal number of long and short positions.

Reaction: A short-term countertrend movement of prices.

Relative Strength Index (RSI) or (RS): A technical momentum indicator that compares the magnitude of recent gains to recent losses in an attempt to determine overbought and oversold conditions of an asset.

Resistance: The price level where a trend stalls. The market stops rising because sellers start to outnumber buyers. The opposite of a support level.

Retracement: In technical analysis, price movement in the opposite direction of the prevailing trend. Also described as a correction.

Retrenchment: A decline in price.

Return on equity: A calculation of a corporation's profitability, specifically its return on assets, calculated by dividing after-tax income by tangible assets.

Reversion to the mean: The concept that most natural fluctuations tend to center around a normal or average value over time.

Risk management: Management to control and monitor the risks of a bank, financial institution, business entity, or individual.

Risk: The potential to lose money.

S

Scalper: A speculator on the trading floor of an exchange who buys and sells rapidly, with small profit or losses, holding positions for only a short time during a trading session.

Seasonal trading: Using the calendar as a fundamental indicator to help predict market trends.

Securities and Exchange Commission (SEC): The Federal agency created by Congress to regulate the securities markets and protect investors.

Security: A note, stock, bond, investment contract, debenture, certificate of interest in profit-sharing or partnership agreement, certificate of deposit, collateral trust certificate, pre-organization certificate, option on a security, or other instrument of investment.

Sell-off: A period of intensified selling in a market that pushes prices sharply lower.

Settlement price: (1) The closing price, or a price within the range of closing prices, which is used as the official price in determining net gains or losses at the close of each trading session. (2) Payment of any amount of money under a contract.

Short covering: Trades that reverse, or close out, short-sale positions.

Short: One who has sold a cash commodity, a commodity futures contract, or other financial instrument; a long, in contrast, is one who has bought a cash commodity or futures contract.

Slippage: The difference between estimated transaction costs and the amount actually paid, usually attributed to a change in the spread.

Speculator: One who attempts to anticipate price changes and make profits through the sale and/or purchase of financial instruments.

Spread: (1) The purchase of one futures contact and the simultaneous sale of another futures contract to take advantage of and profit from the distortions from the normal price relationships that sometimes occur. (2) In a quote, the difference between the bid and the ask prices of a market. (3) The difference between two or more prices.

Spyware: Software that companies place on a user's PC without permission that slows down the computer by collecting data on the user's practices and generating ads.

Stochastics: A technical momentum indicator that compares a security's closing price to its price range over a given time period.

Stop limit: An order that becomes a limit order once the specified price is hit.

Stop order or stop: A dormant order that is triggered and becomes active only when a stock or commodity hits a price specified by the customer. A sell stop is placed below the market; a buy stop is placed above the market. Sometimes referred to as a stop loss order.

Strike price: A specified price at which an investor can buy or sell an option's underlying financial instrument. The exchange rate, interest rate, or market price that is guaranteed by an option transaction.

Straddle: An options strategy of purchasing a put and a call with the same strike price and expiration date. The strategy is generally used if the investor believes the price will move significantly but is unsure of the direction.

Supply: The total amount of a good or service available for purchase by consumers.

Support: A price level at which, historically, a declining market has difficulty falling below. Once this level is reached, the market trades sideways for a period of time or rebounds. It is the opposite of a resistance price range.

Synthetic stop: An order to exit the trade held either on your own computer or an intermediary computer, rather than at the exchange level. When the price touches the level of the stop, the order is then fired off to the exchange server for execution.

System: See Trading System

T

T1: A dedicated phone connection to the Internet supporting fast data transmission rates.

Tail: A chart pattern that shows a long, one-day price spike with a close near the intraday low.

Technical analysis: An approach to analysis of markets that anticipates trends of market prices based on mathematical patterns. Technicians normally examine patterns of price range, rates of change, changes in volume of trading, and open interest. Data are charted to show trends and formations which serve as indicators of likely future price movements.

Technical stop: An order to exit a trade at a predetermined price level that uses technical analysis to determine placement of the level.

Theta: Measures the change in the theoretical value of an option when the outstanding time before it expires is changed.

Tick: A minimum upward or downward movement in the price of securities, futures, or other financial instruments. Also called points.

Traders: Individuals who negotiate prices and execute buy and sell orders, either on behalf of an investor or for their own account.

Trading system: A method of buying and selling stocks according to a screen based on results from predetermined indicators and other criteria.

Trailing stop: An order to exit a trade at a predetermined price level. Trailing stops automatically follow the stock tick-by-tick by a specified amount as the market moves in a trader's favor, ensuring that a winner does not turn into a loser.

Transaction costs: (1) The cost of negotiating, monitoring, and enforcing a contract. (2) The total cost of executing a financial transaction.

Trendline: A line that connects either a series of highs or lows in a trend. The trendline can represent either support (a positive trendline) or resistance (a negative trendline).

V

Vega: The amount that the price of an option changes as compared to a one-percent changes in volatility.

Vertical spread: A simultaneous purchase of one option, hedged by the sale of another option, where the two options have the same expiration month but different striking prices. Also called a bull or bear spread.

Volatility: (1) A measure by which an exchange rate is expected to fluctuate over a given period. (2) A measure of a commodity's tendency to move up and down in price based on its daily price history over a period of time.

Volume: The number of contracts, shares, or other financial instruments traded during a specified period of time.

W

Whipsaw: a short-term trade with a small loss.

Y

Yield: The annual rate of return on an investment, as paid in dividends or interest. It is expressed as a percentage.

CONTRIBUTORS

Nigel Bahadur leads the research and development program for LBRGroup. Prior to this, he was the senior vice president of research and development for EXE Technologies.

Linda Bradford Raschke has been a full-time, professional trader since 1981. She began as a floor trader and later started LBR Group, a professional money management firm (lbrgroup.com). Raschke was recognized in Jack Schwager's book, *The New Market Wizards* (Wiley, 1995).

Thomas Bulkowski is a private investor and author of several books. He was formerly a hardware design engineer at Raytheon and a senior software engineer for Tandy Corporation.

John Carter has been a full time trader for the past decade and is one of the principals at www.tradethemarkets.com, an online trading and financial markets analysis firm and at www.razorforex.com, which focuses on the forex markets.

George Fontanills is the president of Pinnacle Investments of America and president emeritus of Optionetics (www.optionetics.com). He actively trades equity options and stocks and has written several best-selling books.

Philip Gotthelf is publisher of the COMMODEX, the longest-running daily futures trading system published anywhere, and president of EQUIDEX Inc. and EQUIDEX Brokerage Group. He is the author of several books.

Toni Hansen is president of The Bastiat Group, Inc., a company which provides market education to fellow traders. Hansen specializes in trading and investing in stocks, as well as E-mini futures. Her syndicated daily market commentary can be found at www.tonihansen.com.

John Hill is founder and president of Futures Truth Company, an organization that analyzes and rates publicly offered futures trading systems (www.futurestruth.com). He has been a futures trader since 1958.

Michael Kahn is a well respected technical analyst. He writes the Getting Technical column for Barron's Online, the daily Quick Takes Pro technical newsletter and has written two books on technical analysis.

Jim Kharouf is a financial reporter with 16 years experience. He has covered stock, options and futures markets worldwide.

Steven Landis is the founder of Landis Financial & Investment Services and past president and chairman of the National Association of Active Investment Managers (NAAIM), an organization for professional, active investment managers.

Lawrence McMillan is president of McMillan Analysis Corp. (www.option-strategist.com.), which provides educational material on options and manages individual options accounts and a hedge fund. He is the author of several books on options trading.

John "Doctor J" Najarian is the editor of ChangeWave's Options Investor and OptionMONSTER.com. He was a Chicago pit trader for 25 years and founded Mercury Trading, a firm that he sold to Citadel in 2004. He is a frequent media commentator.

David Nassar founded one of the first electronic trading firms and is a New York Times best selling author. Since selling his firm, David formed Cross-Winds Capital, LLC to work directly with high net worth investors and institutions.

William O'Neil is the founder and chairman of Investor's Business Daily (www.investors.com) and developer of the CAN SLIM investing method. He is the author of several books on investing.

Mark Pankin is the founder and owner of MDP Associates LLC. Before becoming a registered investment advisor, he taught math at the university level and worked as an operations research analyst.

George Pruitt is director of research at Futures Truth (www.futurestruth.com). He has co-written two trading books.

Frederic Ruffy is senior writer and index strategist for Optionetics. He specializes in trading options on exchange-traded funds and index products. Prior to working with Optionetics, Ruffy worked for the trading firm Miller Tabak + Co.

Bernie Schaeffer is chairman of Schaeffer's Investment Research (www.schaeffersresearch.com). His approach focuses on stocks with technical and fundamental trends that run counter to investor expectations.

Boris Schlossberg serves as senior currency strategist at FXCM, one of the largest retail forex dealers in the world. He is the recent author of a technical analysis book on the currency market.

Sam Seiden is a trader, research analyst, and instructor with more than ten years of experience. He provides research and guidance to clients through speaking engagements, workshops, magazine articles, and advisory services via www.samseiden.com.

Catherine Shalen is a director in the research and product development department of the Chicago Board Options Exchange. Her contribution was written when she was a senior economist at the Chicago Board of Trade, specializing in equity contracts.

David Silverman spent 16 years on the trading floor of the CME and is a former director of the exchange. He is currently an independent electronic trader and a consultant to brokerage firms, exchanges, and fund managers and author of an online futures trading book.

Phil Tiger was involved in the futures industry for 35 years as a commodity futures specialist and the leading authority on spreads. He developed the Seasonal Spread Index, and it or its variations are used extensively throughout the futures industry today.

Jerry Toepke has been involved in futures markets since 1977 and is editor of Moore Research Center, Inc., (MRCI) publications (www.mrci.com), which analyzes price movement in commodity markets.

Toni Turner is a best-selling author and a popular speaker and educator at financial conferences and forums nationwide. For more information, please go to: www.toniturner.com.

Russell R. Wasendorf, Sr. is CEO of Peregrine Financial Group, Inc., publisher of *SFO* and author of *The Complete Guide to Single Stock Futures* and *All About Futures*.

John Yackley is president and manager of funds at Be Free Investments, a registered commodity trading advisor (www.befreeinvestments.com). He specializes in trading stock index and interest rate futures and options.

INDEX